Advanced

Modular

Mathematics

MECHANICS 3

Stephen Webb

SECOND
EDITION

COLLINS

NATIONAL
EXTENSION
COLLEGE

Unit M3

Published by HarperCollins Publishers Limited
77–85 Fulham Palace Road
Hammersmith
London W6 8JB

www.CollinsEducation.com
On-line Support for Schools and Colleges

© National Extension College Trust Ltd 2000
First published 2000
ISBN 000 322517 8

This book was written by Stephen Webb for the National Extension College Trust Ltd.

British Library Cataloguing in Publication Data
A catalogue record for this publication is available from the British Library.

Original internal design: Derek Lee
Cover design and implementation: Terry Bambrook
Project editors: Hugh Hillyard-Parker and Margaret Levin
Page layout: Stephen Pargeter
Printed and bound: Scotprint, Musselburgh

The authors and publishers thank Dave Wilkins for his comments on this book.

The National Extension College is an educational trust and a registered charity with a distinguished body of trustees. It is an independent, self-financing organisation.

Since it was established in 1963, NEC has pioneered the development of flexible learning for adults. NEC is actively developing innovative materials and systems for distance-learning options from basic skills and general education to degree and professional training.

For further details of NEC resources that support Advanced Modular Mathematics, and other NEC courses, contact NEC Customer Services:

National Extension College Trust Ltd
18 Brooklands Avenue
Cambridge CB2 2HN
Telephone 01223 316644, Fax 01223 313586
Email resources@nec.ac.uk, Home page www.nec.ac.uk

You might also like to visit:

www.fireandwater.com
The book lover's website

UNIT

M3
Contents

Section 1   Variable acceleration   1

Systematic approach   1
Increases in the variables   4
Variable force   6
Proportional forces   7
Newton's Law of Gravitation   10

Section 2   Elastic strings and springs   17

Hooke's Law   17
Energy stored in an elastic string   22
Conservation of energy   23
Catapults   27
Particle on a plane   28
Springs   30

Section 3   Further dynamics   35

What is simple harmonic motion?   35
Speed at any point   36
Velocity and displacement at any time   38
Time for a complete cycle   39
Tides   42
SHM equation   44

Section 4   Uniform circular motion   51

Linear and angular velocity   51
The period of revolution   53
Central force   53
Conical pendulum   55
Motion on a horizontal surface   57
Smooth beads   60
Two strings   62
Two particles   65
Other systems involving circular motion   67
Banked corners   72
Elastic strings   75

Section 5   Motion in a vertical circle   85

Motion in a vertical circle   85
Initial velocity   86
Complete circles   87
Threaded particle   91
Motion inside a smooth sphere   95
Motion on the outer surface of a sphere   98

Section 6   Statics of rigid bodies   105

Finding the centre of mass by integration   105
Volumes of revolution   108
Standard results   109
Objects suspended from strings or pivoted   113
Toppling   115
Particles   118

Practice examination paper   129

Solutions to exercises   131

M3

Advanced Modular Mathematics

FOREWORD This book is one of a series covering the Edexcel Advanced Subsidiary (AS) and Advanced GCE in Mathematics. It covers all the subject material for Mechanics 3 (Unit M3), examined from 2001 onwards.

While this series of text books has been structured to match the Edexcel specification, we hope that the informal style of the text and approach to important concepts will encourage other readers whose final exams are from other Boards to use the books for extra reading and practice. In particular, we have included references to the OCR syllabus (see below).

This book is meant to be *used*: read the text, study the worked examples and work through the Practice questions and Summary exercises, which will give you practice in the basic skills you need for maths at this level. Many exercises, and worked examples, are based on applications of the mathematics in this book. There are many books for advanced mathematics, which include many more exercises: use this book to direct your studies, making use of as many other resources as you can.

There are many features in this book that you will find particularly useful:

- Each **section** covers one discrete area of the new Edexcel specification. The order of topics is exactly the same as in the specification.

- **Practice questions** are given at regular intervals throughout each section. The questions are graded to help you build up your mathematical skills gradually through the section. The **Answers** to these questions come at the end of the relevant section.

- **Summary exercises** are given at the end of each section; these include more full-blown, exam-type questions. Full, worked solutions are given in a separate **Solutions** section at the end of the book.

- In addition, we have provided a complete **Practice examination paper**, which you can use as a 'dummy run' of the actual exam when you reach the end of your studies on M3.

- Alongside most of the headings in this book you will see boxed references, e.g. OCR **M3** 5.9.1 (a) These are for students following the OCR specification and indicate which part of that specification the topic covers.

- Key Skills: because of the nature of mechanics, your work on this book will not provide many obvious opportunities for gathering evidence of Key Skills, and so we have not included any Key Skills references (as we have done in other books in this series).

The National Extension College has more experience of flexible-learning materials than any other body (see p. ii). This series is a distillation of that experience: Advanced Modular Mathematics helps to put you in control of your own learning.

1

Variable acceleration

In Unit M2 we saw how a definition of the acceleration in terms of time could be integrated to find the velocity and then the distance. We shall now extend this to include cases where the acceleration is given in terms of the distance: this leads to the setting up of differential equations similar to the type you may already have met in P3. (If you haven't come across them, you may like to skip this section temporarily.) We then look at the forces that produce such an acceleration; in particular, the gravitational force and applications.

Systematic approach

OCR M3 5.9.5 (a)

By and large, if we're given the acceleration as a function of another variable (which can be velocity, time or displacement), the method of solution can be broken down into fairly well-defined sections. For the moment we'll make a list of these and then look at each in turn:

1 Sign

2 Form

3 Setting up

4 Integrating

5 Values

6 Rearranging.

1st stage: Sign

As in many types of question which deal with **vector** quantities, i.e. where the **direction** is important, we have to choose a positive direction. This often chooses itself – if we are told that a car is moving in a straight line, then obviously we take its direction of motion as positive. There are two cases where you have to be careful, however. If you are told that a force produces a **retardation**, it means that the acceleration will automatically be negative. Alternatively you could be told that a particle is moving in the positive direction of the positive x-axis – if the force on the body is then towards the origin, this will tend to slow the body down and so the acceleration will again be negative.

2nd stage: Form

There are two main forms for the acceleration with which you should be familiar.

$$① \ \frac{dv}{dt} \quad \text{and} \quad ② \ v\frac{dv}{dx} \qquad \begin{array}{l} \text{where } v \text{ is the velocity} \\ x \text{ is the displacement} \end{array}$$

If we start from the definition of acceleration, the rate of change of velocity, we have

$$a = \frac{dv}{dt} \qquad \qquad \dots \text{①}$$

then $\quad a = \dfrac{dv}{dt} = \dfrac{dv}{dx} \times \dfrac{dx}{dt} = \dfrac{dv}{dx} \times v = v\dfrac{dv}{dx} \qquad \dots \text{②}$

(There is a third form, $\dfrac{d^2x}{dt^2}$, but this is not used so much.)

If we're given the acceleration as:

● a function of t, we use $\dfrac{dv}{dt}$

● a function of x, we use $v\dfrac{dv}{dx}$.

3rd stage: Setting up

Having chosen the appropriate form for the acceleration we should have a first-order differential equation with separable variables and we proceed as normal by putting all the terms of one variable on one side and all the terms of the other variable on the other.

It makes integration easier if you leave constants **outside** the integral and on the less cluttered side, e.g. to rearrange

$$\frac{dv}{dt} = \frac{-3v}{5},$$

it might be easier to put $\displaystyle\int \frac{dv}{v} = -\frac{3}{5}\int dt,$

rather than $\displaystyle\int \frac{-5dv}{3v} = \int dt.$

4th stage: Integrating

This is not likely to be too arduous since the syllabus only asks for particular forms for the acceleration which produce reasonable equations – if you intend continuing on to M4 you will meet more complicated functions.

5th stage: Values

Once we've integrated the equation successfully, we have the **general solution**, i.e. we will have an arbitrary **constant** from the integration.
To find the value of this constant we need to know a **pair of values** for the variables in the solution. This pair of values can be written into the question in such a way that they are not immediately obvious, and you have to be able to 'translate' into mathematical symbols. For example:

● 'Initially' means when $t = 0$

● 'Starts from rest' means that $v = 0$ when $t = 0$

● 'Greatest height' means that $v = 0$

● 'Returns to its initial position' means that $x = 0$ (again), and others.

6th stage: Rearranging

Once we've found the solution to the equation, we then have to express it in the required form – again, this is not likely to be a problem with the types of equation we look at. Be careful if you are asked for an expression for v and you have an expression for v^2 to take square roots and think whether to take the positive or negative solution.

That then is the sequence of stages through which the solution of a typical problem might pass. It's not intended as a rigid framework and you'll probably find that the question doesn't fit exactly – but on the whole it gives a fair indication of how to proceed. Let's take a question and see it working.

Example

The acceleration of a particle, moving on the positive x-axis, has magnitude $n^2(3a - x)$, where x is the displacement from the origin O and n and a are positive constants. The direction of the acceleration is towards O. At time $t = 0$, the particle is moving through the point $x = a$ with speed $2na$ away from O. Show that, in the ensuing motion, the speed v of the particle is given by:

$$v = n(3a - x)$$

Hence find x in terms of t.

Sketch the graph of x against t.

Solution

Sign: We're told that the direction of the acceleration is 'towards O', so that it is **negative**, of magnitude $n^2(3a - x)$.

Form: Since the acceleration is given in terms of x, we choose the form
$$v\frac{\mathrm{d}v}{\mathrm{d}x} \ .$$

Setting up: Combining the parts above, we have:

$$v\frac{\mathrm{d}v}{\mathrm{d}x} = -n^2(3a - x)$$

$$\int v\,\mathrm{d}v = \int -n^2(3a - x)\mathrm{d}x$$

$$\int v\,\mathrm{d}v = -n^2\!\int (3a - x)\mathrm{d}x$$

Integrating: No problem in this example, noting that a is constant, so that $3a$ integrates to $3ax$.

$$\frac{v^2}{2} = -n^2\left(3ax - \frac{x^2}{2}\right) + C \qquad \qquad …①$$

Values: We're told that when $x = a$, the speed is $2na$ away from O, i.e. positive and $v = 2na$.

Putting these values into equation ①

$$\frac{(2na)^2}{2} = -n^2\left(3a^2 - \frac{a^2}{2}\right) + C$$

$$2n^2a^2 = -\frac{5a^2n^2}{2} + C \ \Rightarrow \ C = \frac{9a^2n^2}{2}$$

and so $\dfrac{v^2}{2} = -n^2\left(3ax - \dfrac{x^2}{2}\right) + \dfrac{9a^2n^2}{2}$

Rearranging: $\times 2 \quad v^2 = -6n^2ax + n^2x^2 + 9a^2n^2$
$$= n^2(9a^2 - 6ax + x^2) = n^2(3a - x)^2$$

Take square roots $\Rightarrow v = \pm n(3a - x)$

But we know that $v = 2na$ when $x = a$, so we discard the negative solution and

$$v = n(3a - x)$$

The next part of the question is a little twist – we have to use the fact that $v = \dfrac{dx}{dt}$ and then set up a differential equation in x and t.

$$\frac{dx}{dt} = n(3a - x) \Rightarrow \int \frac{dx}{3a - x} = n \int dt$$
$$\Rightarrow -\ln(3a - x) = nt + D$$

But we're told that when $t = 0$, $x = a$ and so $-\ln 2a = D$ for $x < 3a$.
Putting this back in,

$$-\ln(3a - x) = nt - \ln 2a \Rightarrow \ln 2a - \ln(3a - x) = nt$$
$$\Rightarrow \ln \frac{2a}{3a - x} = nt$$
$$\Rightarrow \frac{2a}{3a - x} = e^{nt}$$
$$\Rightarrow (3a - x)(e^{nt}) = 2a$$
$$\Rightarrow 3a - x = \frac{2a}{e^{nt}} = 2ae^{-nt}$$
$$\Rightarrow x = 3a - 2ae^{-nt}$$

Figure 1.1

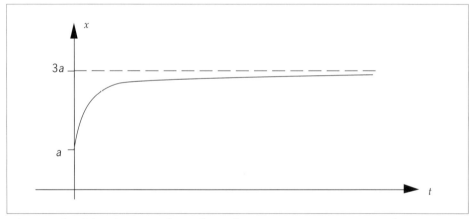

The sketch of this function shows how the distance from O was a when t was 0, and how the distance approaches a **limiting value** of $3a$ as t becomes large and consequently the term $2ae^{-nt}$ becomes very small.

Increases in the variables

OCR M3 5.9.5 (a)

We are frequently asked to find the increase in one variable corresponding to the increase in the other – for example, find the time taken for the particle to move from the point where $x = a$ to the point where $x = 3a$. In this case we measure our time **from the first point,** i.e. we let t be zero when $x = a$.
When we put this pair of values into our general solution we'll find the value of the arbitrary constant and can find the new value of t when $x = 3a$.

Here's an example of this kind where we want to find an increase in time corresponding to a given increase in the speed.

Example	A particle moves with an acceleration of $2e^{-t}$ m s^{-1}. Find the time for the velocity to increase from 6 m s^{-1} to 7.8 m s^{-1}.

Solution

Here we have

$$\frac{dv}{dt} = 2e^{-t}$$

$$\int dv = \int 2e^{-t}\, dt$$

$$\Rightarrow v = -2e^{-t} + C$$

we measure time from when $v = 6$, and so $t = 0$, then,

$$6 = -2 + C \quad \Rightarrow C = 8$$

$$v = 8 - 2e^{-t}$$

when $v = 7.8$, $\quad 7.8 = 8 - 2e^{-t}$

$$2e^{-t} = 8 - 7.8 = 0.2$$

$$e^{-t} = 0.1$$

$$e^{t} = 10 \quad \Rightarrow t = \ln 10 = 2.3 \text{ seconds}$$

Practice questions A

1 A particle moves along Ox in the positive direction. At time $t = 0$, its speed is 8 m s^{-1}. At time t seconds, its acceleration is $3e^{2t}$ m s^{-2} in the positive direction. Calculate, in metres to 3 significant figures, the distance the particle moves in the first 2 seconds.

2 A modern Formula One racing car accelerates in a straight line from a standing start to 86.4 km h^{-1} in 2 seconds.

(a) Show that 86.4 km h^{-1} is equivalent to 24 m s^{-1}.

The acceleration a m s^{-2}, of the racing car, t seconds after starting from rest, is modelled by the equation

$$a = t (16 + kt), 0 \le t \le 2$$

where k is a constant.

(b) Show that $k = -3$.

(c) Calculate, in m, how far the racing car travels as it accelerates from rest to 86.4 km h^{-1}.

3 On joining a motorway, a car accelerates for 8 seconds from a speed of 20 m s^{-1} to reach a top speed of 36 m s^{-1}.

In an initial model of the situation, the acceleration is assumed to be constant.

(a) Estimate the distance, in m, travelled by the car during this 8-second period.

It is noted that the acceleration of the car decreases as its speed increases. A refined model is proposed in which the acceleration of the car, t seconds after it starts to accelerate, is taken to be $k(8 - t)$ m s^{-2}, $0 \le t \le 8$, where k is a positive constant.

(b) Find the value of k.

(c) Find a revised estimate for the distance, in m, travelled by the car during this 8-second period.

4 A particle moves in a straight line away from a fixed point O in the line in such a way that its speed, v m/s, at a distance x metres from O is given by

$$v = \frac{4}{2x + 3}$$

If the particle passes through the point A, where $OA = 5$ m, calculate

(a) the time taken to cover the distance OA

(b) the acceleration of the particle at A

(c) the distance OB, where B is the position of the particle 1 second after leaving O.

5   A particle P moves along the positive x-axis such that when its displacement from the origin O is x m, its acceleration in the positive x direction is $(10x - 2x^3)$ m s^{-2}, The speed of P is $\sqrt{15}$ m s^{-1} when $x = 2$. Find an expression for the speed of P for any value of x.

Determine the values of x for which P comes instantaneously to rest.

6   A particle P, of mass 0.2 kg, moves in a straight line through a fixed point O. At time t seconds after passing through O, the distance of P from O is x metres, the velocity of P is v m s^{-1} and the acceleration of P is $(x^2 + 4)$ m s^{-2}.

(a)   Use the information given to form a differential equation in the variables v and x only for the motion of P.

Given that $v = 2$ when $x = 0$,

(b)   show that $3v^2 = 2x^3 + 24x + 12$

(c)   Find, in J, the work done by P by the force producing its acceleration as P moves from $x = 0$ to $x = 9$.

Variable force

OCR M3 5.9.5 (a)

Instead of an acceleration or retardation, we are sometimes given a force which varies with one of velocity, displacement or time. Apart from some preliminary work, the method is the same as the one we have just been using.

We need a connection between the force applied and the acceleration produced – this comes from Newton's Second Law:

> Newton's Second Law: $F = ma$
>
> where F is the force in Newtons,
>
> m is the mass in kg,
>
> and a is the acceleration in m s^{-2}.

Since the mass can make the working more complicated, the force will usually be given in such a way that m disappears. This can be done either by giving the force in terms of m or, equivalently, by giving the force **per unit mass**, which means that we have to multiply the force by m, the mass of the particle it is acting on. In both these cases, the same m will appear on both sides of the equation and will cancel.

Remember that any force which **resists** the motion in the positive direction, or **opposes** the motion or is given as a retarding force will be **negative**.

Example   A particle of mass m moves along the x-axis under the action of a single force directed towards the origin O. The magnitude of the force is $\dfrac{mk}{(x + 2)^2}$ where k is a positive constant and x is the distance of the particle from the origin O.

The particle is released from rest at a point where $x = 3$ and has a speed of $\dfrac{8}{15}$ where $x = 1$. Find its speed at the origin.

| **Solution** | Since the direction of the force is away from x-increasing, it will be negative, so |

$$F = \frac{-mk}{(x+2)^2}$$

Since $F = ma$,

$$ma = \frac{-mk}{(x+2)^2} \Rightarrow a = \frac{-k}{(x+2)^2}$$

Using $a = v\dfrac{dv}{dx}$,

$$v\frac{dv}{dx} = \frac{-k}{(x+2)^2}$$

Rearranging,

$$\int v\,dv = \int \frac{-k}{(x+2)^2}\,dx$$

$$\frac{v^2}{2} = \frac{k}{(x+2)} + C$$

When $x = 3$, $v = 0 \Rightarrow$

$$O = \frac{k}{5} + C \Rightarrow C = \frac{-k}{5}$$

$$\frac{v^2}{2} = \frac{k}{x+2} - \frac{k}{5}$$

When $x = 1$, $v = \dfrac{8}{15} \Rightarrow$

$$\frac{1}{2} \times \frac{64}{225} = \frac{k}{3} - \frac{k}{5} = \frac{2k}{15}$$

$$\Rightarrow k = \frac{32}{225} \times \frac{15}{2} = \frac{16}{15}$$

i.e.

$$\frac{v^2}{2} = \frac{16}{15}\left(\frac{1}{x+2} - \frac{1}{5}\right)$$

When $x = 0$,

$$\frac{v^2}{2} = \frac{16}{15}\left(\frac{1}{2} - \frac{1}{5}\right)$$

$$= \frac{48}{150} \Rightarrow v = \frac{4}{5}$$

Proportional forces

OCR M3 5.9.5 (b)

In the previous example the expression for the force included the positive constant k. Instead of being given an expression for the force, we can be told that it is **proportional to** some variable term, like v^2 or the square root of the distance. Then we have to rewrite this information in the form of an equation, i.e. $F = kv^2$ or $F = k\sqrt{x}$, and state that k is a positive constant.

| **Example** | A particle of mass m is subject to a force attracting it towards the fixed point O. The magnitude of this force is inversely proportional to the distance of the particle from O. When the particle is at A (where $OA = a$), the magnitude of the force is $\dfrac{4m}{a}$. The particle is projected from A with speed 2 along the line OA in the direction away from O. |

Find the distance, in terms of a, from A when the particle has a speed of $\sqrt{20}$.

Solution   The force is negative, since towards O, and inversely proportional to x, so

$$F = \frac{-k}{x}$$

when $x = a$, $F = \frac{-4m}{a}$ $\Rightarrow \frac{-4m}{a} = \frac{-k}{a}$, $k = 4m$

$$\Rightarrow F = \frac{-4m}{x}$$

$$ma = \frac{-4m}{x}$$

$$\Rightarrow a = \frac{-4}{x}$$

$$v\frac{dv}{dx} = \frac{-4}{x}$$

$$\int v\,dv = \int \frac{-4}{x}\,dx$$

$$\frac{v^2}{2} = -4\ln x + C$$

when $x = a, v = 2, \dfrac{2^2}{2} = -4\ln a + C \Rightarrow C = 2 + 4\ln a$

$$\frac{v^2}{2} = -4\ln x + 2 + 4\ln a$$

$$\frac{v^2}{2} - 2 = 4(\ln a - \ln x) = 4\ln \frac{a}{x}$$

when $v = \sqrt{20}, \dfrac{20}{2} - 2 = 4\ln \dfrac{a}{x}$, $8 = 4\ln \dfrac{a}{x}$, $2 = \ln \dfrac{a}{x}$

$$\frac{a}{x} = e^2 \Rightarrow x = ae^{-2}$$

Practice questions B

1 A particle P of mass 0.4 kg moves along the positive x-axis under the action of a single force of magnitude $\dfrac{12}{x^3}$ newtons, where x metres is the distance of P from the origin O. The force acts along the x-axis in the direction of x increasing. The particle is released from rest at the point where $x = 2$. In the subsequent motion, when P is x metres from O, its speed is v metres per second. Show that

$$v^2 = \frac{15}{2}\left(1 - \frac{4}{x^2}\right)$$

2 A particle of mass 0.5 kg moves on the positive x-axis under the action of a variable force of magnitude $\dfrac{4}{x^3}$ N, where x metres is the distance of the particle from O. The force is directed towards O. The particle is released from rest at a point A, where $OA = 8$ m. The speed of the particle is denoted by v m s^{-1}, Show that

$$v^2 = \frac{64 - x^2}{8x^2}$$

3 A particle of mass m moves on a smooth horizontal table and is attracted towards a fixed point O on the table by a force of magnitude $\dfrac{mk}{x^2}$, where x is the distance of the particle from O and k is a constant. The particle is projected from a point A, where $OA = a$, in the direction OA with an initial speed $\sqrt{\left(\dfrac{k}{a}\right)}$.

Show that the particle first comes to instantaneous rest at a distance $2a$ from O.

4 A particle P of mass 0.7 kg moves along the x-axis under the action of a single force directed towards the origin O. When the distance of P from O is x metres, the magnitude of the force is $0.6\,x^2$ N, and the speed of P is v m s^{-1}. Initially P is at the point where $x = 1$ and is moving away from O with speed 2 m s^{-1}

Show that $7v^2 = 32 - 4x^3$

Find the distance of P from O when P comes to instantaneous rest.

5 A particle starts with speed 20 m s^{-1} and moves in a straight line. The particle is subjected to a resistance which produces a retardation with is initially 5 m s^{-2} and which increases uniformly with the distance moved, having a value of 11 m s^{-2} when the particle has moved a distance of 12 m. Given that the particle has speed v m s^{-1} when it has moved a distance of x m, show that, while the particle is in motion

$$v\frac{dv}{dx} = -\left(5 + \frac{1}{2}x\right)$$

Hence, or otherwise, calculate the distance moved by the particle in coming to rest.

6 A toy car of mass 0.2 kg is driven by a clockwork motor. When fully wound up, the motor runs for 10 s. In a simple model for the motion of the car, the motor is assumed to produce a driving force of $(0.1 - 0.01\,t)$ newtons at time t seconds after the car is released ($0 \leq t \leq 10$). The car is released from rest on a horizontal floor, and its speed at time t seconds is v m s^{-1}.

Assume that all resistances to the motion of the car can be ignored. Write down a differential equation relating v and t, and hence find the speed of the car when $t = 10$.

7 A particle of mass 0.2 kg moving on the positive x-axis has displacement x metres and velocity v m s^{-1} at time t seconds. At time $t = 0$, $v = 0$ and $x = 1$. The particle moves under the action of a force in the direction of x increasing and of magnitude $\frac{4}{x}$ N.

(a) Assuming that no other forces act on the particle, show that $v = \sqrt{40 \ln x}$

(b) Assuming that a constant resisting force of magnitude 2 N acts on the particle whenever the particle is in motion, show that the greatest speed reached by the particle is $\sqrt{20(20 \ln 2 - 1)}$ m s^{-1}.

8 A charged particle P, of mass m kg, is repelled from a fixed point O by a force of magnitude $\frac{25m}{x^2}$ N, where x m is the distance of P from O.

No other forces act on P. The particle is projected, directly towards O, from a point A, where $OA = 0.5$ m, with initial speed 10 m s^{-1}. Obtain a differential equation relating the velocity, v m s^{-1}, of P, to x. Show that P comes to rest at a distance 0.25 m from O. Briefly describe the ensuing motion.

9 A particle P, of mass m, moves along the x-axis under the action of a single force directed towards the origin O. The magnitude of the force is

$$\frac{mk}{2x + c},$$

where k and c are positive constants and x is the distance of P from O. The particle is released from rest at the point A, where $OA = 2c$.

(a) Given that P is moving with speed v when it is at a distance x from O, where $0 \leq x \leq 2c$, show that

$$v^2 = k \ln\left(\frac{5c}{2x + c}\right).$$

(b) Hence, or otherwise, show that when P moves from B to O, where $OB = c$, the work done by the force is $\frac{1}{2}mk \ln 3$.

10 A particle P, of mass m, moves away from the origin O along the positive x-axis under the action of a single force directed towards O of magnitude $\frac{\lambda m}{x^2}$, where λ is a positive constant. At the point C, where $OC = c$, the speed of P is $\sqrt{\left(\frac{\lambda}{c}\right)}$.

(a) Given that P is moving with speed v at the instant when it is at a distance x from O, show that

$$v^2 = \lambda\left(\frac{2c - x}{xc}\right).$$

(b) Hence, or otherwise, find in terms of λ, m and c, the work done when P moves from the point C to the point D, where $OD = \frac{3c}{2}$.

Newton's Law of Gravitation

Newton's Law of Gravitation states that the force of attraction between two particles of masses m_1 and m_2, separated by a distance r, acts along the line between the two particles and has a magnitude F given by

$$F = G \frac{m_1 m_2}{r^2}, \text{ where } G \text{ is a constant.}$$

In particular, if one of the 'particles' is the earth, we can use this equation as an approximate model for the motion of satellites if we remember that the distance r is measured between the *centres*: the difference for the satellite is negligible but we have to include the radius of the earth in our calculations.

| Example | A satellite, of mass m kg, is being launched into space when its rocket malfunctions and causes the satellite to slow down and momentarily come to rest at a height h m above the surface of the earth. The satellite then begins to fall towards the Earth due to the downward gravitational force which is given, in N, by |

$$\frac{mK}{r^2}$$

where r m is the distance of the satellite from the Earth's centre and K is a constant.

(a) (i) Use the given gravitational model to show that the velocity v m s^{-1} of the satellite satisfies the equation

$$v \frac{dv}{dr} = -\frac{K}{r^2}$$

if resistance forces are neglected.

  (ii) Hence show that on collision with the surface, the velocity of the satellite V m s^{-1} is given by

$$V^2 = \frac{2hK}{R(R + h)}$$

where R m is the radius of the Earth.

(b) It is usual to adopt the approximate model that sets the force of gravitational attraction near the Earth's surface as constant and equal to mg N. Use this model to calculate the corresponding value of V at the surface for the same satellite.

| Solution | (a) (i) The force is in the direction of r decreasing, so it is negative |

We have $F = ma = mv \dfrac{dv}{dr} = \dfrac{-mK}{r^2}$

using the model, which simplifies to

$$v \frac{dv}{dr} = \frac{-K}{r^2}$$

(ii) Integrating, $\displaystyle\int v \, dv = \int \frac{-K}{r^2} \, dr$

$$\Rightarrow \quad \frac{v^2}{2} = \frac{K}{r} + C$$

We are told that the satellite is at rest at a height h above the surface of the earth, i.e. that $v = 0$ when $r = R + h$, where R is the radius of the earth. This gives

$$O = \frac{K}{R+h} + C \Rightarrow C = \frac{-K}{R+h}$$

$$\frac{v^2}{2} = \frac{K}{r} - \frac{K}{R+h}$$

when the satellite is in collision with the surface, i.e. when $r = R$, and $v = V$

$$\frac{v^2}{2} = \frac{K}{R} - \frac{K}{R+h} = \frac{Kh}{R(R+h)}$$

$$\Rightarrow V^2 = \frac{2hK}{R(R+h)} \qquad \dots Ⓐ$$

(b)   If the gravitation force, $\frac{mK}{r^2}$ is mg when $r = R$,

$$\frac{mK}{R^2} = mg \Rightarrow K = R^2g$$

Ⓐ becomes $V^2 = \frac{2hR^2g}{R(R+h)} = \frac{2hgR}{R+h} \Rightarrow V = \sqrt{\left(\frac{2hgR}{R+h}\right)}$

Work done

We can use the expression that we found in part (b), i.e. $K = R^2g$ to rewrite the equation for the force as

$$F = \frac{-mgR^2}{r^2} = \frac{-mgR^2}{(R+x)^2}$$

where x is the distance above the earth's surface. We can then find the work done against this force in raising it from the surface, $x = 0$ to a height h, $x = h$.

Using work done against $= \displaystyle\int_{x_1}^{x_2} -F \, dx$, this gives

$$\begin{aligned}
\text{work done} \quad &= \int_0^h \frac{mgR^2}{(R+x)^2} \, dx &&= mgR^2 \left[-\frac{1}{R+x} \right]_0^h \\[2mm]
&= mgR^2 \left[-\frac{1}{R+h} + \frac{1}{R} \right] &&= mgR^2 \left(\frac{h}{R(R+h)} \right) \\[2mm]
& &&= \frac{mghR}{R+h} = mgh \left(\frac{R}{R+h} \right) \\[2mm]
& &&= mgh \left(1 + \frac{h}{R} \right)^{-1}
\end{aligned}$$

In general, we can find the work done by a single force by finding the change in kinetic energy.

Example

A force acting on a particle of mass m produces an acceleration such that the velocity v and distance x from the origin O are connected by $v^2 = 2x + \dfrac{x^2}{4}$.

Find the work done by moving the particle from the point A where $x = 1$ to the point B where $x = 4$.

Solution

At A, $v^2 = 2 + \dfrac{1}{4} = \dfrac{9}{4}$ $\qquad$ At B, $v^2 = 8 + 4 = 12$

Work done is change in KE, i.e. $\dfrac{1}{2} m \left(12 - \dfrac{9}{4}\right) = \dfrac{39m}{8}$

Example

The radius of the earth is R and the acceleration due to gravity at the earth's surface is g. The gravitational force acting on a particle P of mass m, when it is at a distance x, $x \geq R$, from the centre of the earth, is $\dfrac{km}{x^2}$ where k is a constant.

(a)　Find k in terms of R and g.

At time $t = 0$, P is projected vertically upwards from the surface of the earth with speed $\sqrt{(1.6gR)}$. At time t it is at a distance x from the centre of the earth and is moving with velocity v.

Ignoring the effects of air resistance, and the motion of the earth,

(b)　show that $v \dfrac{dv}{dx} = - \dfrac{R^2 g}{x^2}$.

(c)　Hence find, in terms of R, the greatest height of P above the earth's surface.

Solution

(a)　At the earth's surface, i.e. when $x = R$, the gravitational force on a particle of mass m is $- mg$ (towards the centre of the earth, i.e. opposite to the direction in which x is increasing and so negative). This gives

$$- mg = \frac{km}{R^2} \implies k = - gR^2$$

(b)　We now know that the force is $\dfrac{-gR^2 m}{x^2}$ and so

$$F = ma \quad = mv \frac{dv}{dx} \quad = - \frac{mgR^2}{x^2}$$

$$\implies v \frac{dv}{dx} \quad = - \frac{R^2 g}{x^2}$$

(c)　Separating variables, $\displaystyle\int v\,dv = \int - \frac{R^2 g}{x^2}\,dx$

$$\implies \frac{v^2}{2} = \frac{R^2 g}{x} + C$$

when $x = R$, $v^2 = 1.6\,gR \implies 0.8\,gR = Rg + C$, $C = - 0.2\,gR$

$$\frac{v^2}{2} = \frac{R^2 g}{x} - 0.2\,gR$$

When $v = 0$ (greatest height)

$$\frac{R^2 g}{x} = 0.2\,gR \implies x = 5R$$

Practice questions C

1   The magnitude of the gravitational force exerted by the Earth on a particle is proportional to the mass of the particle and inversely proportional to the square of the distance of the particle from the centre of the Earth. The Earth is modelled as a sphere of radius R, and the acceleration due to gravity at the Earth's surface is g.

(a)   Show that, at a distance x from the centre of the Earth, $x \geq R$, the magnitude if the acceleration due to gravity is $\dfrac{gR^2}{x^2}$.

A particle is projected vertically into space from a point on the surface of the Earth with initial speed u.

Ignoring any effect of air resistance,

(b)   find an expression for the speed of the particle when it is at a distance x from the centre of the Earth.

Given that the radius of the Earth is approximately 6.3×10^6 m,

(c)   find an estimate for the minimum initial speed of the particle if it is to continue moving away from the Earth and is never turned back by the Earth's gravitational force.

2   The gravitational force per unit mass at a distance x ($> a$) from the earth's centre is $\dfrac{ga^2}{x^2}$, where a is the radius of the earth, and g is constant. A particle is projected vertically upwards from the earth's surface at A with speed u. Show that if $u^2 < 2ag$, the particle rises to a maximum height $\dfrac{au^2}{(2ag - u^2)}$ above A. What happens if $u^2 > 2ag$?

3   A particle of unit mass moves in a straight line which passes through a fixed point O. The particle is acted on by a force which is directed towards O and is of magnitude kx^{-2}, where k is a positive constant, and x is the displacement of the particle from O. Initially the particle is at a displacement a from O ($a > 0$), and is moving with speed u away from O. Obtain v^2 in terms of x, and show that the loss of kinetic energy as the displacement increases from a to x is

$$k \left(\frac{1}{a} - \frac{1}{x} \right).$$

Find the least value of u if the particle never comes to rest.

If u was half this value, show that the particle will come to rest where $x = \dfrac{4}{3} a$.

4   [The gravitational force of attraction, F, between any two particles of masses m_1 and m_2 separated by a distance d is given by $F = \dfrac{Gm_1 m_2}{d^2}$, where G is a constant.]

O and A are fixed points, and the distance OA is 9 units. A particle of mass $4M$ is fixed at O and a particle of mass M is fixed at A. A particle P of mass m is free to move on the line OA between O and A, and the only forces acting on P are the gravitational attractions towards O and A. Determine the position of the point B on OA at which the resultant force on P is zero.

The particle P is projected with speed u towards A from the point S on OA such that $OS = 1$ unit. In the subsequent motion the velocity of P is v when the displacement of P from O is x. Show that

$$v^2 = u^2 + GM \left(\frac{2}{9 - x} + \frac{8}{x} - \frac{33}{4} \right)$$

and deduce that, for P to reach B, u must not be less than $\dfrac{5}{2} \sqrt{(GM)}$.

SUMMARY EXERCISE

1   A particle moves in a straight line in such a way that its acceleration is $(2 - 2t)$ m s^{-2}, where t is the time in seconds. The velocity is 3 m s^{-1} when $t = 0$. Show that the particle comes instantaneously to rest when $t = 3$.

Find the distance moved between $t = 0$ and $t = 3$.

2   A particle P moves in a straight line. At time t seconds, the acceleration of P is e^{2t} m s^{-2}, $t \geq 0$. When $t = 0$, P is at rest. Show that the speed, v m s^{-1}, of P at time t seconds is given by

$$v = \frac{1}{2} (e^{2t} - 1)$$

3   A particle of mass 2 kg is acted on by a single force of magnitude $8x$ newtons, where x metres is its displacement from a fixed point O. The force is directed away from O. The particle is at rest when it is 2 m from O.

   (a)   Show that $v\dfrac{\mathrm{d}v}{\mathrm{d}x} = 4x$, where v m s^{-1} is the velocity of the particle when its displacement is x metres.

   (b)   Find v in terms of x.

4   A particle P, of mass m, moves along the x-axis under the action of a force directed towards the origin O. The magnitude of the force is mkx^2, where $OP = x$ and k is a positive constant. Given that P is initially at rest at the point C, where $x = c$, find:

   (a)   the speed of P when it first passes through O, giving your answer in terms of c and k,

   (b)   the work done by the force in moving P from C to O, giving your answer in terms of m, c and k.

5   A particle moves along the x-axis, with an acceleration in the positive x direction of

$$k\left[\frac{3a^2}{x^2} - 1\right] ,$$ where k and a are positive

constants. When $x = 2a$ the particle has a

speed $(ka)^{\frac{1}{2}}$ in the positive x direction. Find the speed of the particle in terms of x, a and k and determine the maximum and minimum values of x.

6   A particle of mass m moves along the positive x-axis under the action of a force directed towards the origin O and of magnitude F given by

$$F = \frac{km}{x^2},$$

where k is a constant. The points A, B and C lie on the positive x-axis at distances a, b and c from O, respectively, where $a < b < c$. Show that the work done against the force as the particle moves from A to B is

$$\frac{km(b-a)}{ab}.$$

Given that the particle is projected from A with speed $2u$ towards B and that it passes through B with speed u, find an expression for u in terms of k, a and b.

Given further that the particle comes to rest at C, find c in terms of a and b.

7   A particle of mass m is projected upwards from a point P on the earth's surface. It experiences a force, of magnitude $\dfrac{(mgR^2)}{x^2}$, directed towards the centre O of the earth, where R is the radius of the earth and x is the distance of the particle from O. Given that the particle is projected with speed $\sqrt{gR}$ in the direction OP, find how far it will have travelled when its speed is $\frac{1}{2}\sqrt{gR}$.

8   A particle moves on the positive x-axis. The particle is moving towards the origin O when it passes through the point A, where $x = 2a$, with speed $\sqrt{\left(\dfrac{k}{a}\right)}$, where k is constant. Given

that the particle experiences as acceleration

$\dfrac{k}{2x^2} + \dfrac{k}{4a^2}$ in a direction away from O, show that it comes instantaneously to rest at a point B, where $x = a$. Immediately the particle reaches B the acceleration changes to $\dfrac{k}{2x^2} - \dfrac{k}{4a^2}$ in a direction away from O. Show that the particle next comes instantaneously to rest at A. (Be careful with the signs in this one.)

9   A particle P moves on the x-axis under the action of a force of variable magnitude directed along the axis. At time t seconds the displacement of P from the origin O is x metres, and the velocity and acceleration of P, both in the positive x-direction, are v m s^{-1} and a m s^{-2} respectively.

   (a)   Given that $a = 6x - 4x^3$ and that, when $x = 1$, $v = 0$, show that v is also zero when $x = \sqrt{2}$.

   (b)   Given that $a = -v^4$ and that, when $t = 0$, $x = 0$ and $v = 2$, find x and t in terms of v.

      Show that the average speed $\Big($remember

that average speed $= \dfrac{\text{total distance}}{\text{total time}}\Big)$ over

the time interval in which v decreases from 2 to 1 is $\dfrac{9}{7}$ m s^{-1}.

10

O, B and A are three collinear points on a smooth horizontal table. $OB = 2$ m and $BA = 3$ m. A particle P, of mass 0.5 kg, is attracted towards O by a force of magnitude $\dfrac{k}{x^2}$ newtons, where the distance OP is x metres (see diagram) and k is a positive constant. P is released from rest at A and reaches a speed of 12 m s^{-1} at B.

Calculate the value of k.

SUMMARY

When you have finished, you should:

- be familiar with the general procedure for solving standard differential equations

- know which form of the acceleration to use, depending on the question

- know how to use the given expression for a force to set up and solve the corresponding differential equation

- know about proportional forces and the conditions under which a given force is negative

- be familiar with Newton's Gravitational Law.

ANSWERS

Practice questions A

1 53.9 m

2 (c) $\frac{52}{3}$

3 (a) 224 (b) $k = \frac{1}{2}$ (c) $245\frac{1}{3}$

4 (a) 10 (b) -0.015 m s^{-2} (c) $x = 1$

5 $v = \left[10x^2 - x^4 - 9 \right]^{\frac{1}{2}}$, 1, 3

6 (a) $v\frac{dv}{dx} = x^2 + 4$ (c) 55.8 J

Practice questions B

4 $x = 2$ m

5 20 m

6 $0.2\frac{dv}{dt} = 0.1 - 0.01t$, $v = 2.5$ m s^{-1}

8 $\frac{25}{x^2} = v\frac{dv}{dx}$

10 (b) $\frac{\lambda m}{3c}$

Practice questions C

1 (b) $v = \left[\frac{2gR^2}{x} - 2gR + u^2 \right]^{\frac{1}{2}}$

  (c) 1.1×10^4 m s^{-1}

2 Escapes gravitational field

3 $v^2 = u^2 + 2k\left(\frac{1}{x} - \frac{1}{a}\right)$, $\sqrt{\left(\frac{2k}{a}\right)}$

4 $OB = 6$ units

SECTION

2

Elastic strings and springs

INTRODUCTION

In the models we have used so far, we have assumed that any string is inextensible. We are going to extend this to include cases where the string or spring is elastic: the equations relating to this are derived from Hooke's Law. They will allow us to explore a variety of situations, both static and dynamic; we shall make frequent use of the principle of conservation of mechanical energy.

Hooke's Law

OCR M3 5.9.2 (a)

The fundamental law that applies in work on elastic strings is called **Hooke's Law** and states that the tension is directly proportional to the extension in the string; or in the case of a spring which is compressed, the thrust is directly proportional to the compression.

Hooke's Law

$$T = \frac{\lambda x}{l}$$

where x is the extension/compression, l the natural length
of the elastic string/spring
and λ is a constant for any particular string/spring
called the **modulus of elasticity**.

The equation $T = \frac{\lambda x}{l}$ enables us to find what **mass** suspended on one end of the string will cause a given **extension** and vice versa. Since the tension is directly proportional to the extension, twice the mass will produce twice the extension. Here are some examples which use the basic equation.

Example

An elastic string of natural length 2 m has a modulus of elasticity of $3g$ N. Find the extension when a particle of mass 4 kg is suspended from one end.

Solution

Look at Fig. 2.1.

Figure 2.1

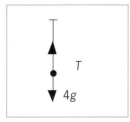

Since the system is in equilibrium,
$$T - 4g = 0 \implies T = 4g$$
But since $T = \frac{\lambda x}{l}$ and $\lambda = 3g$, $l = 2$
$$4g = \frac{3gx}{2} \implies x = \frac{8}{3}$$

17

Example	A mass of 4 kg suspended on one end of an elastic string produces an extension of 2 m. Find the modulus of elasticity if the natural length is 5 m.

Solution	$T = 4g$ and also $T = \dfrac{\lambda x}{l}$.

Since $x = 2$, and $l = 5$ (given), $4g = \dfrac{\lambda \times 2}{5}$

$\Rightarrow \lambda = 10g$, i.e. the modulus is $10g$ N

(Note that the units of the modulus are those of a force, i.e. Newtons)

Example	A spring of natural length 40 cm has been compressed to 30 cm. If the modulus of elasticity of the spring is 80 N, find the force required to maintain it in this position.

Solution	The thrust, $T = \dfrac{\lambda x}{l} = \dfrac{80 \times 0.1}{0.4} = 20$ N exerted by the spring, so we need a force of 20 N in opposition.

Let's have a look now at some questions involving slightly more complicated systems. Here's one where an elastic string passes over a smooth peg.

Example	A light elastic string, of natural length l and modulus of elasticity $4mg$, has one end tied to a fixed point A. The string passes over a fixed smooth peg B and at the other end a particle P, of mass m, is attached. The particle hangs in equilibrium. The distance between A and B is l and AB is inclined at 60° to the vertical as shown in Fig. 2.2.

Figure 2.2	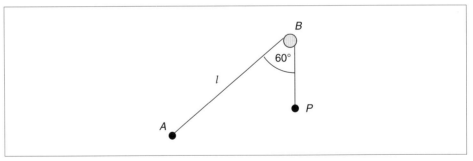

(a) Find, in terms of l, the length of the vertical portion BP of the string.

(b) Show that the magnitude of the force exerted by the string on the peg is $mg\sqrt{3}$.

Solution	(a) Since the peg is smooth, the tension will be the same on either side (see Fig. 2.3).

The system is in equilibrium, so the net force acting on the particle P must be zero, i.e.

$$T - mg = 0 \qquad\qquad \dots \text{①}$$

Figure 2.3

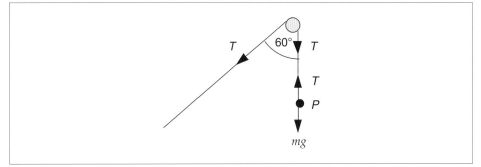

But since the string is elastic, natural length l and $\lambda = 4mg$,

$$T = \frac{\lambda x}{l} = \frac{4mgx}{l}$$ ... ②

Substituting this into ①, $\dfrac{4mgx}{l} - mg = 0$

$$mg\left(\frac{4x}{l} - 1\right) = 0 \quad \Rightarrow \quad \frac{4x}{l} - 1 = 0 \quad \text{since } mg \neq 0$$

$$\Rightarrow x = \frac{l}{4}$$

Since AB is l, the natural length, this extension of $\dfrac{l}{4}$ is the required

length BP.

(b) The force exerted by the string on the peg will be the resultant of the two equal tensions in each part of the string.

Figure 2.4

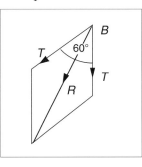

Resolving along the bisector of the angle at B,

$$R = 2T \cos 30° = 2T \times \frac{\sqrt{3}}{2} = T\sqrt{3}$$

But from ①, $T = mg \Rightarrow$ magnitude of the resultant is $mg\sqrt{3}$ as required.

Here are two further examples of a static situation before we look at systems which involve the calculation of the energy stored in an elastic string.

Example

Two light elastic strings AB and CD each have natural length l and an extension of $\dfrac{l}{2}$ is produced in each string by tensions mg and $2mg$ respectively. The strings are joined at their ends B and C and the end A is fastened to a fixed point. From the end D is hung a particle of mass m. Show that, when the mass m hangs at rest vertically below A, the total extension in the combined string $ABCD$ is $\dfrac{3l}{4}$.

Solution

We'll calculate the moduli of elasticity of each string first of all.

$AB:$ $T_1 = \dfrac{\lambda_1 x}{l} \Rightarrow mg = \dfrac{\dfrac{\lambda_1 l}{2}}{l} \Rightarrow \lambda_1 = 2mg$ ... ①

$CD:$ $T_2 = \dfrac{\lambda_2 x}{l} \Rightarrow 2mg = \dfrac{\dfrac{\lambda_2 l}{2}}{l} \Rightarrow \lambda_2 = 4mg$ ... ②

Figure 2.5

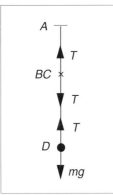

The point is that since the system is in equilibrium, the tension throughout the string is the same. Let this tension be T where $T = mg$.

To find the total extension, we'll find the extension in each part.

$AB:\ \ T = mg = \dfrac{\lambda_1 x_1}{l} = \dfrac{2mg\, x_1}{l}$ using ① $\Rightarrow x_1 = \dfrac{l}{2}$ ...③

$CD:\ \ T = mg = \dfrac{\lambda_2 x_2}{l} = \dfrac{4mg\, x_2}{l}$ using ② $\Rightarrow x_2 = \dfrac{l}{4}$ ... ④

From ③ and ④ the total extension $x_1 + x_2 = \dfrac{l}{2} + \dfrac{l}{4} = \dfrac{3l}{4}$

Example

A thin uniform rod AB, of length 3 m and mass 5 kg, is freely pivoted to a fixed point A. A light elastic string BC, of modulus 30 N, has one end C fixed to a point at the same level as A, where $AC = 5$ m. When the system is in equilibrium, $\angle ABC = 90°$. Calculate:

(a)   the tension, in N, in the string

(b)   the natural length of the string.

Solution

Look at Fig. 2.6

Figure 2.6

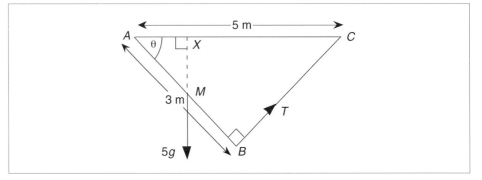

$\triangle ABC$ is $3 - 4 - 5$ and we can call the angle $B\hat{A}C$ θ.

Taking moments about the point A means that we don't have to worry about the reaction at the pivot. Since we are given that $A\hat{B}C = 90°$, the perpendicular distance of the line of action of the tension will be AB,
i.e. 3 m. We now need the perpendicular distance of the line of action of the weight of the rod from A, which is marked AX in the diagram. Since AM will be $\frac{1}{2}AB$ for a uniform rod, $AM = \frac{3}{2}$ m and $AX = \frac{3}{2}\cos\theta$.

Since from the triangle, $\cos\theta = \frac{3}{5}$, $AX = \frac{3}{2} \times \frac{3}{5} = \frac{9}{10}$.

Now we can take moments about A:

$$T \times 3 - 5g \times \frac{9}{10} = 0$$

(a) $3T = 5g \times \frac{9}{10} \Rightarrow 3T = 45$ (taking g to be 10 m s^{-2})

$\Rightarrow T = 15$ N

(b) $T = \frac{\lambda x}{l} \Rightarrow 15 = \frac{30x}{l} \Rightarrow x = \frac{l}{2}$

This is the extension, so the total stretched length, BC, will be $\frac{3l}{2}$.

Since $BC = 4$,

$$\frac{3l}{2} = 4 \Rightarrow l = \frac{8}{3} \text{ m}$$

Practice questions A

In the following questions, λ is the modulus of elasticity, x is the extension/compression and l the natural length

1   Find λ in terms of g when a light elastic string is extended by the given amount supporting a mass of:

(a)   2 kg with $x = 10$ cm, $l = 1$ m

(b)   500 g with $x = 5$ cm, $l = 80$ cm

(c)   80 g with $x = 2$ cm, $l = 40$ cm

(d)   5 kg with $x = 80$ cm, $l = 3.2$ m

2   Find the extension produced when the elastic string supports a mass of:

(a)   3 kg: $\lambda = 40g$ and $l = 0.8$ m

(b)   5m: $\lambda = 10mg$ and $l = 20$ cm

(c)   800 g: $\lambda = 2g$ and $l = 50$ cm

(d)   50 g: $\lambda = 0.5g$ and $l = 1.2$ m

3   A light elastic string of modulus $4g$ supports a mass of 2 kg and the *total* length of the stretched string is 2.4 m. Find the natural length.

4
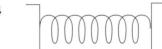

A light elastic spring of modulus of elasticity 80 N and natural length 20 cm is held horizontally in the jaws of a vice, as shown in the diagram. Given that the distance between the jaws is 16 cm, calculate the magnitude of the force exerted by each of the jaws on the spring.

5
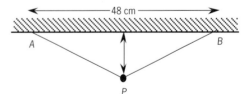

Two light elastic strings each have natural length 24 cm and modulus of elasticity λN. One end of each string is attached to a particle P of mass 0.6 kg, and the other ends are attached to two points A and B on a horizontal beam, where $AB = 48$ cm. The particle hangs in equilibrium, at a distance 10 cm vertically below the beam, as shown in the above figure.

Find the value of λ.

Energy stored in an elastic string

We have already seen how the **tension** in a stretched elastic string is given by the formula:

$$T = \frac{\lambda x}{l}$$

where λ is the modulus of elasticity of the string, x is the extension and l is the natural length.

A certain amount of **work** is necessary to produce this extension and so the **energy** that is stored in the stretched string must have the same magnitude as the work. To find the work done by a variable force, we integrate the force with respect to the distance,

$$\text{i.e. work done} = \text{energy stored} = \int F \, ds$$

Since the force is the tension and the distance expressed in x, the work done in extending from O to x is

$$\int_0^x T \, dx = \int_0^x \frac{\lambda x}{l} \, dx = \frac{\lambda x^2}{2l}$$

This is the result that we shall be using repeatedly in this section:

Energy stored in an elastic string is $\dfrac{\lambda x^2}{2l}$

This energy is termed the **elastic potential energy**, EPE, although it is often shortened to **elastic energy**, EE. When various energies are considered, what is normally termed the potential energy is more properly referred to as **gravitational potential energy**, GPE, to avoid confusion.

Example

Find the energy stored in a light elastic string of modulus $4g$ and natural length 80 cm when it supports a mass of 500 grams and rests in equilibrium.

Solution

We have to find the extension first of all:

$$T = 0.5g = \frac{\lambda x}{l} = \frac{4g \times x}{0.8}$$

$$\Rightarrow \quad 4gx = 0.4g$$

$$\Rightarrow \quad x = 0.1 \text{ m (or 10 cm)}$$

$$\text{Energy is } \frac{1}{2}\frac{\lambda}{l}x^2 = \frac{1}{2} \times \frac{4g}{0.8} \times 0.1^2 = 0.245 \text{ J}$$

Example

Find the work done on an elastic string of modulus 80 N and natural length 0.75 m by increasing the stretched length from 1 m to 1.15 m

---

Solution

Work done is the increase in stored energy. This is:

$$\frac{1}{2}\frac{\lambda}{l}\left(x_2^2 - x_1^2\right) = \frac{1}{2} \times \frac{80}{0.75}\left(0.4^2 - 0.25^2\right) = 5.2 \text{ J}$$

Practice questions B

1   An elastic string of natural length 1 m obeys Hooke's law. When it is stretched to 1.2 m the energy stored in it is 16 J. Find the energy stored in the string when it is stretched to 1.5 m.

2   An elastic string, of natural length 0.6 m, is stretched 8 cm by a mass of 1 kg hanging from it. Find the work done in stretching from a length of 0.65 to 0.7 m.

3   If it requires a force of 20 N to hold a certain spring compressed 1 cm, find how much work is required to compress it another centimetre.

4   One end of a light spring, of modulus of elasticity 50 N and natural length 0.1 m, is attached to a fixed point O of a horizontal table. A horizontal force is applied to the spring at its other end A, in the direction from O to A. Calculate:

  (a)   the elastic potential energy of the spring when its length is 0.25 m

  (b)   the length of the spring when the elastic potential energy is 4 times the value found in (a).

5   A light elastic string has natural length 10 m and modulus of elasticity 130 N. The ends of the string are attached to fixed points A and B, which are at the same horizontal level and 12.6 m apart.

  (a)   Calculate the tension in the string.

An object is attached to the mid-point of the string and hangs in equilibrium at a point 1.6 m below AB. Calculate:

  (b)   the elastic energy in the string when the object is in this position

  (c)   the weight of the object

6   One end of a light elastic spring of natural length 40 cm and modulus of elasticity 10 N is attached to a fixed point O. The spring hangs vertically below O with a particle of mass 0.36 kg attached to its lowest point. The particle hangs freely at rest. Calculate

  (a)   the extension of the spring

  (b)   the elastic potential energy of the spring.

7   One end of a light spring of natural length a and modulus of elasticity $2mg$ is fastened to a fixed point O. The spring hangs vertically and in equilibrium with a particle of mass m attached to its lower end. Write down an expression for the potential energy of the spring.

When a horizontal force F acts on the particle, the system is in equilibrium with the spring inclined at an angle of 45° to the vertical, the particle being below the level of O. Prove that the depth of the particle below O is then $\frac{1}{2} a (\sqrt{2} + 1)$ and that the total potential energy of the particle and the spring has been increased by $\frac{1}{4} mga (5 - 2\sqrt{2})$.

We're going to look now at systems which involve some movement.

Conservation of energy

OCR M3 5.9.2 (c)

If there are no external forces acting on a system and no friction or resistance to overcome, using energy to do so, no energy is lost, i.e. the total amount of energy remains the same. In the systems that we shall be looking at there are three types of energy making up the total energy:

● **kinetic energy**, from the movement of the mass(es)

● **potential energy**, from the position of the mass(es)

● **elastic energy**, stored in the stretched elastic string.

So by the principle of conservation of energy:

> The sum of the kinetic, potential and elastic energies
> at any position of the system is constant.

In practice, we make a table giving these energies at the positions we are interested in and use the principle above to set up our equation(s) in the unknown(s). Let's take a simple example and see how this works.

| **Example** | A particle of mass 2 kg is attached to one end of an elastic string of natural length 2 m and modulus of elasticity 19.6 N. The other end of the elastic string is attached to the point A. If the particle is released from rest at the point A, find the greatest distance it will reach vertically below A. (Take g to be 9.8 m s^{-2}.) |

| **Solution** | When the particle is at A, it is stationary and so it has no kinetic energy. The string is not stretched and so there is no elastic energy stored in the string. Finally, if we take A to be the level from which to measure the potential energy, there will be no potential energy either. |

Figure 2.7

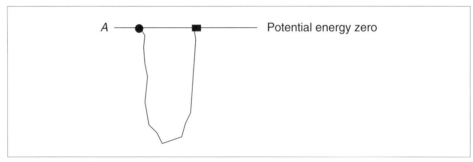

Our table for the energies is very simple!

	KE	PE	EE	Sum
At A	0	0	0	0

Now when the particle is released, it will increase in speed until it reaches the natural length of the string. From then on, there will be an increasing force from the tension in the stretched string which opposes the motion and eventually will bring the particle to a stop. This is the greatest distance it will fall below A – the tension then produces a movement upwards towards A again. To find this greatest distance we find what the energies will be at the instant when the particle comes temporarily to rest – we can call the point it reaches D and the distance AD we can call d.

Figure 2.8

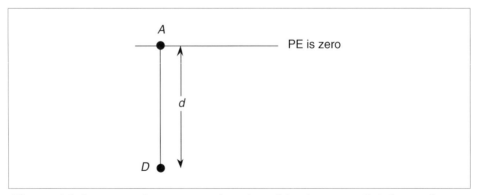

The particle is once again at rest, so there is no kinetic energy. It is **lower** than the zero level at A, so it has **lost** potential energy of magnitude $mgh = 2gd$ in this case. The string has a natural length of 2 m, so a distance of d between its ends represents an extension of $(d - 2)$, and so the elastic energy stored is:

$$\frac{\lambda x^2}{2l} = \frac{19.6 \times (d-2)^2}{4}$$

Our table of energies would be

	KE	PE	EE
At D	0	$-2gd$	$\dfrac{19.6 \times (d-2)^2}{4}$

and the sum of these must be the same as the sum at A, i.e. zero

$$-2gd + \frac{19.6 \times (d-2)^2}{4} = 0$$

$$\frac{19.6(d-2)^2}{4} = 2gd \qquad \text{rearranging}$$

$$(d-2)^2 = \frac{2 \times 9 \cdot 8 \times d \times 4}{19 \cdot 6}$$

i.e. $d^2 - 4d + 4 = 4d$

$d^2 - 8d + 4 = 0$

$$d = \frac{8 \pm \sqrt{64-16}}{2} = 4 \pm \sqrt{12} = 4 \pm 2\sqrt{3}$$

If we take d to be $4 - 2\sqrt{3}$, it would mean that the distance fallen is less than the natural length of the string, which cannot be true. So the greatest distance below A is $(4 + 2\sqrt{3})$ m.

Here is another example with a particle being projected vertically upwards instead of dropping downwards.

Example

A light elastic string of natural length 5 m and modulus 4 N has one end fixed to a point O on level ground. To the other end of the string is attached a ball of mass 0.5 kg, which is projected vertically upwards from O with speed u m s^{-1}.

(a) Find u, given that the ball first comes to instantaneous rest when it reaches a height of 10 m above the ground.

(b) Given that the coefficient of restitution between the ball and the ground is 0.6, show that, after the first bounce at O, the string does not become taut.

Solution

We can fix the zero potential level at ground level, so that if the particle is above this level it has positive potential energy.

So initially, at ground level:

KE	PE	EE	Sum
$\frac{1}{2}mu^2$	0	0	$\frac{1}{2}mu^2$

When it has reached a height of 10 m above the ground,

Figure 2.9

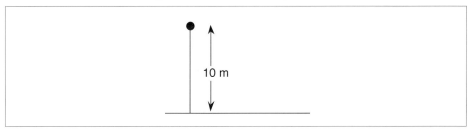

it comes to rest so its kinetic energy is zero. It has **gained** potential energy, $mgh = 0.5 \times g \times 10 = 5g$. It has also **gained** elastic energy. Since the string has a natural length of 5 m, a difference of 10 m between its ends means an extension of 5 m. Then the elastic energy, $\dfrac{1}{2}\dfrac{\lambda x^2}{l} = \dfrac{1}{2} \times \dfrac{4 \times 5^2}{5} = 10$ J

The sum of these energies is $5g + 10$ and since the initial sum of the energies was $\frac{1}{2}mu^2$,

$$\frac{1}{2}mu^2 = 5g + 10 = 59 \quad \text{(taking } g = 9.8 \text{ m s}^{-2}\text{)}$$

$$\Rightarrow u^2 = 4 \times 59 \Rightarrow u = 15.4 \text{ m s}^{-1} \text{ (1 d.p.)}$$

When it returns to ground level it will have this same velocity (only downwards) immediately **before** impact. Immediately **after** impact, its speed will be speed before $\times e = 15.4 \times 0.6 = 9.2$ m s^{-1} (1 d.p.) and so its kinetic energy will be $\frac{1}{2}mv^2 = 21.2$ J (1 d.p.).

In order to change all this kinetic energy to potential energy the particle would have to be at a height h given by

$$mgh = 21.2 \Rightarrow h = \frac{21.2}{mg} = 4.3 \text{ m}$$

At this height, all its kinetic energy would be exhausted, and since the natural length of the string 5 m, is more that this, it would not become taut.

Practice questions C

1 A light elastic string has natural length 1.25 m and modulus of elasticity λ newtons. One end of the string is attached to a fixed point A, and a particle of mass 0.4 kg is attached to the other end. The particle is held at A and is released from rest. It then falls vertically and comes to instantaneous rest at a distance 2 m below A. It may be assumed that any effect of air resistance is negligible.

Using the principle of conservation of energy, or otherwise, find, to 3 significant figures, the value of λ.

2 A particle of mass 0.4 kg is attached to a fixed point O by a light elastic string of natural length 4 m and modulus of elasticity 60 N. The particle is released from rest at O and is allowed to fall freely. Find, correct to 2 decimal places, the length of the string when the particle is at its lowest point.

3 A particle of mass 0.5 kg is suspended from a fixed point O by a light elastic string of natural length 1.5 m and modulus of elasticity 40 N. The particle is released from rest at the point A, which is vertically below O and such that $OA = 1.5$ m. Using the principle of conservation of energy, find the distance

below A at which the particle comes instantaneously to rest for the first time.

4 A particle P of mass m is attached to a fixed point O by a light elastic string of natural length $4a$ and modulus $4mg$. The particle is released from rest at O and allowed to fall freely.

(a) Find the length of the string when P is at its lowest point.

(b) Show that the maximum speed of P occurs when the string has length $5a$. (This is when P passes through the equilibrium position, i.e. when $T = mg$.)

5 One end of a light elastic string of modulus λ is attached to a fixed point A, and the other end is attached to a particle of mass m. The unstretched length of the string is a, and the particle hangs freely in equilibrium at a point B which is at a distance $\frac{5}{4}a$ below A. Prove that

$$\lambda = 4mg.$$

The particle is held at A, and released from rest. Find its velocity as it passes B, and the total distance it falls before coming instantaneously to rest.

6 One end of a light elastic string of natural length l and modulus $4mg$ is attached to a fixed point O. The other end is attached to a particle P of mass m. The particle is projected vertically downwards from O with speed $\sqrt{(4gl)}$. By using the principle of conservation of energy, or otherwise, find the speed of P when P is at a depth x below O, where $x > l$, and show that the greatest depth below O attained by P is $5l/2$. Find also the maximum value of the speed.

Show that the particle subsequently rises to a maximum height $3l/2$ above O.

7

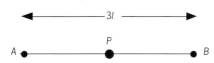

The ends of a light elastic string, of natural length $2l$ and modulus of elasticity λ, are attached to fixed points A and B, where AB is horizontal and $AB = 3l$. A particle P, of mass m, is attached to the mid-point of the string, as shown in the above figure. The particle is held at rest with the string horizontal and is then released. In the subsequent motion air resistance may be neglected.

The particle falls a distance $2l$ before first coming instantaneously to rest.

(a) Show that $\lambda = mg$.

(b) Find the magnitude of the acceleration of P when it first comes to instantaneous rest.

Catapults

OCR M3 5.9.2 (c)

The stored energy in an elastic string can be used to impart kinetic energy to a suitable object, as anyone who has used a catapult could tell you. The system is usually taken to be horizontal and so we have quite a simple conversion from elastic potential to kinetic energies.

Example

Figure 2.10

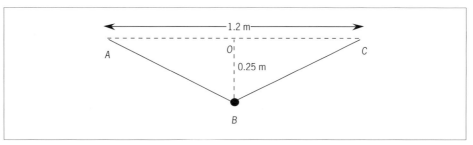

A light elastic string of natural length 1 m has its ends fixed at points A and C on a smooth horizontal plane, where $AC = 1.2$ m. The mid-point B of the string is pulled horizontally in a direction perpendicular to AC, through a distance of 0.25 m. A particle of mass 0.02 kg rests on the plane and is in contact with the string at B (see diagram). The particle and the string are released from rest. The particle remains in contact with the string at B until it reaches O, the mid-point of AC. At this point the speed of the particle is 70 m s^{-1}. Find the modulus of elasticity of the string.

Solution

See Fig. 2.11 on the next page. Note that in the equilibrium position, i.e. when the elastic string is in a straight line between A and C, there is still an extension and so some EPE: the kinetic energy gained is then equated to the difference, i.e. the loss of EPE.

Figure 2.11

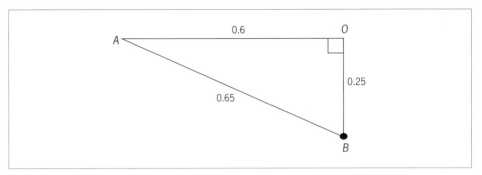

By Pythagoras, $AB = 0.65$ m, and so EPE is $\frac{1}{2} \times \frac{\lambda}{1} \times (2 \times 0.65 - 1)^2$

i.e. $\frac{\lambda \times 0.09}{2}$. When AC is straight, EPE is $\frac{\lambda}{2}(1.2 - 1)^2$

i.e. $\frac{\lambda \times 0.04}{2} \Rightarrow$ loss in EPE is $\frac{\lambda \times (0.09 - 0.04)}{2} = \frac{\lambda \times 0.05}{2}$

Gain in KE is $\frac{1}{2}mv^2 = \frac{1}{2} \times 0.02 \times 70^2 = \frac{\lambda \times 0.05}{2} \Rightarrow \lambda = 1960$ N

Particle on a plane

OCR M3 5.9.2 (c)

Exactly the same principle of conservation of energy applies if the particle, instead of falling vertically downwards, slides down an inclined plane. You have to be careful with the **potential** energy – the h in the formula mgh refers to the **vertical** height and not the distance down the face of the plane. Let's have a look at an example of this.

Example

One end of a light elastic string of modulus $20mg$ and natural length a is attached to a point A on the surface of a smooth plane inclined at an angle of $30°$ to the horizontal. The other end is attached to a particle P of mass m. Initially P is held at rest at A and then released so that it slides down a line of greatest slope of the plane. By use of conservation of energy, or otherwise, show that the speed v of P when $AP = x$, $(x > a)$, is given by

$$v^2 = \frac{g}{a}(41ax - 20a^2 - 20x^2).$$

(a) Find the maximum value of v in the subsequent motion.

(b) Find the maximum value of x in the subsequent motion.

Solution

Fig. 2.12 illustrates this set-up.

Figure 2.12

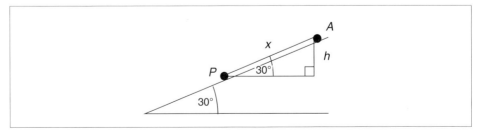

From the right-angled triangle we can find an expression for h, the vertical height fallen, in terms of x, the distance along the plane from A:

$$\sin 30° = \frac{h}{x} \Rightarrow h = x \sin 30° = \frac{x}{2}$$

If we call the potential energy at A zero, then each of the kinetic, potential and elastic energies are zero at A and so at any other point, the sum of these energies must also be zero.

If we call the speed of the particle at P, v, then its kinetic energy at this point will be $\frac{1}{2}mv^2$. There will have been a **loss** of potential energy of magnitude

$mgh = mg\dfrac{x}{2}$ where x is the distance along the plane.

The extension in the string at this point will be $x - a$, where a is the natural length of the string, and so the elastic energy stored in the string will be:

$$\frac{1}{2}\lambda \frac{\text{Extension}^2}{l} \quad \text{i.e.} \quad \frac{1}{2} \times \frac{20mg\,(x-a)^2}{a}$$

The sum of these three energies is zero, i.e.

$$\frac{1}{2}mv^2 - \frac{mgx}{2} + \frac{10mg\,(x-a)^2}{a} = 0$$

Rearranging, and dividing through by m,

$$\frac{1}{2}v^2 \ = \frac{gx}{2} - 10g\,\frac{(x-a)^2}{a}$$

$\times\, 2$ and collecting

$$v^2 \ = g\left[x - 20\frac{(x-a)^2}{a}\right] = \frac{g}{a}\left[ax - 20(x-a)^2\right]$$

$$= \frac{g}{a}\left[ax - 20x^2 + 40ax - 20a^2\right]$$

$$= \frac{g}{a}\left[41ax - 20a^2 - 20x^2\right] \qquad \ldots \,①$$

(a) We want to find the maximum value for v, so we want to find the value of x which makes $\dfrac{dv}{dx}$ zero. If we differentiate equation ① with respect to x, we get

$$2v\frac{dv}{dx} = \frac{g}{a}\left[41a - 40x\right] \quad (a \text{ is constant})$$

and if $\dfrac{dv}{dx}$ is zero, $41a - 40x = 0 \Rightarrow x = \dfrac{41a}{40}$

Putting this value of x into ①,

$$v^2 \ = \frac{g}{a}\left[\frac{(41a)^2}{40} - 20a^2 - 20\left(\frac{41a}{40}\right)^2\right] = \frac{g}{a}\left[\frac{(41a)^2}{40} - 20a^2 - \frac{(41a)^2}{80}\right]$$

$$= \frac{g}{a}\left[\frac{(41a)^2}{80} - 20a^2\right] = \frac{g}{a}\left[\frac{(41a)^2 - 1600a^2}{80}\right]$$

$$= \frac{g \times 81a^2}{80a} = \frac{81ag}{80}$$

Then maximum value of v is $\sqrt{\left(\dfrac{81ag}{80}\right)} = \dfrac{9}{4}\sqrt{\left(\dfrac{ag}{5}\right)}$

(b) The maximum value of x occurs when the **velocity** is zero, i.e. when

$$\frac{g}{a}(41ax - 20a^2 - 20x^2) = 0 \quad \Rightarrow 20x^2 - 41ax + 20a^2 = 0$$

$$(5x - 4a)(4x - 5a) = 0 \quad \Rightarrow x = \frac{4a}{5} \text{ or } x = \frac{5a}{4}$$

since we know that $x > a$, $\quad x = \frac{5a}{4}$

Springs

OCR M3 5.9.2 (c)

The formulae for the tension and the stored energy in an elastic string are also true for springs except that the quantity x, which was just the extension in the elastic string, can now be either the **extension** or the **compression** in the spring. The working in the case of an extension of a spring is exactly the same as that of a string. Here's an example where the spring is compressed.

Example

A trolley of mass m runs down a smooth track of constant inclination $\frac{\pi}{6}$ to the horizontal, carrying at its front a light spring of natural length a and modulus $\frac{mga}{c}$, where c is constant. When the spring is fully compressed it is of length $\frac{a}{4}$, and it obeys Hooke's law up to this point. After the trolley has travelled a distance b from rest the spring meets a fixed stop. Show that, when the spring has been compressed a distance x, where $x < \frac{3a}{4}$, the speed v of the trolley is given by:

$$\frac{cv^2}{g} = c(b + x) - x^2.$$

Given that $c = \frac{a}{10}$ and $b = 2a$, find the total distance covered by the trolley before it momentarily comes to rest for the first time.

Solution

At the start of the motion, the kinetic and elastic energies are zero, and so if we take this to be the level from which we measure the potential energy, the total of the three energies will be zero.

Figure 2.13

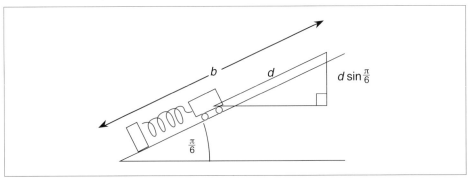

When it has travelled a distance d down the slope, the corresponding vertical distance is $d \sin\frac{\pi}{6} = \frac{d}{2}$ and so the loss in potential energy in this case will be $\frac{mgd}{2}$.

It meets the stop after it has travelled a distance of b down the slope and the spring is then compressed a further distance x, so the total distance travelled down the slope is $b + x$.

This means a loss in potential energy of $\dfrac{mg(b + x)}{2}$ from the result in the previous paragraph with $d = b + x$.

The gain in elastic potential energy is $\dfrac{1}{2} \times \dfrac{x^2}{l}$, i.e. $\dfrac{1}{2} \times \dfrac{mga}{c} \times \dfrac{x^2}{a} = \dfrac{mgx^2}{2c}$.

The gain in kinetic energy is $\dfrac{1}{2}mv^2$, and so, using the fact that the sum of the energies is zero,

$$-\dfrac{mg(b + x)}{2} + \dfrac{mgx^2}{2c} + \dfrac{mv^2}{2} = 0$$

Rearranging, $\qquad \dfrac{v^2}{2} = \dfrac{g(b + x)}{2} - \dfrac{gx^2}{2c} \qquad$ multiplying by $\dfrac{2c}{g}$

$$\dfrac{cv^2}{g} = c(b + x) - x^2$$

When it comes to rest, $v = 0 \implies c(b + x) - x^2 = 0$.

$c = \dfrac{a}{10}$ and $b = 2a \implies \dfrac{a}{10}(2a + x) - x^2 = 0$

$2a^2 + ax - 10x^2 = 0$

$10x^2 - ax - 2a^2 = 0$

$(5x + 2a)(2x - a) = 0 \implies x = \dfrac{a}{2}$, taking the positive solution,

and total distance, $b + x$ is $\dfrac{5a}{2}$

Practice questions D

1

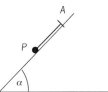

One end of a light elastic string, of natural length 1.5 m and modulus of elasticity 30 N, is attached to a fixed point A of an inclined plane. The other end of the string is attached to a particle P of weight 25 N which lies on the plane. The plane makes an angle α with the horizontal, where

$\tan \alpha = \dfrac{3}{4}$, and the string is parallel to a line of greatest slope of the plane (see diagram). The coefficient of friction between P and the plane is 0.15.

(a) P is in equilibrium, and the extension of the string is x metres. Find the greatest and least possible values of x.

(b) P is released from rest in the position where $AP = 2$ m. By considering energy and work, find the distance AP when P first comes to rest.

SUMMARY EXERCISE

1 Find the extension when a particle of mass 2 kg is suspended on one end of an elastic string of natural length 3 m and modulus of elasticity $12g$ N.

2 Find the modulus of elasticity of an elastic string of natural length 0.5 m if a mass of 500 g suspended on one end produces an extension of 0.05 m.

3 The figure shows an elastic string AB, of natural length $4l$. The end A is fixed and the other end B carries a particle of mass m. The particle is held at a horizontal distance $4l$ from the vertical through A by a horizontal force kmg, which acts in the vertical plane through the stretched string.

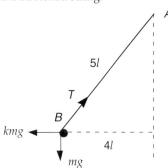

When the particle rests in this position, the length of the string is $5l$. Show that the modulus of elasticity of the string is $\dfrac{20mg}{3}$ and calculate the tension in the string and the numerical value of k.

4 Two light elastic strings AB and CD, each with the same natural length c, have moduli of elasticity $9mg$ and $12mg$ respectively. The ends B and C are joined together, the end A is tied at a fixed point and a particle of mass M is attached to D. The particle hangs in equilibrium with the strings vertical. Find, in terms of c the length of AD.

5 A light elastic string, of natural length c and modulus of elasticity $4\,mg$, is attached at one end to a fixed point A. A particle of mass m is tied to the other end B of the string.
(a) If the particle hangs in equilibrium, calculate the length AB of the extended string.
(b) If the particle is held at A and allowed to fall vertically, use the principle of conservation of energy to find the greatest distance between A and B in the ensuing motion.

6 A particle of mass m is suspended from a fixed point O by a light elastic string of natural length l. When the mass is hanging freely at rest the length of the string is $\dfrac{13l}{12}$. The particle is allowed to fall from rest at O. Find the greatest extension of the string in the subsequent motion. Show that the maximum kinetic energy of the particle during this fall occurs when it passes through the equilibrium position.

7 One end of a light elastic string, of natural length a and modulus of elasticity $3mg$, is fixed at a point A and the other end carries a particle P of mass m. The particle is held at A and then projected vertically down with speed $\sqrt{3ga}$. Find the distance AP when the acceleration of the particle is instantaneously zero.

Find also the maximum speed attained by the particle during its motion.

8 Show that the work done in stretching a light elastic string by a length x from its natural length a is $\tfrac{1}{2}Tx$,

where T is the final tension in the string.
One end A of a light elastic string AB of natural length a is attached to a fixed point at a height $a + b$ above a horizontal floor, where $b > 0$. To the other end B is attached a small spherical ball of mass m.
The modulus of elasticity of the string is $\dfrac{mga}{b}$.

(a) Show that in equilibrium under gravity the ball is just in contact with the floor.
(b) The ball is released from rest at A. Show that it strikes the floor with speed v, given by
$$v^2 = (2a + b)g.$$

When the ball strikes the floor the elastic string breaks and the ball rebounds to a height a.

(c) Find, in terms of a and b, the coefficient of restitution between the ball and the floor.

9 A particle P of mass m lies at rest at a point A on a rough horizontal table. The particle is attached to one end of a light elastic spring of natural length a and modulus of elasticity $2mg$. The other end of the spring is attached to a fixed point O of the table. The coefficient of friction between P and the table is μ.

Given that P remains at rest when $OA = \dfrac{7}{8}a$,

(a) show that $\mu \geq \dfrac{1}{4}$.

P is now moved along the table towards O until $OP = \dfrac{1}{2}a$ and released from rest.

(b) Given that $\mu = \dfrac{3}{8}$, find, in terms of a, how far P moves before first coming to rest again.

10

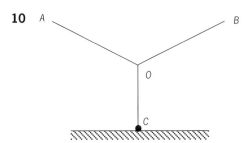

The diagram shows three identical elastic strings OA, OB and OC, each of natural length a and modulus λ. The strings are joined at O, and A and B are fixed to points in a horizontal line at a distance $2a$ apart. String OC is vertical and has a particle of mass m attached to the end C. The system is in equilibrium with the particle resting in a horizontal table.

Given that OA and OB are each inclined at $60°$ to the vertical, show that

(a) the magnitudes of the tension in each string are equal

(b) $OA = \dfrac{2a}{\sqrt{3}}$

(c) the magnitude of the tension in each string is equal to

$$\dfrac{\lambda(2 - \sqrt{3})}{\sqrt{3}}.$$

Find, in terms of m, g and λ, an expression for the magnitude of the reaction exerted on the particle by the table.

Deduce that $\lambda \leq \dfrac{mg\sqrt{3}}{2 - \sqrt{3}}$.

11 A climber of mass M kg falls vertically from a climbing wall. He is fastened to one end of an elastic rope which has natural length 4 m and modulus of elasticity $12Mg$ newtons. He falls from rest at the point where the rope is attached to the climbing wall. The climber is modelled as a particle and the rope is modelled as a light string. It is assumed that the only forces acting on the particle are its weight and the force due to tension. Given that the climber does not reach the ground,

(a) find, in m, how far he falls before coming momentarily to rest.

(b) Find, in m, the extension of the rope when the tension in the rope is Mg newtons.

(c) Find his speed at the instant when the tension in the rope is Mg newtons, giving your answer in m s^{-1} to 3 s.f.

(d) State one physical force that has been ignored in this model.

12 A small catapult consists of a light elastic string fastened to two fixed points A and B, with the line AB horizontal and the distance $AB = 30$ cm. The natural length of the string is 20 cm. When the string forms a straight line between A and B, the tension in the strength is 150 N.

(a) Find, in N, the modulus of elasticity of the string.

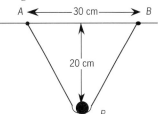

A small light leather pouch P is fixed to the mid point of the string. The pouch is now pulled back horizontally a distance of 20 cm in a direction perpendicular to AB, so that A, B and P all lie in the same horizontal plane. The above figure shows a view of the catapult *from above*.

(b) Find the magnitude of the horizontal force required to hold the pouch in equilibrium in this position.

A small stone of mass 0.1 kg is placed in the pouch and held in the position shown in the figure. The pouch is then released from this position. By considering the energy of the system

(c) find, in m s^{-1}, the horizontal speed which the stone has when it crosses the line AB.

(Any vertical motion of the stone can be assumed to be so small that it may be neglected.)

13 A small cubical block of mass $8m$ is attached to one end A of a light elastic spring AB of natural length $3a$ and modulus of elasticity $6mg$. The spring and block are at rest on a smooth horizontal table with AB equal to $3a$ and lying perpendicularly to the face to which A is attached. A second block of equal physical dimensions, but of mass m, moving with a speed $(2ga)^{\frac{1}{2}}$ in the direction parallel to BA impinges on the free end B of the spring.

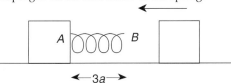

Assuming that the heavier block is held fixed and that AB remains straight and horizontal in the subsequent motion, determine the maximum compression of the spring.

33

SUMMARY When you have finished, you should:

- know the formula for the tension or thrust in an elastic string/spring

- be able to use this to find unknowns in related situations

- know the formula for the elastic potential energy in an elastic string/spring

- know how to relate this to work done in increasing this energy

- know that the sum of EPE, GPE and KE is constant if no external force, e.g. air resistance, is acting

- relate this to examples where particles are allowed to fall or are projected upwards on one end of an elastic string or spring

- know that the maximum velocity in such a fall occurs when the particle passes through the static equilibrium position

- be able to find the speed of a particle attained by the release of EPE.

ANSWERS

Practice questions A

1 (a) $20g$ (b) $8g$ (c) $1.6g$ (d) $20g$

2 (a) 6 cm   (b) 10 cm   (c) 20 cm   (d) 12 cm

3 1.6 m

4 16 N

5 91.7 N (3 s.f.)

Practice questions B

1 100 J

2 0.46 J

3 0.3 J

4 (a) 5.625 J (b) 0.4 m

5 (a) 33.8 N   (b) 58.5 J (c) 19.2 N

6 (a) 14 cm (nearest)   (b) 0.25 J

7 $\frac{1}{4}mga$

Practice questions C

1 34.8 N

2 5.73 m

3 37 cm (nearest)

4 (a) $8a$

5 $\frac{3}{2}\sqrt{ga}$, $2a$

6 $\sqrt{\left(10\,gx - \frac{4gx^2}{l}\right)}$, $\frac{5}{2}\sqrt{gl}$

7 (b) $\frac{7g}{5}$

Practice questions D

1 (a) 0.9 m and 0.6 m   (b) $AP = 2.2$ m

3

Further dynamics

INTRODUCTION In the first section we looked at the motion of particles when the acting force was a function of the velocity or distance. We are now going to look in some detail at one particular example of this where the force is proportional to the distance of the particle from a central point and is always directed towards this point. This type of motion is called Simple Harmonic Motion and is the underlying structure behind very many naturally occurring phenomena.

What is simple harmonic motion?

OCR M3 5.9.6 (a)

When a particle is fastened to one end of an elastic string (the other end of which is fixed), it will rest in an equilibrium position when lowered slowly.

Figure 3.1

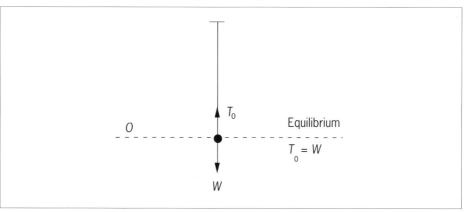

If the particle is moved away from this position, the two forces produce a resultant force which tends to bring it back. See Fig. 3.2.

Figure 3.2

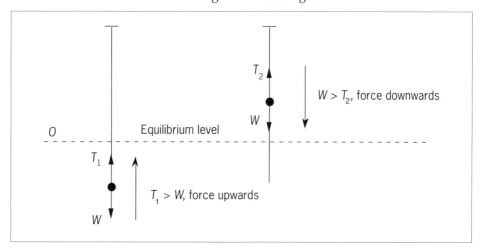

Taking displacements to be positive above the equilibrium level and negative below, we can see that the force is upwards (positive) when the displacement is negative and downwards (negative) when the displacement is positive. In fact, as we will show later, the force is directly proportional to the displacement away from the central point and since it has the opposite sign to the displacement , we can write

Force = $-kx$

where k is a positive constant and x is the displacement. Since force is mass × acceleration, we can use the form $\dfrac{d^2x}{dt^2}$ for the acceleration and write

$$-kx = m\,\frac{d^2x}{dt^2}$$

$$\Rightarrow \frac{d^2x}{dt^2} = -\frac{k}{m}\,x$$

It turns out, since we shall be taking square roots later on, that the most convenient form for the positive constant $\dfrac{k}{m}$ is ω^2, and so we then have:

$$\frac{d^2x}{dt^2} = -\omega^2 x$$

This is the defining equation for this particular type of motion, called *Simple Harmonic Motion* (written SHM from now on). We shall be looking a little later on at the typical systems which have this type of motion, but for the moment we shall take this equation which relates the acceleration and distance and see what relationships we can deduce between these and the other variables, velocity and time.

Speed at any point

OCR M3 5.9.6 (a)

Since the force acting on the particle is always directed towards O, the central point of the motion, the speed of the particle starts to decrease as soon as it passes O. At some point it will come to instantaneous rest and start back towards the centre, pass through this, slow down and stop and so on.

In this way it oscillates about the central point O, reaching a maximum positive position of a and a minimum position of $-a$ relative to O. This maximum displacement a from the central point is called the amplitude.

Figure 3.3

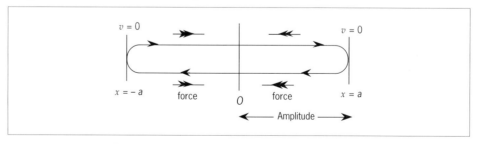

To find a relationship between the velocity and displacement we are going to write $v\,\dfrac{dv}{dx}$ in place of the acceleration $\dfrac{d^2x}{dt^2}$ in the defining equation, which becomes:

$$v\,\frac{dv}{dx} = -\omega^2 x$$

i.e. $\displaystyle\int v\,dv = \int -\omega^2 x\,dx$

$\Rightarrow \quad \dfrac{v^2}{2} = -\omega^2\,\dfrac{x^2}{2} + C$ ... ①

For our pair of values of v and x, we know that the particle is temporarily at rest at the greatest positive distance, i.e. $x = a$. Putting these values into ①

$$0 = -\frac{\omega^2 a^2}{2} + C \;\Rightarrow\; C = \frac{\omega^2 a^2}{2} \qquad \text{and ① becomes}$$

$$\frac{v^2}{2} = \frac{-\omega^2 x^2}{2} + \frac{\omega^2 a^2}{2} \qquad\qquad \text{$\times$ by 2 and factorising,}$$

$$v^2 = \omega^2(a^2 - x^2)$$

From this equation, we can see that the maximum speed occurs when $x = 0$, i.e. the particle is at O, and then $v^2 = \omega^2 a^2$,

$$V_{max} = \omega a$$

Example

A particle is moving with SHM and has acceleration 2.4 m s^{-2} when at a distance of 0.6 m from its mean position O. If the amplitude is 1.5 m, find:

(a) the speed when the particle is 1.2 m from O

(b) the distance from O when its velocity is 2.4 m s^{-1}

(c) the maximum speed

(d) the magnitude of the maximum acceleration.

Solution

We are given that $a = 1.5$ and the acceleration is $+2.4$ m s^{-2} when $x = -0.6$ m (opposite sign, so negative).

Using $\quad \dfrac{d^2 x}{dt^2} = -\omega^2 x \qquad$ with $\quad \dfrac{d^2 x}{dt^2} = 2.4$ and $x = -0.6$

$$2.4 = -\omega^2 \times (-0.6)$$
$$\omega^2 = 4 \;\Rightarrow\; \omega = 2 \quad (\text{since } \omega \geq 0)$$

(a) Using the equation $\quad v^2 = \omega^2\,(a^2 - x^2)$, with $\omega = 2$, $a = 1.5$ and $x = 1.2$

$$v^2 = 2^2\,(1.5^2 - 1.2^2)$$
$$= 3.24 \;\Rightarrow\; v = 1.8 \text{ m s}^{-1}$$

(b) Same equation, with $v = 2.4$, $\omega = 2$ and $a = 1.5$

$$2.4^2 = 2^2\,(1.5^2 - x^2)$$
$$x^2 = 1.5^2 - 1.2^2 \;\Rightarrow\; x = \pm\,0.9 \text{ m s}^{-1}$$

(Can be to the left or right of 0, moving in a positive direction.)

(c) maximum speed is $\omega a = 2 \times 1.5 = 3$ m s^{-1}

(d)   maximum acceleration at the extreme positions of the motion, i.e. $x = \pm a$

Using $\dfrac{\mathrm{d}^2 x}{\mathrm{d}t^2} = -\omega^2 x,$

magnitude of maximum acceleration is $\left| -\left(2^2\right) \times 1.5 \right| = 6 \text{ m s}^{-2}.$

Practice questions A

1   A particle moving with SHM has a maximum speed of 1.8 m s^{-1} and the acceleration is 5.4 m s^{-2} when the distance from the central point 0 is 0.6. Find:

(a) ω

(b)   the amplitude a

(c)   the speed when $x = 0.36$ m

(d)   the distance from 0 when the speed is 1.08 m s^{-1}

(e)   the acceleration when $x = 0.2$ m.

2   A particle is moving with SHM and at a particular instant the displacement, velocity and acceleration are respectively

7.5 cm, 7.5 cm s^{-1}, 7.5 cm s^{-2}

Find:

(a) ω

(b) a

(c)   the maximum speed (to 2 d.p.)

3   A particle is moving with SHM and has speeds of 1.2 m s^{-1} and 0.9 m s^{-1} when at distances of 0.9 m and 1.2 m from the central point 0. Find:

(a)   the amplitude a

(b) ω

(c)   the magnitude of the maximum acceleration.

Velocity and displacement at any time

OCR M3 5.9.6 (a)

If we take the square root of the equation:

$$v^2 = \omega^2 (a^2 - x^2)$$

we have $v = \pm \omega \sqrt{(a^2 - x^2)}$

and writing v as $\dfrac{\mathrm{d}x}{\mathrm{d}t}$ we have the differential equations:

$$\frac{\mathrm{d}x}{\mathrm{d}t} = \pm \omega \sqrt{(a^2 - x^2)}$$

The solution of these equations is beyond the scope of our technique at the moment (it is covered in Unit P4). We can show that it leads to:

$$\frac{x}{a} = \sin (\omega t + C) \text{ for the positive square root}$$

and $\dfrac{x}{a} = \cos (\omega t + C)$ for the negative square root.

Since generally we measure the time either from when the particle is at the centre of the motion, i.e. $x = 0$ or at one extreme position, i.e. $x = a$, the value of C in both cases turns out to be zero. We then have the pair of equations:

$x = a \sin \omega t$	(starting at $x = 0$)
and	
$x = a \cos \omega t$	(starting at $x = a$)

Differentiating these for the velocity at any time

$$v = a\omega \cos \omega t \qquad \text{(starting at } x = 0)$$

$$\text{and}$$

$$v = -a\omega \sin \omega t \qquad \text{(starting at } x = a)$$

Note that the velocity in the last case is negative since it is returning to 0 from $x = a$.

Time for a complete cycle

OCR M3 5.9.6 (b)

Both of the expressions for the distance involve periodic functions, sine and cosine, with a period of 2π. In the first expression, x will have the value of a when

$$a = a \sin \omega t \quad \Rightarrow \quad \sin \omega t = 1$$

$$\Rightarrow \quad \omega t = \frac{\pi}{2}$$

This is the first positive solution, but there will be further solutions whenever $\sin \omega t$ has the value of 1, i.e. at $\frac{5\pi}{2}, \frac{9\pi}{2}, \frac{13\pi}{2}$ ... etc., where each solution is 2π more than the last.

The time T, called the **period** of the motion, between successive times at which $x = a$ is given by $\omega T = 2\pi$

$$T = \frac{2\pi}{\omega}$$

It's important to know these equations – you will frequently find that you will be able to answer questions with just this knowledge and an ability to solve and rearrange.

Here is a summary of the ones we have found so far.

$$\text{Acceleration} = \frac{d^2x}{dt^2} = -\omega^2 x$$

$$v^2 = \omega^2(a^2 - x^2), \quad a \text{ is amplitude}$$

$$V_{MAX} = \omega a$$

$$x = 0 \text{ when } t = 0 \quad \Rightarrow \quad x = a \sin \omega t, \; v = a\omega \cos \omega t$$

$$x = a \text{ when } t = 0 \quad \Rightarrow \quad x = a \cos \omega t, \; v = -a\omega \sin \omega t$$

$$\text{Period, } T = \frac{2\pi}{\omega}$$

Example

A particle is describing simple harmonic motion in a straight line about a point O as centre. At a particular instant its displacement from O, its speed and the magnitude of its acceleration are 3 cm, 6 cm s^{-1} and 12 cm s^{-2} respectively.

Find:

(a) the greatest speed of the particle, and

(b) the period of its motion.

Solution $x = 3$, $|v| = 6$ and $|\text{acceleration}| = 12$

Since acceleration is $-\omega^2 x$, $|-\omega^2 x| = |-3\omega^2| = 3\omega^2 = 12$

i.e. $\omega^2 = 4$ and $\omega = 2$, since $\omega > 0$

$$v^2 = \omega^2(a^2 - x^2) \quad \Rightarrow \quad 36 = 4(a^2 - 9)$$
$$\Rightarrow 9 = a^2 - 9 \quad \Rightarrow a^2 = 18$$
$$\Rightarrow a = 3\sqrt{2}, \text{ since } a > 0$$

(a) $v_{\text{MAX}} = \omega a = 2 \times 3\sqrt{2} = 6\sqrt{2}$ cm s^{-1}

(b) $T = \dfrac{2\pi}{\omega} = \dfrac{2\pi}{2} = \pi$ seconds

---

Here's another slightly more involved example.

Example   A particle P of mass 8 kg describes simple harmonic motion with O as centre and has a speed of 6 m s^{-1} at a distance of 1 m from O and a speed of 2 m s^{-1} at a distance of 3 m from O.

(a)   Find:

   (i)   the amplitude of the motion

   (ii)   the period of the motion

   (iii)   the maximum speed of P

   (iv)   the time taken to travel from O directly to one extreme point B of the motion.

(b)   Determine the magnitude of:

   (i)   the acceleration of P when at a distance of 2 m from O

   (ii)   the force acting on P when at a distance of 2 m from O.

(c)   Write down an expression for the displacement of P from O at any time t, given that P is at O at $t = 0$. Hence, or otherwise, find the time taken to travel directly from O to a point C between O and B and at a distance of 1 m from O. Find also the time taken to go directly from C to the point D between O and B and at a distance of 2 m from O.

Solution   (a)   (i)   We are going to use the equation $v^2 = \omega^2(a^2 - x^2)$ and substitute the pairs of values $v = 6$ when $x = 1$

and $v = 2$ when $x = 3$

First pair: $36 = \omega^2(a^2 - 1)$ ... ①

Second pair: $4 = \omega^2(a^2 - 9)$ ... ②

① ÷ ② gives $9 = \dfrac{a^2 - 1}{a^2 - 9}$

$$\Rightarrow 9a^2 - 81 = a^2 - 1$$
$$8a^2 = 80$$
$$a^2 = 10 \quad \Rightarrow a = \sqrt{10} \text{ m, the amplitude}$$

(ii) The period $T = \dfrac{2\pi}{\omega}$, so we need ω. Putting the value $a = \sqrt{10}$ into ①

gives $36 = \omega^2(10 - 1) \Rightarrow 9\omega^2 = 36$

$\omega^2 = 4 \Rightarrow \qquad \omega = 2$ (taking positive value)

The period T is then $\dfrac{2\pi}{\omega} = \dfrac{2\pi}{2} = \pi$ seconds.

(iii) The maximum speed is given by $v_{\text{MAX}} = \omega a = 2\sqrt{10}$ m s^{-1}

(iv) The time for O to B is a quarter of the period, i.e. $\dfrac{\pi}{4}$ s.

(b) (i) Since the acceleration is $-\omega^2 x$, when $x = 2$ and $\omega = 2$, this will be -8, i.e. *magnitude* of 8 m s^{-2}

(ii) Force $F = $ mass $\times$ acceleration $\Rightarrow F = 8 \times 8 = 64$ N

(c) When the motion starts at O, the central point, we use

$$x = a \sin \omega t, \quad v = a\omega \cos \omega t$$

Since $a = \sqrt{10}$ and $\omega = 2$, we have the distance x given by

$$x = \sqrt{10} \sin 2t$$

Time for O to C, $x = 1$

$\Rightarrow \quad 1 = \sqrt{10} \sin 2t \quad \Rightarrow \quad \dfrac{1}{\sqrt{10}} = \sin 2t$

$\Rightarrow \quad t = 0.1609$ (remember to use radians)

Time for O to D, $x = 2$

$\Rightarrow \quad 2 = \sqrt{10} \sin 2t \Rightarrow t = 0.3424$

So time for C to D is the difference of these times,

i.e. $0.3424 - 0.1609 = 0.18$ seconds (2 d.p.)

Here are some questions for you to try. You may find it helpful when the situations become more complicated to sketch the path of the particle, marking in distances and velocities.

Practice questions B

1 A particle P performs simple harmonic oscillations of amplitude 4 cm and period 8 seconds.

Find:

(a) the maximum speed of P

(b) the maximum magnitude of the acceleration of P

(c) the speed of P when it is 2 cm from the centre of the oscillations.

2 A particle describes simple harmonic motion with period $\frac{1}{2}\pi$ seconds about a point O as centre and the maximum speed in the motion is 20 m s^{-1}.

Find:

(a) the amplitude of the motion

(b) the speed of the particle when at a point Q distance 2 m from O

(c) the time taken to travel directly from O to Q.

3 A particle of mass 4 kilograms executes simple harmonic motion with amplitude 2 metres and period 10 seconds. The particle starts from rest at time $t = 0$. Find its maximum speed and the time at which half the maximum speed is first attained. Find also the maximum value of the magnitude of the force required to maintain the motion. (Leave your answers in terms of π.)

4 A particle moves along a straight line with simple harmonic motion of amplitude 0.5 m and of period 4 seconds. Find the maximum speed in m/s and the maximum acceleration in m/s² of the particle. Find also in m/s the speed of the particle when it is 0.25 m from its central position. (Answers may be left in terms of π.)

Find also the least time which elapses between two instants when the speed of the particle is half its maximum speed.

5 A particle C moving along the x-axis describes simple harmonic motion about the point $x = 1$ m as centre of oscillation. The period of the motion is π seconds and C has a speed of 3 m s⁻¹ when $x = 3$ m. Find the amplitude of the motion. At time $t = 0$ seconds, C is passing through the centre of oscillation and is moving in the positive x direction. Obtain an expression to determine the position of C at any time t seconds.

6 A particle moves on a straight line with simple harmonic motion whose centre is O. The speed at distance d from O is $3V$, and the speed at distance $2d$ from O is V. Find the amplitude and the period of the motion.

7 A particle moves on the line Ox so that after time t its displacement from O is x, and

$$\frac{d^2x}{dt^2} = -9x.$$

When $t = 0$, $x = 4$ and $\frac{dx}{dt} = 9$.

Find the maximum displacement of the particle from O.

8 A particle P moves in a straight line so that its acceleration is always directed towards a point O in its path and is of magnitude proportional to the distance OP. When P is at the point A, where $OA = 1$ m, its speed is $3\sqrt{3}$ m/s and when P is at the point B, where $OB = \sqrt{3}$ m, its speed is 3 m/s. Calculate the maximum speed attained by P and the maximum value of OP.

Show that P takes $\pi/18$ seconds to move directly from A to B. Find, in m/s correct to 2 significant figures, the speed of P one second after it passes O.

9 A particle of mass m moves in simple harmonic motion about O in a straight line, under the action of a restoring force of magnitude proportional to the distance from O. At time $t = 0$ the speed of the particle is zero. After 1 second the speed of the particle is 2 m s⁻¹, after a further second the speed is $2\sqrt{3}$ m s⁻¹ and subsequently the particle passes through O for the first time. Show that the speed of the particle when it passes through O is 4 m s⁻¹ and find:

(a) the period and amplitude of the motion,

(b) the time at which the speed of the particle is equal to 2 m s⁻¹ after it first passes through O.

10 A particle P of mass 0.04 kg describes simple harmonic motion about a point O as centre. When P is at a distance of 3 m from O its acceleration is of magnitude 48 m s⁻² and its kinetic energy is 5.12 J. Find the amplitude of the motion.

11 A particle moves in a straight line through a fixed point O. At time t seconds its displacement from O is x metres and its equation of motion is

$$\frac{d^2x}{dt^2} = -36x.$$

It is given that when $t = 0$, $x = 4\sqrt{2}$ and $\frac{dx}{dt} = 0$. Find the total distance moved by the particle in the interval from $t = 0$ to $t = \frac{\pi}{6}$.

Tides

OCR M3 5.9.6 (b)

One naturally occurring example of simple harmonic motion (at least approximately) is the height of tidal water between the low and high tide marks. The centre of the motion will be the average of these heights. Here's an example of this.

| Example | On a certain day the depth of water in a harbour entrance at low tide at 1200 hours is 5 m. At the following high tide at 1815 hours the depth of water is 15 m. In order to enter this harbour safely, a ship needs a minimum depth of 12 m of water. Given that the rise of the water level between low and high tides is simple harmonic, find: |

(a) the earliest time during this tide at which the ship can safely enter the harbour

(b) the rate, in cm s^{-1}, at which the water level is rising at this earliest time.

| Solution | The centre will be $\frac{5+15}{2} = 10$ m depth, and so the amplitude, a, is $10 - 5 = 5$ m. Since half the period, from low to high tide, takes $6\frac{1}{4}$ hours, the period will be 12.5 hours, |

i.e. $\frac{2\pi}{\omega} = 12.5 \Rightarrow \omega = \frac{4\pi}{25}$

If we measure time from one of the extremes, low tide, we use the forms

$x = a \cos \omega t$ and $v = -a\omega \sin \omega t$

(a) We have to be careful with the signs – when $t = 0$, $x = -5$, i.e. 5 m below the central point so we need to put $a = -5$, giving $x = -5 \cos \omega t$.
We need the time when the height is 12 m, i.e. 2 m above the central point. We find this from

$2 = -5 \cos \omega t \Rightarrow \frac{-2}{5} = \cos \omega t$

and $\omega t = \cos^{-1}\left(\frac{-2}{5}\right) \Rightarrow t = \frac{1}{\omega}\cos^{-1}\left(\frac{-2}{5}\right) = \frac{25}{4\pi} \times (1.982)$ [in *radians*]

$= 3.944$ hours $= 3$ hrs 56.6 mins

Since low tide is at 1200, the earliest time is 1557 (to nearest minute)

(b) At this time, using $v = 5\omega \sin \omega t$ and the fact that $\cos \omega t = -\frac{2}{5}$

$\Rightarrow \sin \omega t = \sqrt{(1 - \cos^2 \omega t)} = \sqrt{\left(1 - \frac{4}{25}\right)} = \frac{\sqrt{21}}{5}$

we have $v = 5 \times \frac{4\pi}{25} \times \frac{\sqrt{21}}{5} = 2.303$ m h^{-1} $= 0.064$ cm s^{-1}

Practice questions C

1   A ship is to enter a harbour. It needs a minimum depth of water of 11 m in order to ensure a safe passage into the harbour. At low tide, which occurs at 4 pm, the depth of water in the harbour is 10 m, and at high tide, which next occurs at 10 pm, the depth of water in the harbour is 16 m.

By modelling the rise and fall of the surface of the water in the harbour as simple harmonic motion:

(a) write down the amplitude and the period of the motion

(b) find, to the nearest minute, the earliest time after 4 pm at which it is safe for the ship to enter the harbour.

(c) Assuming that the ship enters the harbour at this time, find, to the nearest minute, the latest time before the next low tide at which it is safe for the ship to leave the harbour.

SHM equation

The standard equation for SHM is

$$\frac{d^2x}{dt^2} = -\omega^2 x \qquad \dots \text{Ⓐ}$$

and conversely; if the equation of motion is of this form then the motion is simple harmonic. Since we have to have a restoring force of some sort or another, there is a limited choice of situation for simple examples. For one force, we generally have the tension in an elastic spring or string and for two forces, the tensions in two elastic strings or two opposing attraction or repulsion forces.

To show that the motion of a particle is simple harmonic we find all the forces acting and set up the equation of motion, which after simplification should look like the equation Ⓐ above. We can then immediately find ω and deduce the period of the motion. To be able to say anything more about it, we need additional information.

Example

A light elastic spring of natural length 80 cm has one end A attached to a fixed point. A particle P, of mass 0.1 kg, is attached to the other end of the spring. When P hangs in equilibrium vertically below A, the extension of the spring is 20 cm.

(a) Find the modulus of elasticity of the spring.

The spring is now placed on a smooth horizontal table and the end A is fixed. The particle P is pulled away from A to a point B on the table, where $AB = 1$ m, and released from rest.

(b) Show that P performs simple harmonic motion with period $\frac{2\pi}{7}$ seconds.

(c) Find the greatest speed of P during the motion.

The point C on the table lies between A and B, with $AC = 70$ cm.

(d) Find the time taken by P to reach C from B for the first time.

Solution

Figure 3.4

(a)

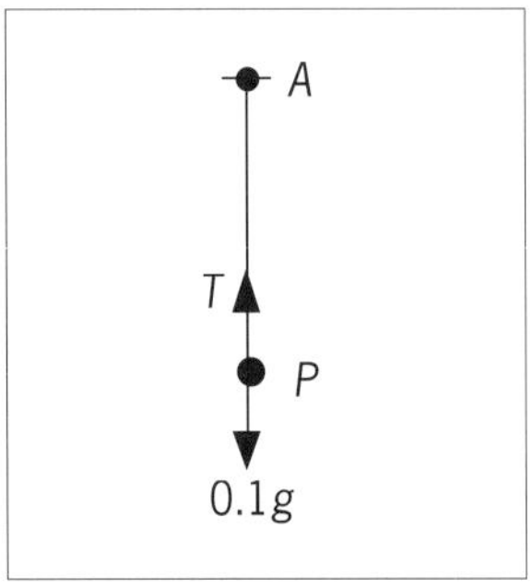

In equilibrium, $T = 0.1\,g$

But for an elastic spring, $T = \dfrac{\lambda x}{l}$

$\Rightarrow \dfrac{\lambda \times 0.2}{0.8} = 0.1g \Rightarrow \lambda = 0.4g$ N

(Note that we put distances in metres.)

(b)

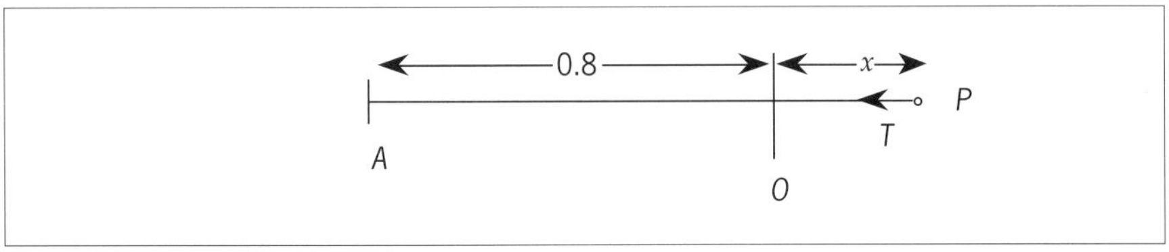

On a table, the particle on a spring oscillates about the point O, where AO is its natural length. (This only works with a *spring*: an elastic *string* would become slack and the equations of SHM would not apply.) We'll call the distance OP x metres – this can be negative, which would mean that the spring was under compression. The equation of motion is then:

$$m \frac{d^2x}{dt^2} = -\frac{\lambda x}{l} = -\frac{0.4gx}{0.8}$$

$$\Rightarrow \quad 0.1 \frac{d^2x}{dt^2} = -\frac{gx}{2} \quad \Rightarrow \quad \frac{d^2x}{dt^2} = -5gx$$

This is the equation of SHM with $\omega^2 = 5g \Rightarrow \omega = 7$,

and the period is $\dfrac{2\pi}{\omega} = \dfrac{2\pi}{7}$ seconds as required.

(c) Since no external forces are acting, the particle will oscillate back and forth from its original position B, where $x = 1 - 0.8 = 0.2$, i.e. amplitude is 0.2 m.

Greatest speed is $\omega a = 7 \times 0.2 = 1.4$ m s^{-1}

(d)

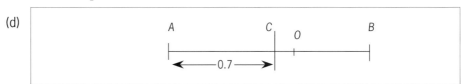

At C, there is a compression of 0.1 m. i.e. $x = -0.1$

Using the equation $x = a \cos \omega t$ since $x = a$ when $t = 0$.

$$-0.1 = 0.2 \cos 7t \Rightarrow \cos 7t = -0.5$$

First positive solution of this is $120°$, i.e. $\dfrac{2\pi}{3}$ in radians,

$$\Rightarrow \quad 7t = \frac{2\pi}{3}, \; t = \frac{2\pi}{21} \text{ seconds.}$$

Example

Two points A and B on a smooth horizontal table are a distance 1.6 m apart. A particle P of mass 0.5 kg is attached to one end of each of two light elastic strings, each of which has natural length 0.6 m and modulus of elasticity 1.35 N. The other ends of the two strings are attached to A and B respectively. The mid-point of AB is O. The particle P is released from rest at a point C on the table between A and B, where $BC = 0.6$ m. At subsequent time t seconds, the distance of P from O is x metres.

(a) Write down the extension of each string in terms of x.

(b) Show that P performs simple harmonic motion with period $\dfrac{2\pi}{3}$ seconds.

(c) Find the greatest speed of P during the motion.

The point D lies between A and B, with $AD = 0.7$ m.

(d) Find the time taken for P to reach D for the first time.

Solution

Figure 3.5

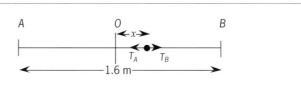

(a) $AO = \dfrac{1}{2} \times 1.6 = 0.8$, so extension in string attached to A is

$$(0.8 + x) - 0.6 = 0.2 + x$$

Extension in string attached to B is $(0.8 - x) - 0.6 = 0.2 - x$

(b) Force on particle, in direction of x increasing is

$$T_B - T_A \quad = \frac{\lambda (0.2 - x)}{l} - \frac{\lambda (0.2 + x)}{l}$$

$$= \frac{\lambda}{l} (-2x) \quad = \frac{1.35 (-2x)}{0.6} = -\frac{9x}{2}$$

$$F = ma \quad \Rightarrow \quad -\frac{9x}{2} = \frac{1}{2} \frac{d^2x}{dt^2}$$

i.e. $\dfrac{d^2x}{dt^2} = -9x$

This is the equation of SHM, with $\omega^2 = 9$.

Period is $\dfrac{2\pi}{\omega} = \dfrac{2\pi}{\sqrt{9}} = \dfrac{2\pi}{3}$, as required.

(c) Initially, $BC = 0.6 \Rightarrow x = 0.2$ and this will be the amplitude of the SHM, i.e. $a = 0.2$.

Max. speed is $\omega a = 3 \times 0.2 = 0.6 \text{ m s}^{-1}$.

(d) When $t = 0$, $x = a \Rightarrow$ equation connecting distance and time is

$$x = a \cos \omega t, \text{ i.e. } x = 0.2 \cos 3t$$

At D, $x = -0.1$ (relative to initial position)

Figure 3.6

$$\Rightarrow \quad -0.1 = 0.2 \cos 3t$$

$$\cos 3t = -0.5$$

$$3t = \frac{2\pi}{3} \text{ (in radians)}$$

$$t = \frac{2\pi}{9} \text{ seconds (or 0.70, to 2 d.p.)}$$

Example	A particle of mass m moves on a straight line between two points A and B which are a distance $12a$ apart. When the particle is at a general point P, it is attracted to both A and B by forces of magnitude mk^2d and $3mk^2(12a - d)$ respectively, where $d = AP$ and k is a positive constant. Given that the particle is in equilibrium at a point O, show that $AO = 9a$.

When the particle moves in the line AB and performs small oscillations about O, show that the motion is simple harmonic with period $\frac{\pi}{k}$.

The particle is released from rest at the point C where $AC = 11a$ and $BC = a$. In the subsequent motion find, in terms of a, k and time t, expressions for

(a) the distance of the particle from A

(b) the maximum speed of the particle

(c) the magnitude of the maximum acceleration of the particle.

Solution	
Figure 3.7	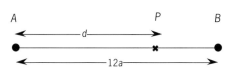

If the particle is in equilibrium, the forces of attraction are equal, i.e.

$$mk^2d = 3mk^2(12a - d)$$
$$\Rightarrow \quad d = 3(12a - d) \quad \Rightarrow 4d = 36a$$
$$d = 9a \quad \text{i.e. } AO = 9a$$

Figure 3.8	

Suppose the particle is at the general point Q, with $OQ = x$ between O and B. The force of attraction from A is then $mk^2(9a + x)$ and from B is

$$3mk^2(12a - (9a + x)).$$

Taking the direction OB as positive, this gives the equation of motion

$$\frac{md^2x}{dt^2} = -mk^2(9a + x) + 3mk^2(3a - x), \quad \text{i.e.} \quad \frac{d^2x}{dt^2} = -4k^2x$$

This is in the required form, i.e. SHM with $\omega^2 = 4k^2 \Rightarrow \omega = 2k$.

The period is $\frac{2\pi}{w} = \frac{2\pi}{2k} = \frac{\pi}{k}$ as required.

(a) The amplitude will be $11a - 9a = 2a$ and we are starting from an extreme, so we take the form $x = [\text{amplitude}] \cos(\omega t) = 2a \cos(2kt)$.

From A, the distance will be $9a + 2a \cos(2kt)$.

(b) Amplitude is $2a \Rightarrow$ max. speed is $2a\omega = 4ak$

(c) Max. acceleration at an extreme, magnitude is $4k^2 \times 2a = 8k^2a$.

Practice questions D

1 An elastic string of natural length $2a$ and modulus λ has its ends attached to two points A, B on a smooth horizontal table. The distance AB is $4a$ and C is the mid-point of AB. A particle of mass m is attached to the mid-point of the string. The particle is released from rest at D, the mid-point of CB.

Denoting by x the displacement of the particle from C, show that the equation of motion of the particle is

$$\frac{d^2x}{dt^2} + \frac{2\lambda}{ma}x = 0$$

Find the maximum speed of the particle and show that the time taken for the particle to move from D directly to the mid-point of CD is

$$\frac{\pi}{3}\left(\frac{ma}{2\lambda}\right)^{\frac{1}{2}}.$$

2 An elastic rope has natural length 20 cm and modulus of elasticity 40 N. One end of the rope is attached to a fixed point and a particle, of mass 200 grams, hangs from the other end.

(a) Find the extension of the rope when the mass is at rest.

Assume that when the mass moves, it always travels along a vertical line that passes through the point of suspension.

(b) At time t seconds, the displacement of the mass from its equilibrium position is x metres. Find the tension in the rope in terms of x, and show that $\dfrac{d^2x}{dt^2} = -1000x$.

3 When a particle of mass 2 kg is suspended from a light elastic string, the extension is 5 cm.

The particle is then pulled down a further 2 cm and released. Show that it performs SHM with period $\dfrac{\pi}{7}$ seconds.

4 A light spiral spring is carrying a weight of mass 6 kg; it extends 5 cm when an extra weight of mass 1.5 kg is placed on it. The extra weight is removed suddenly. Find the period of oscillation of the 6 kg weight, and the tension in the spring and the velocity of the weight when it is 2.5 cm above its lowest point.

SUMMARY EXERCISE

1 A particle P describes simple harmonic oscillations of amplitude 7 cm and period 4 seconds. Find the maximum speed of P and its speed when at a distance of 3 cm from the centre of oscillation.

2 A particle moves with simple harmonic motion along a straight line. At a certain instant it is 9 m away from the centre O of its motion and has a speed of 6 m s^{-1} and an acceleration of $\dfrac{9}{4}$ m s^{-2}. Find:

(a) the period of the motion

(b) the amplitude of the motion

(c) the greatest speed of the particle.

3 (a) A particle of mass 0.2 kg is performing five complete oscillations per second in simple harmonic motion between A and B, where AB is 0.1 m. Find the maximum speed of the particle and the greatest force exerted on it.

(b) While at A the particle is struck a blow in the direction BA to double the amplitude without altering the frequency. Show that the speed of the particle immediately after the blow is approximately 2.7 m s^{-1}.

4 A particle is moving with simple harmonic motion in a straight line between the extreme points A and B; O is the centre of the oscillations. When the particle is 4 m from O, its speed is 4 m s^{-1}, and when the particle is 2 m from O, its speed is 8 m s^{-1}. Calculate the distance AB and the time taken by the particle for one oscillation.

If the particle is of mass 2 kg, find its kinetic energy when it is 2 m from A.

Find the time taken by the particle to travel directly from A to M, where M is the mid-point of OB.

5 A particle of mass 2 kg is acted upon by a variable force which makes it move in simple harmonic motion about O on the straight line Ox. Given that the maximum speed attained is 0.5 m s^{-1} and the maximum acceleration is 0.1 m s^{-2}, find the period of the motion. Show that the amplitude of the motion is 2.5 m.

6 A particle of mass m is suspended from a fixed point O by a light elastic string of natural length l and modulus λ. When the mass is hanging freely at rest the extension of the string is a. Find λ in terms of m, g, l and a.

Suppose that the particle is pulled down a small vertical distance from its equilibrium position and then released from rest. Show that its subsequent motion is simple harmonic with period

$$2\pi \sqrt{\left(\frac{a}{g}\right)}$$

7 A light elastic string of natural length l has one end fastened to a fixed point O. The other end of the string is attached to a particle of mass m. When the particle hangs in equilibrium the length of the string is $\frac{7}{4}l$. The particle is displaced from equilibrium so that it moves vertically with the string taut. Show that the motion is simple harmonic with period $\pi \sqrt{\left(\frac{3l}{g}\right)}$.

At time $t = 0$ the particle is released from rest at a point A at a distance $\frac{3}{2}l$ vertically below O. Find:

(a) the depth below O of the lowest point L of the motion

(b) the time taken to move from A to L

(c) the depth below O of the particle at time

$$t = \frac{1}{3}\pi \sqrt{\left(\frac{3l}{g}\right)}$$

8 In a certain tidal estuary the water level rises and falls with simple harmonic motion. On a particular day a marker indicates that the depths of water at low and high tides are 4 m and 10 m and that these occur at 1100 and 1720 respectively. Calculate:

(a) the speed, in m h^{-1}, at which the water level is rising at 1235

(b) the time, during this tide, at which the depth of water is $8\frac{1}{2}$ m.

9 (a) The natural length and modulus of a light elastic spring AB are l_0 m and λ N respectively. The end A of the spring is fixed. When a particle of mass M kg is attached to

the spring at B and hangs freely under gravity, the extension of the spring is 0.2 m. The mass is pulled down through a further small distance so that the spring is extended, and then released from rest. Show that the subsequent motion is simple harmonic of period $\frac{2\pi}{7}$ seconds.

(b) A particle moves with simple harmonic motion along the x-axis about the origin O, of period $\frac{2\pi}{\omega}$ and amplitude a.

(i) Write down expressions giving the acceleration and speed at a point distance x from O. At a certain time, $x = 3$ m and the speed and the acceleration of the particle are equal in magnitude. Given further that the maximum speed in the motion is 2 m s^{-1}, show that the period and amplitude of the motion are $2\sqrt{3}\pi$ seconds.and $2\sqrt{3}$ m respectively.

(ii) Two particles A and B move in simple harmonic motion about O with amplitude $2\sqrt{3}$ m and period $2\sqrt{3}\pi$ s. A is released from rest at time $t = 0$ from the extreme point P where $x = 2\sqrt{3}$. Particle B is released from P at time $t = \frac{\sqrt{3}}{2}\pi$ seconds.

Show that the particles will collide $\frac{3\sqrt{3}}{4}\pi$ seconds after the release of B. Find how far from O the collision will occur.

10 A particle P of mass m lies on a smooth horizontal table and is attached by two light elastic springs, AP and BP, to the table at two fixed points A and B. Each of the springs AP and BP has natural length l and modulus of elasticity $4mg$. The distance AB is $4l$.

Show that any oscillation of the particle in the line AB has a periodic time $\pi \sqrt{\left(\frac{l}{2g}\right)}$.

The particle is released from a point on the line AB at a distance $\frac{5l}{3}$ from B. Obtain, in terms of g and l

(a) the greatest speed of the particle

(b) the speed at the point C at a distance $\frac{9l}{5}$ from B

(c) the shortest time to reach C.

SUMMARY

When you have finished you should:

● know what is meant by SHM and be familiar with its defining equation

● be familiar with the standard equations connecting the variables

● know the alternative forms for the displacement and velocity at any time depending on the initial condition

● be able to show that a given system moves with SHM and be able to derive the period of the motion.

ANSWERS

Practice questions A

1 (a) 3   (b) 0.6 m   (c) 1.44 m s^{-1}
   (d) 0.48 m   (e) -1.8 m s^{-2}

2 (a) 1   (b) $\frac{3\sqrt{2}}{40}$ m   (c) 0.11 m s^{-1}

3 (a) 1.5 m   (b) 1   (c) 1.5 m s^{-2}

Practice questions B

1 (a) π cm s^{-1} (b) $\frac{\pi^2}{4}$ cm s^{-2} (c) $\frac{\pi\sqrt{3}}{2}$ cm s^{-1}

2 (a) 5 m   (b) $4\sqrt{21}$ m s^{-1} (c) 0.103 seconds

3 $\frac{2\pi}{5}$ m s^{-1}, $\frac{5}{6}$ s, $\frac{8\pi^2}{25}$ N

4 $\frac{\pi}{4}$ m s^{-1}, $\frac{\pi^2}{8}$ m s^{-2} : $\frac{\pi\sqrt{3}}{8}$ m s^{-1} : $\frac{2}{3}$ seconds

5 2.5 m, $x = 1 + 2.5 \sin 2t$

6 $d\sqrt{\left(\frac{35}{8}\right)}$, $\frac{\pi d}{v}\sqrt{\left(\frac{3}{2}\right)}$

7 5

8 6 m s^{-1}, 2 m : 5.9 m s^{-1}

9 (a) 12 seconds, $\frac{24}{\pi}$ m   (b) 5 seconds

10 5 m

11 $8\sqrt{2}$ m

Practice questions C

1 (a) 3 m, 12 hrs
   (b) 5 : 36 pm
   (c) 2 : 24 am

Practice questions D

1 $\sqrt{\left(\frac{2\lambda a}{m}\right)}$

2 (a) 0.98 cm

4 $\frac{2\pi}{7}$ seconds : $\frac{27g}{4}$ N : 0.3 m s^{-1}

4

Uniform circular motion

INTRODUCTION In this section we are going to look at the motion of a particle that describes a horizontal circle and the force that is necessary to keep it in this path. This is quite a large topic because there are so many variations on a basic theme, although you will find that they all come down to a very few basic principles even when the application may be as different as a car travelling fast round a banked corner or a satellite circling the earth.

Linear and angular velocity

OCR M2 5.8.4 (a)

The speed of the particle travelling round the circle can be measured in two ways – either the familiar **linear** measure, i.e. so many centimetres or metres in a second, or **angular** measure, i.e. so many **revolutions** per second (rev s^{-1}) or so many **radians** per second (rad s^{-1}).

The conversion from revolutions to radians per second and vice versa is quite straightforward – since there are 2π radians in one revolution, we divide or multiply by the factor 2π as appropriate. For example:

$$4 \text{ rev s}^{-1} \equiv 8\pi \text{ rad s}^{-1}$$

$$\frac{3}{\pi} \text{ rev s}^{-1} \equiv \frac{3}{\pi} \times 2\pi = 6 \text{ rad s}^{-1}$$

and conversely

$$2 \text{ rad s}^{-1} \equiv \frac{2}{2\pi} = \frac{1}{\pi} \text{ rev s}^{-1}$$

$$10\pi \text{ rad s}^{-1} \equiv 5 \text{ rev s}^{-1}$$

To convert between linear, e.g. m s^{-1}, and angular, rad s^{-1}, we have to remember the formula for arc length, i.e. arc length $= r\theta$ where r is the radius in metres and θ the angle in radians. This is illustrated in Fig. 4.1.

Figure 4.1

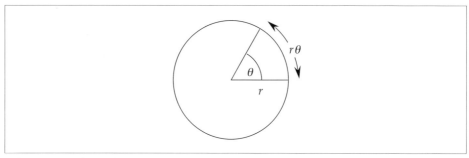

This means that when the particle has turned through an angle of θ radians, it has travelled a distance around the circle of $r\theta$, i.e.

$$\text{Angular } \theta \text{ rad s}^{-1} \equiv \text{linear } r\theta \text{ m s}^{-1}$$

Conventionally we use the Greek letter ω for angular velocity just as we usually use v for linear velocity, and then in appropriate units

$$v = r\omega$$

This means that the linear velocity increases as the radius of the circle increases – so that, for example, you have to run faster on the outside of a running track to keep up with someone on the inside lane.

Example

Find the speed in m s^{-1} of a particle moving in a circular path of radius 50 cm with an angular speed of:

(a) 5 rad s^{-1}

(b) 10 rev s^{-1}

(c) 200 rev min^{-1}

Solution

$v = r\omega \Rightarrow$

(a) $r = 0.5$, $\omega = 5 \Rightarrow v = 2.5$ m s^{-1}

   [Note that we convert the radius to metres.]

(b) $r = 0.5$, $\omega = 2\pi \times 10 \Rightarrow v = 10\pi$ m s^{-1}

(c) 200 rev min$^{-1} = \dfrac{200}{60}$ rev sec$^{-1} = \dfrac{200}{60} \times 2\pi$ rad s^{-1}

$\Rightarrow v = \dfrac{200}{60} \times 2\pi \times \dfrac{1}{2} = \dfrac{10\pi}{3}$ m s^{-1}

Example

Find the radius of the circular path if a woman is running with a speed of 7.5 m s^{-1} and an angular speed of 0.15 rad s^{-1}.

Solution

$v = r\omega \Rightarrow 7.5 = r \times 0.15 \Rightarrow r = 50$ m

Practice questions A

1 Express in rad s^{-1} (in terms of π if necessary)

(a) 2 rev s^{-1} (b) $\dfrac{4}{\pi}$ rev s^{-1}

(c) 180 rev min^{-1}

2 Convert the following to m s^{-1}

(a) $\omega = 2$ rad s^{-1},   radius = 2 m

(b) $\omega = 0.2$ rad s^{-1},   radius = 50 m

(c) $\omega = 4$ rad s^{-1},   radius = 20 cm

(d) $\omega = 30$ rev min^{-1},   radius = 3 m

3 Convert the following to rad s^{-1}

(a) $v = 10$ m s^{-1},   radius = 20 m

(b) $v = 0.1$ m s^{-1},   radius = 5 cm

(c) $v = 60$ m s^{-1},   radius = 100 m

(d) $v = 2$ m s^{-1},   radius = 50 cm

The period of revolution

OCR M2 5.8.4 (a)

The period of revolution is the term that describes how long it takes to go once round the circle.

1   If the speed is given as R rev s^{-1}, then the time for
    1 revolution is simply $\frac{1}{R}$ seconds.

2   If the speed is given as ω rad s^{-1}, we want the time for
    1 revolution, i.e. 2π radians, which will be:

$$\frac{2\pi}{\omega} \text{ seconds} \left(\text{as in Time} = \frac{\text{Distance}}{\text{Speed}} \right)$$

3   If the speed is given as v m s^{-1}, we want the time for one **circumference** of
    the circle, i.e. $2\pi r$, where r is the radius, which will be:

$$\frac{2\pi r}{v} \text{ seconds}$$

Practice questions B

1   Find the time for one revolution of a circle of 10 m when the particle is moving at:

(a) 4 rev s^{-1} (b) 3 rad s^{-1} (c) 4π rad s^{-1} (d) 5 m s^{-1} (e) 7π m s^{-1}

Central force

OCR M2 5.8.4 (b)

Unless a force of some kind is acting, a particle in motion will continue at the same velocity along a straight line. When a particle is moving in a circle it's being forced all the time inwards, away from a straight path.

In Fig. 4.2, the particle at P_1 would keep going in a straight line if there were no force acting, but it continues along the circle to P_2 under the action of the central force, F. This force has to continue to act for the particle to pass around the circle to P_3 and so on.

Figure 4.2

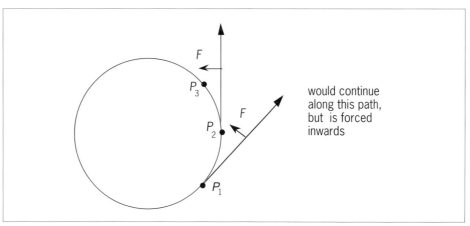

would continue
along this path,
but is forced
inwards

> The **magnitude** of this force has to be
>
> $$mr\omega^2 \quad \text{or} \quad \frac{mv^2}{r}$$
>
> and it is always directed towards the **centre** of the circle.

This means that if we know two of (a) the force, (b) the radius and (c) the speed, we can calculate the value of the remaining unknown quantity.

Example

A particle of mass m kg is moving in a horizontal circle under the action of a force of magnitude $45m$ N directed towards the centre of the circle. If the radius of the circle is 5 m, find the angular velocity.

Solution

We have to examine the question first of all to find out which of the forms for the force is applicable. Here we want **angular** velocity, so we use the formula $F = mr\omega^2$.

Then

$$mr\omega^2 = 45m \quad \text{and } r = 5$$
$$5\omega^2 = 45$$
$$\omega^2 = 9 \quad \Rightarrow \quad \omega = 3 \text{ rad s}^{-1}$$

Example

A force of 12.5 N acts on a particle of mass 2 kg in such a way that the particle describes a horizontal circle of radius 4 m with constant speed. Find the time for 1 revolution correct to 1 decimal place.

Solution

We can use either of the forms in this case. Taking the one for linear speed,

$$F = \frac{mv^2}{r} = 12.5$$

Putting $m = 2$ and $r = 4$,

$$\frac{2v^2}{4} = 12.5$$
$$\Rightarrow v^2 = 25 \text{ and } v = 5 \text{ m s}^{-1}$$

Since the circumference is $2\pi r = 8\pi$, it will take

$$\frac{8\pi}{5} = 5.0 \text{ seconds (1 d.p.)}$$

Practice questions C

1   Find the force acting when a particle of mass 2 kg describes a circle of radius

   (a)   2 m, speed of 5 m s^{-1}

   (b)   20 cm, angular speed of 1 rad s^{-1}

   (c)   50 m, speed of 20 m s^{-1}

   (d)   10 m, angular speed of 2 rev s^{-1}.

2   A particle of mass 3 kg is moving in a horizontal circle under the action of a force of magnitude 4.8 N. If the speed of the particle is 4 m s^{-1}, find the radius of the circle.

3   Find the force necessary to keep a mass of 2 kg moving round a horizontal circle at the rate of 3 rev s^{-1} if the radius of the circle is 0.5 m.

Now let's have a look at different systems where the force inwards can be provided by the tension in a string or the reaction between the particle and the surface on which it is rotating.

Conical pendulum

OCR M2 5.8.4 (c)

When a particle is attached to one end of a string, the other end of which is fixed, and the particle describes a horizontal circle, the string traces out the shape of a cone and the system is called a **conical pendulum**.

Figure 4.3

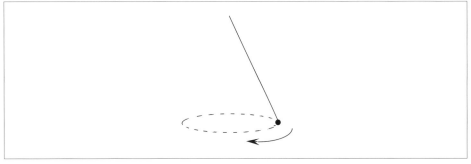

A typical system will have a string of length *l* and a particle of mass *m* at one end. To simplify matters, we can draw it in two dimensions, and then mark in the forces that are acting on the particle. To complete the diagram we can draw in the vertical from the fixed end and call the angle the string makes with this vertical θ.

Figure 4.4

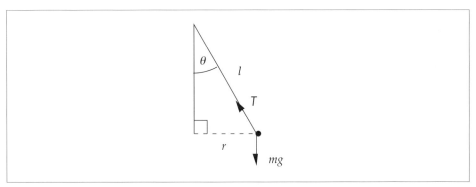

We can then generally find any unknowns in the system from **three** equations:

   ①   vertical

   ②   horizontal

   ③   triangle

and we'll look at each of these in turn.

Since the particle is moving in a **horizontal** circle there is no movement vertically, and so the vertical forces are in equilibrium, i.e.

$$T \cos \theta - mg = 0 \qquad \qquad \dots ①$$

Also, since the motion is in a circle, there must be a force towards the centre of this circle of $\frac{mv^2}{r}$ (or $mr\omega^2$) and since the only force acting towards the centre is $T \sin \theta$,

$$T \sin \theta = \frac{mv^2}{r} \qquad \qquad \dots ②$$

Finally, from the triangle,

$$\sin \theta = \frac{r}{l} \qquad \qquad \text{... ③}$$

In fact, until we come to circular motion with **elastic** strings, these three basic equations, i.e. vertical, horizontal and triangle, will still be sufficient even when the system becomes more complicated. For the moment though, let's have a look at an example.

Example

A conical pendulum consists of a light inextensible string of length l with a particle of mass m attached to its free end. The particle describes a horizontal circle with angular speed ω and the string makes an angle of 60° with the vertical. Express l in terms of g and ω.

Solution

Drawing a diagram and marking in the information given, the tension T and the radius r of the horizontal circle, we get Fig. 4.5.

Figure 4.5

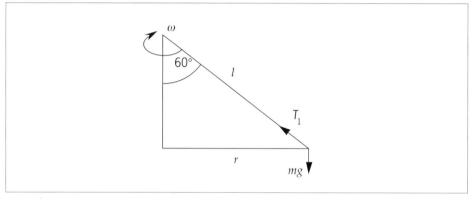

Our three equations are:

Vertical: $T_1 \cos 60° = mg$ ... ①
Horizontal: $T_1 \sin 60° = mr\omega^2$ ... ②

$\Delta :$ $\sin 60° = \dfrac{r}{l}$ ... ③

From ①, since $\cos 60° = \dfrac{1}{2}$, $\dfrac{T_1}{2} = mg \Rightarrow T_1 = 2mg$ and substituting this into ② gives:

$2mg \sin 60° = mr\omega^2$ and since $\sin 60° = \dfrac{\sqrt{3}}{2}$

$mg \sqrt{3} = mr\omega^2 \quad \Rightarrow \quad r = \dfrac{g\sqrt{3}}{\omega^2}$ ... ④

Using $\sin 60° = \dfrac{\sqrt{3}}{2}$ and putting ④ into ③ :

$\dfrac{\sqrt{3}}{2} = \dfrac{\frac{g\sqrt{3}}{\omega^2}}{l} \quad \Rightarrow \quad \dfrac{l}{2} = \dfrac{g}{\omega^2} \quad \Rightarrow \quad l = \dfrac{2g}{\omega^2}$ ... ⑤

Practice questions D

1 One end of a light inelastic string of length a is attached to a particle P of mass m, and the other end of the string is attached to a fixed point O. P moves with constant speed in a horizontal circle whose centre C is a fixed point vertically below O. If the angular velocity at which CP rotates is ω, show that $OC = \dfrac{g}{\omega^2}$.

2 A particle is attached at one end of a light string, the other end of which is fixed. When the particle moves in a horizontal circle with speed 2 m s^{-1}, the string makes an angle $\tan^{-1}\dfrac{5}{12}$ with the vertical. Show that the length of the string is approximately 2.5 m.

3 A particle P is attached by a light inextensible string of length l to a fixed point O. The particle is held with the string taut and OP at an acute angle a to the downward vertical, and is then projected *horizontally* at right angles to the string with speed u chosen so that it describes a circle in a horizontal plane. Show that
$$u^2 = gl \sin a \tan a.$$

4 A conical pendulum consists of a light inextensible string of length l with a particle of mass m attached to its free end. The particle describes a horizontal circle with angular speed ω and the string makes an angle of 60° with the vertical.

(a) Express l in terms of g and ω.

A second conical pendulum consists of a light inextensible string of length L with a particle of mass M attached to its free end. The particle describes a horizontal circle with angular speed $\dfrac{1}{2}\omega$ and the string makes an angle of 30° with the vertical.

(b) Find the value of the fraction $\dfrac{l}{L}$, leaving your answer in surd form.

5 A particle P is attached to one of a light inextensible string of length 0.125 m, the other end of the string being attached to a fixed point O. The particle describes with constant speed, and with the string taut, a horizontal circle whose centre is vertically below O. Given that the particle describes exactly two complete revolutions per second find, in terms of g and π, the cosine of the angle between OP and the vertical.

Motion on a horizontal surface

OCR M2 5.8.4 (c)

A possible question here is that of a particle on a rough horizontal turn-table, with the friction being the central force.

Example

A coin is placed on the edge of a horizontal turntable with the centre of the coin 20 cm from the axis of rotation. The turntable is rotating at the rate of 45 revs per minute. By modelling the coin as a particle, calculate the least possible value for the coefficient of friction between the coin and the turntable.

Solution

A suitable diagram is shown in Fig. 4.6.

Figure 4.6

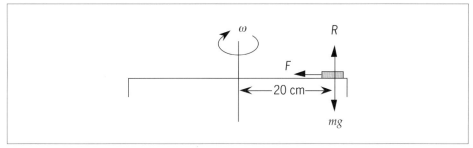

We first of all convert the rate of rotation into rads per second.

$$\omega = 45 \text{ revs min}^{-1} \equiv \frac{45}{60} \times 2\pi \text{ rads sec}^{-1}$$

i.e. $\omega = \frac{3\pi}{2} \text{ rads sec}^{-1}$ ... ①

Resolving vertically, $R = mg$ ... ②

Resolving horizontally, $F = mr\omega^2$ ... ③

Since $F \le \mu R$, $mr\omega^2 \le \mu mg$

$\Rightarrow$ $r\omega^2 \le \mu g$

$\Rightarrow$ $\mu \ge \dfrac{r\omega^2}{g} = \dfrac{0.2 \times \left(\frac{3\pi}{2}\right)^2}{9.8} = 0.45$

Apart from examples like this, the surface will be **smooth** in the questions you are likely to encounter for this module and so the only addition is a normal reaction from the surface which changes the equation for the vertical forces. A possible question in connection with this is to find the maximum speed for which the particle remains in contact with the table, i.e. find the condition that the normal reaction is greater than zero. Let's have a look at an example of this.

Example

As shown in Fig. 4.7, a particle A of mass m is in contact with a smooth horizontal plane, and is attached by means of a light inextensible string to the fixed point O, which is at a height h above the plane. A moves in uniform circular motion in contact with the plane, and with the string taut. Prove that the angular speed, ω, of the motion satisfies $\omega^2 < \dfrac{g}{h}$.

Figure 4.7

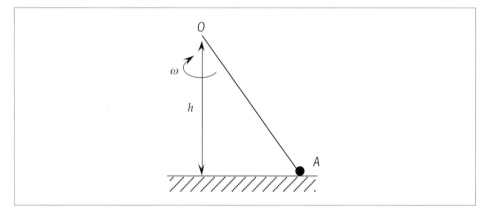

Solution

Redrawing the diagram with the forces acting on the particle A, marking the radius r of the circle and putting in θ, the angle the string makes with the downward vertical, we get Fig. 4.8.

The three equations are:

Vertical: $R + T \cos \theta = mg$ ... ①

Horizontal: $T \sin \theta = mr\omega^2$ ... ②

Δ: $\tan \theta = \dfrac{r}{h}$ ... ③

Note the addition of the normal reaction R in equation ①.

Rearranging ① to give $T \cos \theta = mg - R$ and dividing this into ② gives:

$$\frac{T \sin \theta}{T \cos \theta} = \frac{mr\omega^2}{mg - R}$$

Figure 4.8

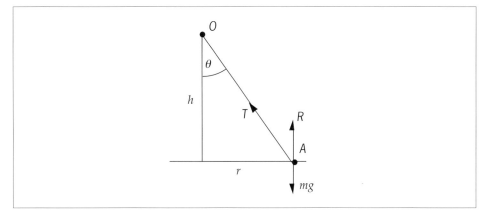

i.e. $\quad \tan \theta = \dfrac{mr\omega^2}{mg - R}$ ... ④

With ③, this becomes $\quad \dfrac{r}{h} = \dfrac{mr\omega^2}{mg - R}$

which becomes $\quad mg - R = mh\omega^2 \quad \Rightarrow \quad R = mg - mh\omega^2$ ... ⑤

Now we apply the condition that the particle should remain on the table, i.e. $R > 0$ and then

$$mg - mh\omega^2 > 0 \quad \Rightarrow \quad mh\omega^2 < mg$$

i.e. $\quad \omega^2 < \dfrac{g}{h} \qquad$ since $h > 0 \;$ and $\; m > 0$

Practice questions E

1 One end of a light inextensible string of length a is attached to a fixed point A which is at a height h above a smooth horizontal table where, $h < a$. A particle P of mass m is attached to the other end of the string and lies on the table with the string taut. The particle is projected so that it moves on the table in a circle at constant angular speed ω. Show that the tension in the string is $ma\omega^2$.

Find, in terms of m, g, h, and ω, the reaction exerted on P by the table.

2 One end of a light inextensible string of length $5a$ is tied at a fixed point A which is at a distance $3a$ above a smooth horizontal table. A particle of mass m, which is tied at the other end of the string, rotates with constant speed in a circle on the table. If the reaction between the particle and the table is R, find the tension in the string when:

(a) $R = 0$ (b) $R = \dfrac{3mg}{4}$.

Show that the respective times of one revolution for these two values of R are in the ratio $1 : 2$.

3 A particle P of mass m is attached to one end of a light inextensible string of length d. The other end of the string is fixed at a height h, where $h < d$, vertically above a point O on a smooth horizontal table. The particle describes a circle, centre O, on the surface of the table, with constant angular speed ω.

Find expressions, in terms of m, d, h, ω and g as appropriate, for:

(a) the tension in the string

(b) the magnitude of the force exerted on P by the plane.

(c) Hence show that:

$$\omega \le \sqrt{\left(\tfrac{g}{h}\right)}.$$

The angular speed of P is now increased to $\sqrt{\left(\tfrac{3g}{h}\right)}$, and P now describes a horizontal circle, centre Q, *above* the surface of the table, with this constant angular speed.

(d) Determine, in terms of h, the distance OQ.

4   One end of a light inextensible string of length a is attached to a fixed point O which is at a height $\frac{a}{3}$ above a smooth horizontal table.

A particle P of mass m is attached to the other end of the string and rests on the table with the string taut. The particle is projected so that it moves in a circle on the table with constant speed v.

Show that the tension in the string is $\frac{9mv^2}{8a}$.

Find in terms of m, g, a and v the reaction exerted on P by the table. Show that $v^2 \le \frac{8ga}{3}$.

Smooth beads

OCR M2 5.8.4 (c)

We are now going to look at slightly more involved systems where the particle, a bead or ring for example, is free to slide along a single string. We'll look at the former case first.

When the bead is **smooth** and can take any position on the string, the tension throughout the string is the same. The three equations that we used for the previous examples are still usually sufficient to solve the new system – there will be slight changes to the vertical and horizontal equations since there may be a component from *each* of the strings in these directions. There can be a little extra geometry involved sometimes to find the fraction of the string on either side of the bead. Let's have a look at a typical problem of this sort.

Example

One end of a light inextensible string of length $2c$ is attached at a fixed point A and the other end is attached at a fixed point B, where B is at a distance c vertically above A. A smooth ring of mass m is threaded on the string and made to rotate in a horizontal circle, centre A, with constant speed. Show that the tension in the string is $\frac{5mg}{4}$ and calculate the speed of the ring.

Solution

Be careful to read the question carefully with examples of this kind – it's very easy to misinterpret the information given and start off with the wrong diagram.

Figure 4.9

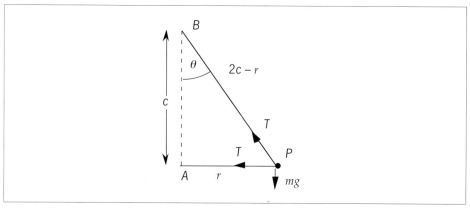

Since the length of the string is $2c$, if we call AP r then BP will be $2c - r$.

Vertically: $T \cos \theta - mg = 0$ ... ①

Horizontally: $T + T \sin \theta = \dfrac{mv^2}{r}$ ... ②

Δ: $\cos \theta = \dfrac{c}{2c - r}$ ... ③

There is actually an additional equation from the triangle in this case. Using Pythagoras,

$$(2c - r)^2 = c^2 + r^2$$

$$4c^2 - 4cr + r^2 = c^2 + r^2$$

$$3c^2 - 4cr = 0 \quad \Rightarrow \quad r = \frac{3c}{4}$$

$$\dots \text{④}$$

Putting this back into ③, $\cos\theta = \dfrac{c}{2c - \dfrac{3c}{4}} = \dfrac{c}{\dfrac{5c}{4}} = \dfrac{4}{5}$ $\quad\dots$ ⑤

and this into ① gives $T \times \dfrac{4}{5} - mg = 0$

$$\Rightarrow \quad T = \frac{5mg}{4} \qquad \dots \text{⑥}$$

If $\cos\theta = \dfrac{4}{5}$ 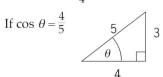 $\sin\theta = \dfrac{3}{5}$

and ② becomes $T + T \times \dfrac{3}{5} = \dfrac{mv^2}{r}$

Putting in the values of T and r from ④ and ⑥,

$$\frac{5mg}{4}\left(1 + \frac{3}{5}\right) = \frac{mv^2}{\dfrac{3c}{4}}$$

$$v^2 = \frac{3c}{4} \times \frac{5g}{4}\left(\frac{8}{5}\right) = \frac{3cg}{2}$$

i.e. $v = \sqrt{\left(\dfrac{3gc}{2}\right)}$

Practice questions F

1 The ends of a light inextensible string of length $2a$ are attached to fixed points A and B which are a distance a apart with A vertically above B. A small smooth ring P of mass m is threaded on to the string and moves in a horizontal circle, centre B, with constant speed, the portions AP, PB of the string being taut.

Find the tension in the string and show that the speed of the particle is

$$\sqrt{\left(\tfrac{3}{2}ga\right)}.$$

2

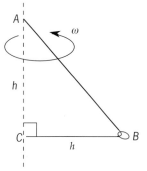

A light inextensible string is threaded through a small smooth ring B, and the ends of the string are attached to the fixed points A and C, as shown in the diagram. The mass of the ring is m and the point A is at a height h vertically above C. The ring moves in a horizontal circle with centre C and radius h, and CB has constant angular velocity ω.

Find ω^2 in terms of g and h.

3

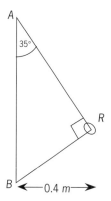

A small smooth ring R, of mass 0.4 kg, is threaded on a light inextensible string. The ends are attached to two fixed points A and B, where A is vertically above B. The system rotates about AB. The ring R moves with constant speed in a horizontal circle of radius 0.4 m. Angle ARB is 90° and angle BAR is 35° (see diagram).

(a)   Find the tension in the string.

(b)   Find the speed of the ring.

4   A smooth ring R of mass 0.3 kg is free to slide along a light inextensible string. The ends of the string are attached to fixed points A and B, where A is a distance 2.1 metres vertically above B. The ring is moving in a horizontal circle about AB with the string taut.

Angle ARB is a right angle and angle BAR is θ, where $\sin\theta = \frac{3}{5}$, as shown in the figure below.

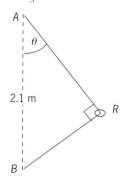

(a)   Find the tension in the string.

(b)   Find the speed of the ring.

Two strings

OCR M2 5.8.4 (c)

There is little difference if the particle is supported by two strings – the same three basic equations are enough to solve the system. Remember that the tensions in the two strings are *different*, so they should be labelled T_1 and T_2, for example (as opposed to the previous section where the tensions either side of a smooth bead were the same).

Example

Fig. 4.10 shows a particle of mass m which is attached to fixed points A and B by means of two light inextensible strings of lengths l and $l\sqrt{3}$ respectively. B is a distance l vertically above A. The system rotates with constant angular speed ω about AB, and both strings are taut.

Figure 4.10

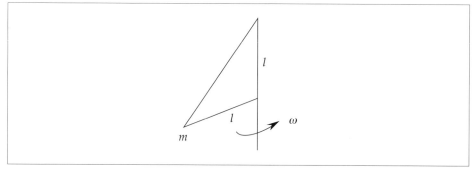

(a)   Show that the strings make angles of 60° and 30° with the vertical.

(b)   Find expressions in terms of m, g, ω and l for the tensions in the strings.

(c)   Show that $\frac{2g}{3l} < \omega^2 < \frac{2g}{l}$.

Solution	Putting in all the information, we get Fig. 4.11:

Figure 4.11

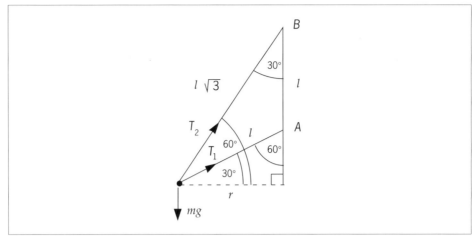

(a) By the cos rule, $\cos \hat{B} = \dfrac{l^2 + 3l^2 - l^2}{2 \times l \times l\sqrt{3}} = \dfrac{3}{2\sqrt{3}} = \dfrac{\sqrt{3}}{2} \Rightarrow \hat{B} = 30°$

Since the upper triangle is isosceles, the obtuse angle at A will be 120° and so the angle that the lower string makes will be 180° − 120°, i.e. 60°.

(b) Forces on the particle,

vertical : $T_2 \cos 30° + T_1 \cos 60° - mg = 0$ ... ①

horizontal : $T_2 \sin 30° + T_1 \sin 60° = mr\omega^2$ ... ②

lower Δ : $\cos 30° = \dfrac{r}{l}$ ... ③

Using $\cos 30° = \dfrac{\sqrt{3}}{2}$, ③ becomes $r = \dfrac{l\sqrt{3}}{2}$ and putting this into ② together with the values for the trig. ratios

$T_2 \times \dfrac{1}{2} + T_1 \times \dfrac{\sqrt{3}}{2} = m \times \dfrac{l\sqrt{3}}{2} \times \omega^2$

i.e. $T_2 + T_1 \sqrt{3} = ml\omega^2\sqrt{3}$ ... ④

and similarly ① becomes $T_2 \times \dfrac{\sqrt{3}}{2} + T_1 \times \dfrac{1}{2} - mg = 0$

i.e. $T_2 \sqrt{3} + T_1 = 2mg$ ... ⑤

$T_2 \sqrt{3} + 3T_1 = 3ml\omega^2$

$2T_1 = 3ml\omega^2 - 2mg$ ④ $\times \sqrt{3}$ −⑤

i.e $T_1 = \dfrac{m}{2}\left[3l\omega^2 - 2g\right]$ and this into ⑤ gives

$T_2 \sqrt{3} = 2mg - \dfrac{3ml\omega^2}{2} + mg = \dfrac{3m}{2}\left[2g - l\omega^2\right]$

i.e. $T_2 = \dfrac{m\sqrt{3}}{2}\left[2g - l\omega^2\right]$

(c) Since both strings are taut, T_1 and T_2 are greater than zero

$$T_1 > 0 \implies \frac{m}{2}\left[3l\omega^2 - 2g\right] > 0$$

$$\implies 3l\omega^2 - 2g > 0 \implies \omega^2 > \frac{2g}{3l}$$

$$T_2 > 0 \implies \frac{m\sqrt{3}}{2}\left[2g - l\omega^2\right] > 0$$

$$\implies 2g - l\omega^2 > 0 \implies \omega^2 < \frac{2g}{l}$$

Combining these two, $\dfrac{2g}{3l} < \omega^2 < \dfrac{2g}{l}$

Practice questions G

1 A light inextensible string of length $3a$ has one end fixed at a point A and the other end fixed at a point B which is vertically below A and at a distance $2a$ from it. A small ring R of mass m is threaded on the string.

(a) If R is fixed to the mid-point of the string and moves in a horizontal circle with speed $\sqrt{(5\,ga)}$, find the tensions in the parts AR and BR of the string.

(b) If R is free to move on the string and moves in a horizontal circle centre B with the string taut, show that $BR = \dfrac{5a}{6}$ and find the speed of R.

2

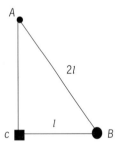

The ends of a light inextensible string ABC of length $3l$ are attached to fixed points A and C, C being vertically below A at a distance $\sqrt3 l$ from A. At a distance $2l$ along the string from A a particle B of mass m is attached. When both portions of the string are taut, B is given a horizontal velocity u, and then continues to move in a circle with constant speed. Find the tensions in the two portions of the string and show that the motion is possible only if

$$u^2 \geq \frac{1}{3}gl\sqrt{3}.$$

3

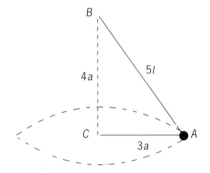

The above figure shows two light inextensible strings, AB and AC, of lengths $5a$ and $3a$ respectively, each attached at A to a particle of mass m. The ends B and C are fixed with B vertically above C, where $BC = 4a$. With both strings taut, the particle moves in a horizontal circle with constant angular speed ω.

(a) Find, in terms of m and g, the tension in the string AB.

(b) Find, in terms of m, g, a and ω, the tension in the string AC.

(c) Hence show that

$$\omega^2 > \frac{g}{4a}.$$

4

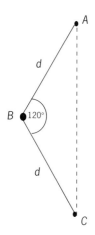

The above figure shows two light inextensible strings *AB* and *BC*, each of length *d*, attached at *B* to a particle of mass *m*. The other ends *A* and *C* are fixed to points in a vertical line with *A* above *C*. With both strings taut and ∠ *ABC* = 120°, the particle moves in a horizontal circle with constant angular speed ω.

Find, in terms of *m*, *g*, *d* and ω

(a)   the tension in string *AB*

(b)   the tension in string *BC*

(c)   Show that

$$\omega^2 \geq \left(\frac{2g}{3d}\right)\sqrt{3}$$

Two particles

OCR M2 5.8.4 (c)

The final variation on this type of system where the string is **inelastic** is the addition of an extra particle fastened on to the other end of the string.

Questions can be set where the string has a particle at each end, one of which is stationary and the other of which is describing a horizontal circle. The force on the stationary particle which opposes the tension and maintains equilibrium comes either from its weight if hanging or from friction if supported by a rough horizontal plane.

Figure 4.12

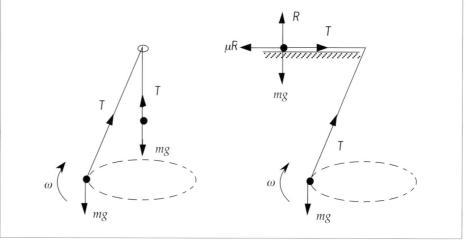

We will need at least one, and possibly two, additional equation(s) which come from looking at the equilibrium of the stationary particle. Here's an example of the first type, where the stationary particle is hanging.

Example

A light inextensible string, of length 2 m, passes through a small fixed smooth ring *R* and carries particle *A*, of mass 2*M*, at one end and particle *B*, of mass *M*, at the other end. The particle *A* is at rest vertically below *R*. The particle *B* moves in a horizontal circle, the centre of which is vertically below *R*, with constant angular speed 4 rad s⁻¹. Given that the string remains taut, calculate the distance *AR*. (Take *g* as 10 m s⁻².)

Solution	It's quite easy to make mistakes in questions of this kind, so once you've drawn your diagram, check back that the information in the question fits. We'll mark in θ, the angle that the string makes with the downward vertical, as in Fig. 4.13.

Figure 4.13

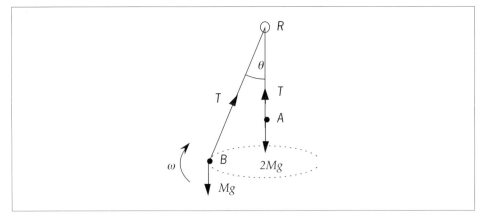

Since A is stationary, the forces in A are in equilibrium, i.e.

$$T - 2Mg = 0 \qquad \dots \text{①}$$

For the particle B,

Vertically: $T \cos \theta - Mg = 0$ $\qquad \dots \text{②}$

Horizontally: $T \sin \theta = Mr\omega^2$ $\qquad \dots \text{③}$

From the triangle shown in Fig. 4.14, $\sin \theta = \dfrac{r}{l}$. $\qquad \dots \text{④}$

Figure 4.14

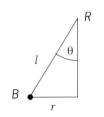

In fact, in this example we don't need all these equations. Combining ③ and ④,

$$\frac{Tr}{l} = Mr\omega^2 \;\Rightarrow\; l = \frac{T}{M\omega^2} \qquad \dots \text{⑤}$$

But from ①, $T = 2Mg$ and so

$$l = \frac{2Mg}{M\omega^2} \quad \text{and since } \omega = 4 \text{ (given)}$$

$$l = \frac{2g}{16} = \frac{5}{4} \text{ m}$$

This is the distance BR, so $AR = 2 - \dfrac{5}{4} = \dfrac{3}{4}$ m

Practice questions H

1

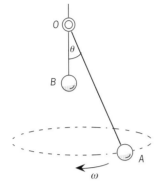

Two small spheres, *A* and *B*, of mass 0.8 kg and 1 kg respectively, are attached to the ends of a light inextensible string which passes through a small smooth ring at the fixed point *O*, as shown in the above figure. The ring is free to turn about a vertical axis. Sphere *A* describes a horizontal circle with constant angular speed ω rad s^{-1}. The portion of the string between *O* and *A* makes a constant θ with the vertical, and the portion *OB* is vertical. Sphere *B* remains in equilibrium.

(a)   Find the value of cos θ.

Given that *A* makes one complete revolution per second:

(b)   state the value of ω, giving your answer in terms of π

(c)   find the length of string between *O* and *A*, giving your answer in cm to the nearest cm.

2   Two equal particles are attached to the ends *A* and *B* of a light inextensible string, which passes through a small hole at the apex *C* of a hollow, right, circular cone fixed with its axis vertical and apex uppermost. The semi-vertical angle of the cone is θ. The particle at *A* moves in a horizontal circle with constant angular velocity ω on the smooth surface of the cone, while the other particle hangs at rest inside the cone. If *CA* = *a*, prove that

$$\omega^2 = \frac{g}{a\,(1 + \cos\theta)}$$

and deduce that $\dfrac{g}{2\omega^2} < a < \dfrac{g}{\omega^2}$.

Other systems involving circular motion

OCR M2 5.8.4 (c)

We are now going to look at three other types of system which appear very different but where, in fact, the same general principles can be carried over with little change necessary in the basic equations.

Bead in a bowl

The first of these is where the particle is moving in a horizontal circle around the inside of a hemispherical shape, a bowl for instance, and the force towards the centre of the circle is provided by the component of the normal reaction in this direction.

Figure 4.15

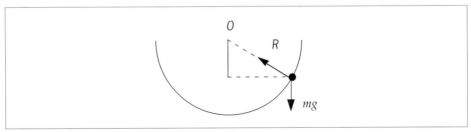

There is in fact very little difference between this and a conical pendulum – the same three equations apply, with the normal reaction (which passes through the centre of the circle) appearing instead of a tension. Here's an example.

Example	A particle P, moving on the smooth inside surface of a fixed hemispherical bowl, of radius r, describes a horizontal circle at depth $\frac{r}{2}$ below the centre of the bowl. Show that P takes time $\pi\sqrt{\frac{2r}{g}}$ to complete one revolution of its circular path.

Solution	If we call the mass of the particle m and the normal reaction of the particle on the smooth surface R, we have the following system:

Figure 4.16	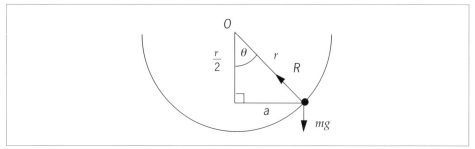

Vertically: $R \cos \theta = mg$ ... ①

Horizontally: $R \sin \theta = ma\omega^2$ ... ②

Δ: $\cos \theta = \dfrac{\frac{r}{2}}{r} = \dfrac{1}{2}$, i.e. $\theta = 60°$ ... ③

Putting this into ①, $R \cos 60° = mg \Rightarrow R = 2mg$ ... ④

Also from the triangle, $\sin \theta = \dfrac{a}{r}$, and putting this together with ④ into ②,

$$2mg \times \frac{a}{r} = ma\omega^2 \;\Rightarrow\; \omega^2 = \frac{2g}{r}$$

$$\therefore \quad \omega = \sqrt{\frac{2g}{r}} \text{ rad s}^{-1}$$

The time for 1 revolution, i.e. 2π radians, will be:

$$\frac{2\pi}{\sqrt{\frac{2g}{r}}} = \pi\sqrt{\frac{2r}{g}}$$

Practice questions I

1   A particle moves in a horizontal circle with angular velocity ω on the smooth inner surface of a hollow sphere of internal radius a. Find the depth of the circle below the centre of the sphere.

2   A particle moves with constant angular ω in a horizontal circle of radius a on the inside of a fixed smooth hemispherical bowl of internal radius $2a$. Show that

$$\omega^2 = \frac{g}{a\sqrt{3}}$$

Here's another example of circular motion, this time on a slightly larger scale.

Satellites in orbit

When an object like a satellite is orbiting the earth, the force that stops it flying out into space is the gravitational 'pull' of the earth. If we know an expression for this, we can connect the height and speed of the object and find the time for one revolution.

Example

The motion of an artificial satellite may be assumed to be uniform motion in a circle whose centre is at the centre of the earth, and the centre of the earth may be regarded as a fixed point. The gravitational force exerted by the earth on any object of mass m is inversely proportional to the square of the distance of the object from the centre of the earth, and at the earth's surface this force is mg.

Prove that a satellite orbiting at a height h above the earth's surface completes one revolution in time T, where

$$T^2 = \frac{4\pi^2(R + h)^3}{gR^2}$$

and where R is the radius of the earth.

Solution

The distance of the centre of the earth from the satellite is $R + h$
(see Fig. 4.17) and so the gravitational force of the earth on the satellite will be:

$$F = \frac{k}{(R + h)^2} \qquad \qquad \dots \text{①}$$

Figure 4.17

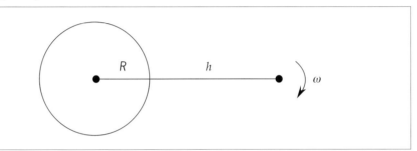

But we're told that on the surface of the earth, i.e. $h = 0$, this force is mg, i.e.

$$mg = \frac{k}{(R + 0)^2} = \frac{k}{R^2} \Rightarrow k = mgR^2 \qquad \qquad \dots \text{②}$$

Putting this back into ①

$$F = \frac{mg\,R^2}{(R + h)^2} \qquad \qquad \dots \text{③}$$

But this force is responsible for the circular motion, i.e. $F = mr\omega^2$, where r is the radius of the circle. But this is $R + h$ and so

$$F = m(R + h)\omega^2 \qquad \qquad \dots \text{④}$$

Equating ③ and ④,

$$\frac{mgR^2}{(R + h)^2} = m(R + h)\omega^2$$

i.e. $\omega^2 = \dfrac{gR^2}{(R + h)^3} \qquad \qquad \dots \text{⑤}$

But the time T for one revolution is $\dfrac{2\pi}{\omega}$,

$$T = \frac{2\pi}{\omega} \Rightarrow T^2 = \frac{4\pi^2}{\omega^2} \qquad \qquad \dots \text{⑥}$$

Inserting ⑤ into ⑥,

$$T^2 = \frac{4\pi^2(R + h)^3}{gR^2}$$

For the final of these three variants of circular motion, we move back down to a smaller scale.

Bead on a rotating wire

If a bead is threaded on a circular wire and the wire rotates around a vertical diameter, the bead will describe a circle provided that it stays in the same place relative to the wire.

Figure 4.18

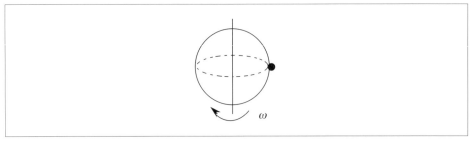

If the wire is smooth the force towards the centre will be provided by the normal reaction between the bead and the wire, which passes through the centre of the wire circle. For the bead to remain stationary relative to the wire, the vertical component of the reaction and the weight have to balance.

Figure 4.19

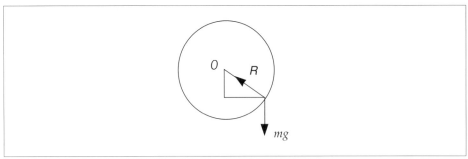

With a **rough** wire, the friction can act in either of two ways. If the angular velocity is not very large, the bead will tend to drop towards the bottom of the wire and the friction, opposing this tendency, will act **upwards**. As the angular velocity increases there will be a speed at which the bead remains in equilibrium relative to the wire.

A further increase in angular velocity means that the bead will tend to slip upwards and the friction will then act **downwards**.

Practice questions J

A miscellaneous selection, with some combinations of types.

1   One end of a light inextensible string of length a is fixed at a point vertically above the centre of a fixed smooth sphere and a particle of mass m is attached to the other end of the string. The particle moves with constant angular velocity ω in a horizontal circle on the surface of the sphere, with the string taut and making an angle 30° with the vertical.

Find the tension in the string in terms of m, g, a and ω.

Show that, if the particle is on the point of leaving the sphere, $\omega^2 = \dfrac{2g}{(a\sqrt{3})}$.

2

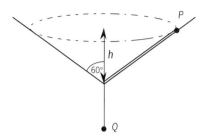

A smooth hollow cone of semi-vertical angle 60° is fixed with its axis vertical and vertex downwards, as shown in the diagram. A light inextensible string passes through a small smooth hole at the vertex and particles of equal mass m are attached to the two ends of the string. The lower particle Q hangs at rest while the upper particle P moves with constant speed v in a horizontal circle on the inner surface of the cone. The circle is at a height h above the vertex of the cone.

Show that the reaction of the cone on P is of magnitude $\sqrt{3}\,mg$, and find h in terms of v and g.

3

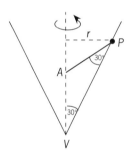

A hollow circular cone is fixed with its axis vertical and its vertex V downwards. A particle P, of mass m, is attached to a fixed point A on the axis of the cone by means of a light inextensible string of length equal to AV.

The particle moves with constant speed v in a horizontal circle on the smooth inner surface of the cone, with the string taut. The radius of the circle is r, and angles APV and AVP are each 30° (see diagram).

(a) Find the expression, in terms of m, g, v and r, for the tension in the string.

(b) Deduce that $\dfrac{v^2}{gr} > \sqrt{3}$

4 A right circular cone of semi-vertical angle α, where $\alpha < \frac{1}{4}\pi$, is fixed with its axis vertical and its vertex V upwards. One end of a light inextensible string of length l is attached to V. A particle of mass m is attached to the other end of the string. The particle moves on the smooth outer surface of the cone in a horizontal circle with constant angular velocity ω. Find the tension in the string and the magnitude of the reaction between the cone and the particle.

Deduce that $\omega^2 \leq \dfrac{g}{l\cos\alpha}$

Given that ω_1 is the value of ω for which the particle just remains on the surface of the cone, and that ω_2 is the constant angular velocity with which the particle moves in a horizontal circle when the string makes an angle 2α with the vertical, show that

$$\left(\frac{\omega_1}{\omega_2}\right)^2 = \frac{\cos 2\alpha}{\cos\alpha}.$$

5 A fixed hollow smooth sphere, of external radius a and centre O, has a small hole at the highest point. A light inextensible string passes through the hole and carries a particle of mass $2m$ which hangs freely, at rest, inside the sphere. A particle P, of mass $3m$, is attached to the other end of the string and moves on the outer surface of the sphere in a horizontal circle of radius $\frac{1}{2}a$ with angular velocity ω.

Show that

$$\frac{a\omega^2}{g} = \frac{2\sqrt{3}}{9}$$

6 The ends of a light inextensible string are fixed to two points A and B in the same vertical line with A above B. A small particle of mass m is fastened at a point P of the string and made to rotate, with both parts of the string taut and with angle APB a right angle, about AB in a horizontal circle of radius r. The angle BAP and the angular speed are denoted by θ and ω respectively. Show that the tension in BP is $m(r\omega^2\cos\theta - g\sin\theta)$ and find the corresponding expression for the tension in AP.

Given that $AB = 5a$, $AP = 4a$ and that the string has a breaking tension of $6\,mg$, find, in terms of a and g, the range of possible values of ω^2.

7

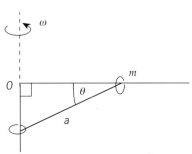

A small ring of mass M is threaded on to the vertical wire, and a small ring of mass m is threaded on to the horizontal wire. The two rings are joined by a light inextensible string of length a. The system rotates with constant angular velocity ω about a vertical axis through O, with the string taut and making a constant acute angle θ with the horizontal.

Show that $Mg < ma\omega^2$.

The diagram shows two smooth straight wires, one vertical and one horizontal, fixed together at O.

Banked corners

OCR M2 5.8.4 (c)

When modern motorways are built, you can see that they are made so that the outer edges of bends are higher than the inner edges – this is even more obvious if you see an indoor cycle track, where this phenomenon, called *banking*, is very prominent. We're going to look at the forces acting as the cars or cycles go round the circular path and see the advantages of this construction.

We can simplify the analysis if we suppose that the car can be treated as a particle performing horizontal circular motion. If the track is banked at an angle θ, we have the situation shown in Fig. 4.20.

Figure 4.20

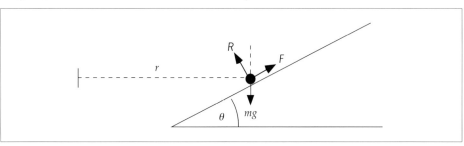

Since the particle is not in equilibrium, we can't resolve parallel and perpendicular to the plane very easily, so instead we resolve vertically and horizontally as we have in previous situations of circular motion. This gives:

Vertically:	$R \cos \theta + F \sin \theta$	$= mg$	... ①
Horizontally:	$R \sin \theta - F \cos \theta$	$= \dfrac{mv^2}{r}$	... ②
① × sin θ, ② × cos θ	$R \sin \theta \cos \theta + F \sin^2\theta$	$= mg \sin \theta$	... ③
	$R \sin \theta \cos \theta - F \cos^2\theta$	$= \dfrac{mv^2}{r} \cos \theta$	... ④
③ − ④	$F (\sin^2\theta + \cos^2\theta)$	$= mg \sin \theta - \dfrac{mv^2}{r} \cos \theta$	
i.e.	$F = m(g \sin \theta - \dfrac{v^2}{r} \cos \theta)$	since $\sin^2\theta + \cos^2\theta = 1$	

Now everything in this equation is constant except the speed, v. So as v increases from zero, there will be some value at which the expression in the bracket is zero, when

$$g \sin \theta - \frac{v^2}{r} \cos \theta = 0 \qquad \Rightarrow \frac{v^2}{r} \cos \theta = g \sin \theta$$

i.e. $v^2 = \dfrac{gr \sin \theta}{\cos \theta} = gr \tan \theta$

When we increase the speed further, the term in the bracket is negative which means that the friction is negative – it now acts in the opposite direction, i.e. downwards. If you have ever been in a car which has taken a corner too fast you will have experienced this – the car is forced outwards and the friction acts towards the centre of the bend as a counter: this can be hard on the tyres. Hence the banking of the curve – instead of the friction from the tyres providing the force inwards, we have the component of the weight which makes for a much smoother ride.

Example

A circular track is banked at an angle α to the horizontal, where $\tan \alpha = \dfrac{3}{4}$.

A woman cycles round the track in such a way that she moves at constant speed in a horizontal circle of radius 25 m. In an initial model of the situation it is assumed that the track is smooth, the woman and the cycle together constitute a particle, and the resistance motion from non-gravitational forces is negligible.

(a)   Find, in m s^{-1} to 1 decimal place, the speed of the woman.

The model is refined to allow for the fact that the track is rough, the coefficient of friction between the cycle and the track being assumed to be $\dfrac{1}{3}$. The resistance from non-gravitational forces opposing the circular motion is still assumed to be negligible.

(b)   Using this model, find, in m s^{-1} to one decimal place, the maximum speed at which the woman could cycle round the track on the same path as before without the cycle slipping sideways.

Solution

(a)

Figure 4.21

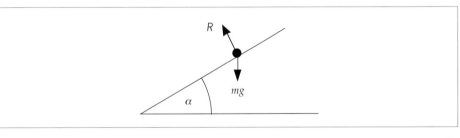

Vertically: $R \cos \alpha = mg$ $\qquad \qquad$ ... ①

Horizontally: $R \sin \alpha = \dfrac{mv^2}{r}$ $\qquad \qquad$ ... ②

$② \div ① \quad \Rightarrow \quad \dfrac{R \sin \alpha}{R \cos \alpha} = \dfrac{mv^2}{r} \times \dfrac{1}{mg} \quad \Rightarrow \quad \tan \alpha = \dfrac{v^2}{gr}$

Since $r = 25$, $\tan \alpha = \dfrac{3}{4}$, $v^2 = \dfrac{3}{4} \times 9.8 \times 25$

$\Rightarrow v = 13.6$ m s^{-1} (1 d.p.)

Figure 4.22

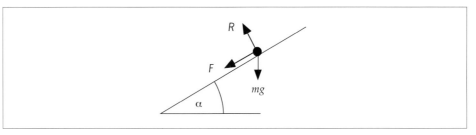

(b) Vertically: $R \cos \alpha - F \sin \alpha = mg$ ... ③

Horizontally: $R \sin \alpha + F \cos \alpha = mv^2$ ... ④

$$F = \mu R \quad ... ⑤$$

Since $\tan \alpha = \dfrac{3}{4}$, $\sin \alpha = \dfrac{3}{5}$, $\cos \alpha = \dfrac{4}{5}$

③ becomes $\dfrac{4}{5} R - \left(\dfrac{1}{3}R\right)\left(\dfrac{3}{5}\right) = mg \quad \Rightarrow \quad \dfrac{3}{5}R = mg, R = \dfrac{5mg}{3}$

③ then becomes $\dfrac{5mg}{3}\left(\dfrac{3}{5}\right) + \dfrac{1}{3}\left(\dfrac{5mg}{3}\right)\left(\dfrac{4}{5}\right) = \dfrac{mv^2}{25}$

$$\dfrac{13\,mg}{9} = \dfrac{mv^2}{25}$$

$$\Rightarrow v^2 = \dfrac{25 \times 13g}{9} \quad \Rightarrow v = 18.8 \text{ m s}^{-1} \ (1 \text{ d.p.})$$

Practice questions K

1 The car, shown in the figure below, is travelling round a circular bend on a road banked at an angle α to the horizontal. The car may be modelled as a particle moving in a horizontal circle of radius 120 metres.

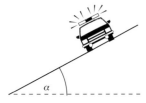

When the car is moving at a constant speed of 20 m s^{-1} there is no frictional force up or down the slope.

Find the angle α, giving your answer in degrees correct to one decimal place.

2 A car, of mass 1200 kg, travels round a bend, of radius 50 m, at a constant speed of 20 m s^{-1}. Model the car as a particle and assume that there is no air resistance acting on it.

(a) A simple model assumes that the road is horizontal. Find the magnitude of the friction force acting on the car.

(b) In reality the road is banked at 2° to the horizontal, as shown in the diagram.

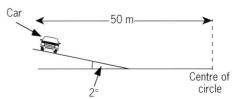

Draw and label a diagram to show the forces on the car and find a revised value for the magnitude of the friction force that takes account of the banking.

3

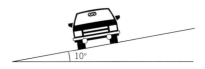

A car is travelling round a circular bend on a road which is banked at an angle of 10° to the horizontal, as shown in the above figure. The car is modelled as a particle moving in a horizontal circle of radius 80 m. When the car is moving at a constant speed of v m s^{-1} there is no sideways frictional force acting on the car.

Find, to 3 significant figures, the value of v.

Elastic strings

A common variant of the situations that we looked at in the previous sections is where the inelastic string is replaced by an elastic string. This doesn't make much difference to the working: we can find an expression for the tension from the formula for an elastic string, $T = \dfrac{\lambda x}{l}$ and this, together with the usual equations for circular motion, should mean that we can solve the system.

Let's have a look at a couple of examples of this, the first of which is quite straightforward.

Example

A particle is suspended from a fixed point by a light elastic string of natural length a. In equilibrium the length of the string is $\dfrac{3a}{2}$. The particle is set rotating in a horizontal circle with uniform speed, the string being at a constant angle to the vertical and extended to a length $2a$. Find the speed of the particle.

Solution

We're not told the mass of the particle nor the modulus of elasticity of the string, so we'll call them m and λ as usual. Our first equation comes from looking at the particle in equilibrium, as shown in Fig. 4.23.

Figure 4.23

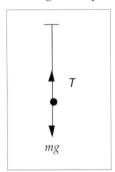

i.e. $T - mg = 0$ ... ①

Also, since the string is elastic,

$$T = \frac{\lambda x}{l} \qquad \text{... ②}$$

and we're told that the length is now $\dfrac{3a}{2}$, i.e. $x = \dfrac{a}{2}$ and $l = a$

so that ② becomes:

$$T = \frac{\lambda}{a} \times \frac{a}{2} = \frac{\lambda}{2} \qquad \text{... ③}$$

Since from ①, $T = mg$, we have:

$$mg = \frac{\lambda}{2} \implies \lambda = 2mg \qquad \text{... ④}$$

Now when the string is rotating, we have the situation shown in Fig. 4.24.

Figure 4.24

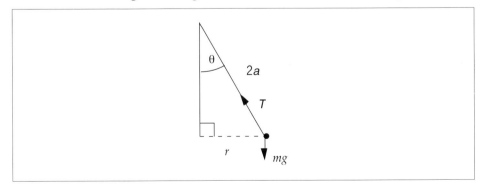

Vertically: $\quad T\cos\theta - mg = 0$ $\qquad\qquad$ ... ⑤

Horizontally: $\quad T\sin\theta = \dfrac{mv^2}{r}$ $\qquad\qquad$ ... ⑥

$\Delta:\qquad\qquad \sin\theta = \dfrac{r}{2a}$ $\qquad\qquad$ ... ⑦

Elasticity: $\quad T = \dfrac{\lambda x}{a}$ $\qquad\qquad$ ... ⑧

Since from ④, $\lambda = 2mg$ and we're told that the new length is $2a$, i.e. $x = a$, ⑧ becomes:

$$T = \frac{2mga}{a} = 2mg \qquad\qquad\text{... ⑨}$$

From ⑤ $\quad T = \dfrac{mg}{\cos\theta} \;\Rightarrow\; \dfrac{mg}{\cos\theta} = 2mg \;\Rightarrow\; \cos\theta = \dfrac{1}{2}$

$$\Rightarrow\; \theta = 60°$$

From ⑥ $\quad v^2 = \dfrac{T\sin\theta \times r}{m}$ and from ⑦, $r = 2a\sin\theta$, so

$$v^2 = \frac{T\sin\theta \times 2a\sin\theta}{m} \text{ and since } T = 2mg \text{ and } \sin\theta = \frac{\sqrt{3}}{2}$$

$$= 3ag \text{ then } v = \sqrt{3ag}$$

Here's another example, this time with the particle resting on a smooth table.

Example

A light elastic string, of natural length l and modulus $3mg$, has one end A attached to a fixed point O on a smooth horizontal table. A particle of mass m is attached to the other end of the string. The particle moves in a horizontal circle, centre O, so that the string rotates with constant angular velocity $\sqrt{\left(\frac{2g}{l}\right)}$.
Find the radius of the circle.

The end A of the string is now raised vertically a distance $\frac{1}{2}l$ and held fixed.
The particle P moves on the table in a circle, with OP having constant angular velocity $\sqrt{\left(\frac{g}{l}\right)}$ Show that the radius of the circle is $l\sqrt{2}$ and that the tension in the string is $\frac{3}{2}mg$. Find the magnitude of the reaction between the particle and the table.

Solution

Sometimes with these questions, you have to read carefully otherwise you might assume that, in the first part, the end of the string is *above* the table, which of course it isn't.

Figure 4.25

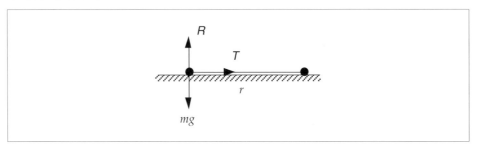

The force for the circular motion is coming entirely from the tension, and so with $\omega = \sqrt{\left(\frac{2g}{l}\right)}$

$$T = mr\omega^2 = mr\frac{2g}{l} \qquad \dots \text{①}$$

Since the string is elastic, we have also that, with an extended length of r, i.e. extension $(r - l)$

$$T = \frac{\lambda x}{l} = \frac{3mg(r - l)}{l} \qquad \dots \text{②}$$

Equating these two, $\qquad \dfrac{2mgr}{l} = \dfrac{3mg(r - l)}{l}$

$$2r = 3(r - l) = 3r - 3l$$

$$r = 3l$$

We need a new diagram for the next part.

Figure 4.26

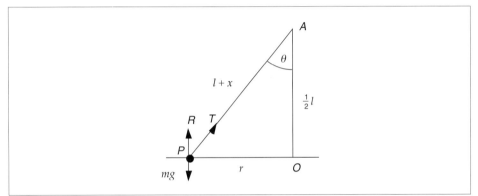

Vertically: $\qquad T\cos\theta + R - mg = 0 \qquad \dots \text{③}$

Horizontally: $\quad T\sin\theta = mr\omega^2 \qquad\qquad \dots \text{④}$

Δ: $\qquad\qquad \sin\theta = \dfrac{r}{l + x} \qquad\qquad \dots \text{⑤}$

Elasticity: $\qquad T = \dfrac{\lambda x}{l} \qquad\qquad\qquad \dots \text{⑥}$

(We want to avoid using ③ if possible since it contains an R and at this stage we have no means of finding what this is or eliminating it.)

Since $\lambda = 3mg$, ⑥ becomes $T = \dfrac{3mgx}{l}$ and since $\sin\theta = \dfrac{r}{l + x}$

④ becomes $T \times \dfrac{r}{l + x} = mr\omega^2 \Rightarrow T = m\omega^2(l + x)$

Equating these two expressions for T,

$$\frac{3mgx}{l} = m\omega^2(l + x) \text{ and since } \omega^2 = \left(\sqrt{\left(\frac{g}{l}\right)}\right)^2 = \frac{g}{l}$$

$$\frac{3mgx}{l} = m\frac{g}{l}(l + x)$$

$$3x = l + x$$

$$\Rightarrow \quad 2x = l$$

$$\Rightarrow \quad x = \frac{l}{2}$$

From the right-angled Δ,

$$(l + x)^2 = \left(\tfrac{1}{2}l\right)^2 + r^2$$

$$\Rightarrow \quad r^2 = \left(l + \tfrac{l}{2}\right)^2 - \left(\tfrac{1}{2}l\right)^2 = 2l^2$$

$$\Rightarrow \quad r = l\sqrt{2}$$

Putting $x = \dfrac{l}{2}$ into ⑥, $\quad T = \dfrac{3mg \times \tfrac{1}{2}}{l} = \dfrac{3mg}{2}$

Now from ③ $\quad R = mg - T \cos \theta$

$$= mg - \dfrac{3mg}{2} \times \dfrac{\tfrac{1}{2}l}{\tfrac{3}{2}l}$$

$$= mg - \dfrac{mg}{2} = \dfrac{mg}{2}$$

Practice questions L

1 A particle is suspended from a fixed point by a light elastic string of natural length a.

In equilibrium the length of the string is $\dfrac{3a}{2}$.

The particle is set rotating in a horizontal circle with uniform speed, the string being at a constant angle to the vertical and extended to a length $2a$. Find the speed of the particle.

2

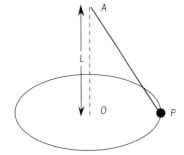

A particle P of mass m is attached to one end of a light elastic string with natural length L and modulus of elasticity $4\,mg$. The other end of the string is attached to a fixed point A. The particle describes a horizontal circle with constant speed v. The centre of this circle is the point O, where O is vertically below A and the distance $OA = L$, as shown in the above figure.

(a) Show that the extension of the string is $\dfrac{L}{3}$.

(b) Show that $v = \dfrac{1}{3}\sqrt{(7gL)}$.

3 A particle of mass m is attached to one end of a light inextensible string of length l, the other end of which is attached to a fixed point O at a height h above a smooth horizontal table. With the string taut the particle describes a circle on the table, at a constant angular speed ω. The centre of the circle is vertically below O. Find the tension in the string and the magnitude of the reaction of the table. Determine the greatest value of ω^2 for which such a motion is possible.

The inextensible string is now replaced by a light elastic string of modulus mg and natural length a and the table is removed. Find the greatest and least values of ω^2, in terms of g and a, such that P can still describe horizontal circles with constant angular speed ω.

4 A particle P of mass m is attached to one end of a light elastic string of natural length a and whose other end is fixed. In the equilibrium position with the string vertical the extension is $\dfrac{1}{4}a$. The string is then moved out of the vertical position and P is projected so that it describes a horizontal circle with constant angular speed and period T. The length of the string during this motion is $a + x$. Write down the equations of motion of P and show that the motion is only possible for $x > \dfrac{1}{4}a$.

Obtain expressions in terms of x, a and g for the angular speed and hence find T.

5

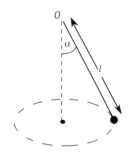

The above figure shows a model of a fairground swing in which a particle of mass m is attached to one end of a light inextensible rope of length l. The other end of the rope is attached to a fixed point O. The particle moves in a horizontal circle with constant angular speed $\sqrt{\left(\frac{5g}{4l}\right)}$. The rope is inclined at a constant angle α to the vertical.

(a) Find the value of α, giving your answer in degrees to one decimal place.

The model is refined so that the rope is now assumed to be elastic, with natural length l and modulus of elasticity $200mg$.
Given that the angular speed remains the same as before, and that the rope is now inclined at a constant angle β to the vertical,

(b) find the value of β, giving your answer in degrees to one decimal place.

6 A particle of mass m is suspended from a fixed point A by a light inextensible string of length l. The particle moves in a horizontal circle, whose centre is vertically below A, with constant angular speed ω and with the string taut and inclined at an angle θ to the downward vertical through A.

(a) Show that $\omega^2 l \cos \theta = g$.

The string is replaced by a light elastic string of natural length a and modulus of elasticity λ. The particle now moves in a horizontal circle, whose centre is vertically below A, with constant angular speed 2ω. The elastic string makes the same angle θ with the downward vertical.

(b) Show that $\dfrac{1}{4a} - \dfrac{1}{l} = \dfrac{m\omega^2}{\lambda}$.

7 The fixed points A and B are in the same vertical line, and B is at a distance a above A. The ends of a light elastic string are fixed at A and B, and a small smooth ring P, of mass m, is threaded on the string. The unstretched length of the string is a, and the modulus of elasticity of the string is mg.

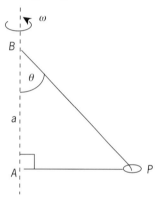

When the ring moves with constant speed in a horizontal circle with centre A, the angular velocity of the system is ω and angle ABP is θ (see diagram).

Show that $\theta = 45°$, and that $\omega^2 = \dfrac{g}{a}(1 + \sqrt{2})$.

SUMMARY EXERCISE

1

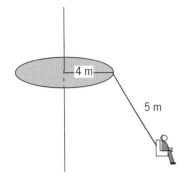

In a fun ride at a theme park, children sit in seats attached by chains of length 5 m to points on the rim of a horizontal circular disc of radius 4 m which rotates at a constant angular speed round a vertical axis through its centre, as shown in the above figure. Safety rules specify that, when the disc rotates during the ride, the chains must not make an angle greater than α to the vertical, where $\tan \alpha = \frac{3}{4}$.

The chains are modelled as light, inextensible strings which lie in a vertical plane containing the axis. A child and a seat are modelled together as a single particle, and any effect of air resistance is ignored.

Find the maximum angular speed with which the disc can rotate in order to comply with the safety rules, giving your answer in rad s^{-1} to 3 significant figures.

2   A particle is attached to one end of a light string, the other end of which is fixed. When the particle moves in a horizontal circle with speed 2 m s^{-1}, the string makes an angle $\tan^{-1}\left(\frac{5}{12}\right)$ with the vertical. Show that the length of the string is approximately 2.5 m.

3   A particle P is attached to one end of a light inextensible string of length 0.125 m, the other end of the string being attached to a fixed point O. The particle describes with constant speed, and with the string taut, a horizontal circle whose centre is vertically below O. Given that the particle describes exactly two complete rev s^{-1} find, in terms of g and π, the cosine of the angle between OP and the vertical.

4   One end of a light inextensible string of length $5a$ is tied at a fixed point A which is at a distance $3a$ above a smooth horizontal table.

A particle of mass m, which is tied at the other end of the string, rotates with constant speed in a circle on the table. If the reaction between the particle and the table is R, find the tension in the string when:

(a) $R = 0$

(b) $R = \frac{3mg}{4}$

Show that the respective times of one revolution for these two values of R are in the ratio 1:2.

5   One end of a light inextensible string of length $8a$ is attached to the point A. The other end is attached to the point B vertically below A, where $AB = 4$a. A small smooth bead of mass m is threaded on the string and moves in a horizontal circle, with centre B and radius $3a$, with constant speed v. Find, in terms of m and g, the tension in the string and show that $v^2 = 6ga$.

6

A light inextensible string AB, of length $4a$, passes through a small, fixed, smooth ring O. Particles of mass m and M are attached to the ends A and B of the string respectively. The mas m hangs at rest with OA vertical and the mass M moves with constant speed in a horizontal circle with centre A. Find, in terms of m and M, an expression for the cosine of the angle AOB. Hence deduce that the motion is only possible when $m > M$.

Given that $m = 3M$ and that the mass M has speed u, show that:

(a) $OA = a$

(b) $u^2 = 8\,ag$

At a given instant the string breaks and the particles move freely under gravity, until they collide with a horizontal table which is a distance $2a$ below O. Explain why the particles collide with the horizontal plane at the same time.

Find, in terms of a and g, the time interval which elapses between the string breaking and the particles colliding with the horizontal plane.

7

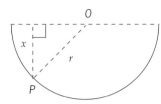

A particle P of mass m is moving in a horizontal circle with uniform speed v on the inner surface of a smooth fixed hemisphere which has centre O and radius r. If the vertical distance of P below the level of O is x, find expressions, in terms of m, g, r and x for v and for the reaction of the surface on P.

A light inextensible string is now attached to P. The string passes through a small hole at the lowest point of the hemisphere, and a particle of mass m hangs in equilibrium at the end of the string, so that the tension in the string is mg. Show that, if P moves on the surface in a horizontal circle with uniform speed v and with $x = \frac{1}{2}r$, then $v^2 = 3rg$.

8 An elastic string of length l and modulus $3mg$ has one end fixed to a point O. A particle of mass m is attached to the other end of the string and hangs in equilibrium. Find the stretched length of the string.

The particle is set in motion and describes a horizontal circle with constant angular speed ω. Given that the centre of the circle is at a distance l vertically below O, show

(a) that the stretched length of the string is $\frac{3l}{2}$

(b) that $\omega^2 l = g$.

(In this question take g to be 9.8 m s^{-2}.)

9 A light elastic string of natural length 0.2 m has one end attached to a fixed point O and a particle of mass 5 kg is attached to the other end.

When the particle hangs at rest vertically below O, the string has length 0.225 m. Find the modulus of elasticity of the string.

The particle is made to describe a horizontal circle whose centre is vertically below O. The string remains taut throughout this motion and is inclined at an angle θ to the downward vertical through O.

(a) Given that the tension in the string is 98 N, find θ and the angular speed of the particle.

(b) Given that the string breaks when the tension in it exceeds 196 N, find the greatest angular speed which the particle can have without the string breaking.

10 A car moves with constant speed in a horizontal circle of radius r on a track which is banked at an angle α to the horizontal, where $\tan \alpha = \frac{3}{4}$. The coefficient of friction between the tyres and the track is $\frac{1}{2}$. Find, in terms of r and g, the range of speeds at which the car can negotiate this bend without the tyres slipping on the road surface. Show that the greatest possible speed is $\sqrt{11}$ times the least possible speed. (It may be assumed that the car will not overturn at these speeds.)

11 A particle, of mass m, is attached by a light inextensible string, of length l, to the top of a smooth cone. The particle is set into motion so that it describes a horizontal circle on the outer surface of the cone as shown in the diagram below.

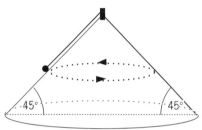

(a) Show that the tension in the string has magnitude $m \left(\frac{v^2}{l} + \frac{g}{\sqrt{2}} \right)$, when the particle describes a circle at a constant speed v.

(b) Find the magnitude of the normal reaction force that the cone exerts on the particle.

(c) What will happen if $v^2 > \frac{gl}{\sqrt{2}}$?

Justify your answer.

12 A satellite S moves in a circular orbit about the centre O of the earth. The earth is to be assumed to be a sphere of radius R and the height of the satellite above the earth's surface is denoted by h. The acceleration due to gravity at a distance r from O is given by $\frac{k}{r^2}$ where k is a constant, and g is the value of this acceleration at the earth's surface. Assuming that the force of gravity acts along SO express k in terms of g and R and show that the angular speed of the satellite is:

$$\left(\frac{gR^2}{(R+h)^3} \right)^{\frac{1}{2}}$$

Given that $R = 6400$ km and $g = 9.8$ m s^{-2} find, to the nearest minute, the period of the satellite when its height above the earth is 1600 km and deduce that this period is approximately 2 hours.

13 A light elastic string of natural length 3 m and modulus of elasticity 180 N is attached at one end to a fixed point O on a smooth horizontal plane. A particle of mass 3 kg is attached to the other end of the string. The particle moves on the plane in a circle, centre O, with angular speed 2 rad s^{-1}. Find the extension of the string.

Given that the string will break if the tension reaches 120 N, find the maximum angular speed of the particle.

14 A light elastic string AB has natural length l m and modulus of elasticity λ N. The end A is attached to a fixed point. When B is held at rest at a distance 0.6 m from A, the tension in the string is 3 N.

(a)   Find an equation relating λ and l.

When B is held at rest at a distance 0.7 m from A, the elastic energy in the string is 0.6 J.

(b)   Show that $l = 0.5$ and find the value of λ.

A particle, of mass 0.2 kg, is attached to the string at B with the end A still fixed. The particle B moves at constant speed in a circular path whose centre is vertically below A, so that the string AB traces out the curved surface of a cone. Given that the tension in the string is 3.92 N, calculate:

(c)   the angle between AB and the downward vertical at A

(d)   length of AB in this case, giving your answer in m to 2 decimal places.

(e)   the speed of B, giving your answer in m s^{-1} to 2 decimal places.

SUMMARY   When you have finished, you should:

- be able to convert from angular to linear speed and vice versa

  know how to find the time for one revolution

- know that a force of $\dfrac{mv^2}{r}$ or $mr\omega^2$ is required towards the centre to maintain circular motion

  know that three equations are generally required to solve a system: horizontal and vertical forces and the geometry

- be able to apply these equations to a conical pendulum

  know that for an object to be in contact with a surface, the contact force $R > 0$

- know that for a string to be taut, the tension $T > 0$

  know that for a smooth threaded bead, the tensions in both parts of the string are the same

  know that for a bead tied to a string, the tensions are not in general the same

  know that for a particle describing circles inside a hemispherical bowl, the reaction takes the place of the tension in a string

  know that the gravitational force provides the central force for a satellite in orbit

  know that the friction on a car rounding a banked curve can act in either direction depending on the speed.

ANSWERS

Practice questions A

1 (a) 4π rad s^{-1} (b) 8 rad s^{-1}
   (c) 6π rad s^{-1}

2 (a) 4 m s^{-1} (b) 10 m s^{-1}
   (c) 0.8 m s^{-1} (d) 3π m s^{-1}

3 (a) 0.5 rad s^{-1} (b) 2 rad s^{-1}
   (c) 0.6 rad s^{-1} (d) 4 rad s^{-1}

Practice questions B

1 (a) $\frac{1}{4}$ second   (b) $\frac{2\pi}{3}$ seconds

   (c) 0.5 second   (d) 4π seconds

   (e) $\frac{20}{7}$ seconds

Practice questions C

1 (a) 25 N   (b) 0.4 N
   (c) 16 N   (d) $320\pi^2$ N

2 10 m   **3** 355.3 N

Practice questions D

4 (a) $\frac{2g}{\omega^2}$ (b) $\frac{l}{L} = \frac{\sqrt{3}}{4}$ **5** $\frac{g}{2\pi^2}$

Practice questions E

1 $mg - m\omega^2 h$

2 (a) $\frac{5mg}{3}$ (b) $\frac{5mg}{12}$

3 (a) $md\omega^2$ (b) $m(g - h\omega^2)$ (d) $\frac{2h}{3}$

4 $R = mg - \frac{3mv^2}{8a}$

Practice questions F

1 $\frac{5mg}{4}$ **2** $\frac{g}{h}(1 + \sqrt{2})$

3 (a) 15.96 N   (b) 4.72 m s^{-1}

4 (a) 14.7 N   (b) 8.32 m s^{-1}

Practice questions G

1 (a) $\frac{15mg}{4}$, $\frac{9mg}{4}$ (b) $\frac{1}{2}\sqrt{5\,ga}$

2 $T_{AB} = \frac{2mg}{\sqrt{3}}$, $T_{BC} = \frac{mu^2}{l} - \frac{mg}{\sqrt{3}}$

3 (a) $\frac{5}{4}mg$ (b) $3\,ma\omega^2 - \frac{3}{4}mg$

4 (a) $\frac{md\omega^2}{2} + \frac{mg}{\sqrt{3}}$ (b) $\frac{md\omega^2}{2} - \frac{mg}{\sqrt{3}}$

Practice questions H

1 (a) 0.8   (b) 2π (c) 31 cm

Practice questions I

1 $\frac{g}{\omega^2}$

Practice questions J

1 $T = \frac{m}{4}(2\sqrt{3}\,g + a\omega^2)$

2 $h = \frac{v^2}{3g}$

3 (a) $m\left(\frac{v^2}{r\sqrt{3}} - g\right)$

4 $T = mg\cos\alpha + ml\omega^2\sin^2\alpha$
   $R = mg\sin\alpha - ml\omega^2\cos\alpha\sin\alpha$

6 $m(\omega^2 r\sin\theta + g\cos\theta)$ $\frac{5g}{16a} \le \omega^2 \le \frac{65g}{18a}$

Practice questions K

1 18.8°   **2** (a) 9600 N (b) 9184 N   **3** 11.8 m s^{-1}

Practice questions L

1 $\sqrt{3\,ga}$

3 $ml\omega^2$, $m(g - \omega^2 h)$, $\sqrt{\left(\frac{g}{h}\right)}$: $\frac{g}{2a} \le \omega^2 \le \frac{g}{a}$

4 $\frac{4mgx\cos\theta}{a} = mg$, $\frac{4mgx\sin\theta}{a} = mr\omega^2$

   $\sqrt{\left(\frac{4\,gx}{a(a + x)}\right)}$, $\pi\sqrt{\left(\frac{a(a + x)}{gx}\right)}$

5 (a) 36.9   (b) 37.3

5

Motion in a vertical circle

INTRODUCTION We have already used the principle of conservation of mechanical energy when we looked at dynamic systems involving elastic strings or springs. We are now going to look at some different applications of this principle, where combined with the knowledge of the force required for circular motion we can analyse systems where particles are describing vertical circles.

Motion in a vertical circle

OCR M3 5.9.4 (b)

We have looked at different systems of an object moving in a **horizontal** circle. In this section we're going to look at the motion of a particle which moves in a **vertical** circle and the conditions which are necessary for this motion to be possible.

Basic equations

There are two main ways of looking at the system and both give an equation – from these two equations we can generally solve the motion. The two ways are:

(a) conservation of energy

(b) circular motion.

From (a) we know that the sum of the kinetic and potential energies at any point is constant, so we have an equation linking velocities and position.

From (b) we know that there must be a force with a component of $\dfrac{mv^2}{r}$ acting towards the centre, and so we obtain an equation which links the velocity to a force, usually a tension if on a string or a normal reaction.

We can apply this pair of determining equations to a number of situations: where the particle is:

- suspended at the end of a fixed inelastic string

- threaded on a smooth hoop

- on the inner surface of a spherical or cylindrical shell

- on the outer surface of a sphere or cylinder.

In all cases the analysis is very similar and even identical except that a different letter appears in the equations.

Before we start a detailed analysis, we'll have a look at different types of motion dependent upon the initial conditions.

Initial velocity

OCR M3 5.9.4 (b)

The initial velocity given to the particle is important since it determines the kind of path taken subsequently. If we look at the case of a particle inside a cylindrical shell we can distinguish three different cases. We are assuming that the particle starts from the bottom of the shell.

Figure 5.1

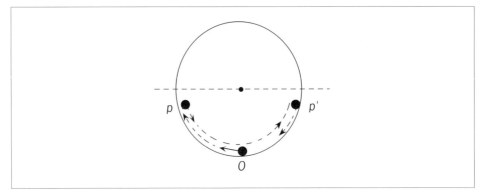

Low initial velocity: the particle reaches a point p below the level of the centre of the circle, stops, returns to O and continues to a corresponding point p' on the opposite side of the circle. With no friction, this will continue indefinitely.

Figure 5.2

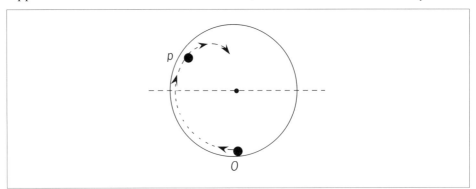

Medium initial velocity: the particle reaches a point p above the level of the centre and then loses contact with the surface. It continues as a projectile.

Figure 5.3

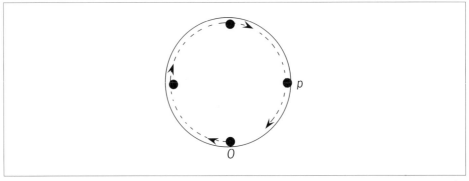

High initial velocity: the particle reaches the top of the circle still in contact with the surface. It continues indefinitely describing complete circles if there is no friction. We'll have a closer look at this particular case.

Complete circles

At the bottom of the circle, the velocity of the particle is greatest

Figure 5.4

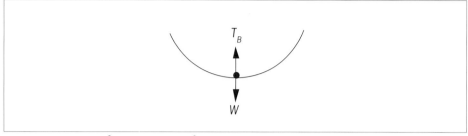

$$T_B - W = \frac{mv_B^2}{a} \;\Rightarrow\; T_B = \frac{mv_B^2}{a} + W \qquad \dots \text{Ⓐ}$$

and at the top, the velocity is least

Figure 5.5

$$T_T + W = \frac{mv_T^2}{a} \;\Rightarrow\; T_T = \frac{mv_T^2}{a} - W \qquad \dots \text{Ⓑ}$$

and you can see by comparing the expressions Ⓐ and Ⓑ for the tensions at the top and bottom that the greatest tension corresponds to the greatest velocity, at the bottom, and similarly the least tension with the least velocity at the top.

We can use equation Ⓑ as a quick way of finding the condition for a particle on the end of a string to describe complete circles. If the velocity at the bottom is V, then by energy

$$\tfrac{1}{2} mv_T^2 + mg(2a) = \tfrac{1}{2} mV^2$$

$$\Rightarrow \quad mv_T^2 = mV^2 - 4mga$$

Substitute this into Ⓑ to give

$$T_T = \frac{mV^2}{a} - 4mg - mg = \frac{mV^2}{a} - 5mg$$

For complete circles, $T_T \ge 0 \;\Rightarrow\; \dfrac{mV^2}{a} \ge 5mg$

$$\Rightarrow \quad V^2 \ge 5ag$$

If we are interested in the speed or tension at some intermediary stage, things become a little more complicated, but basically we still rely on the two sources for our equations: conservation of energy and circular motion.

Example

A particle P of mass m is attached to one end of a light inextensible string of length a. The other end of the string is attached to a fixed point O. When P is at rest vertically below O, it is given a horizontal speed u.

(a) Find the tension in the string when OP makes an angle θ with the *upward* vertical.

(b) Hence, show that P will leave its circular path if $2ga < u^2 < 5ga$.

87

Solution

Fig. 5.6 represents the initial position of the particle and the subsequent position when *OP* makes an angle θ with the upward vertical, *P* being at a vertical height *h* above the initial position.

Figure 5.6

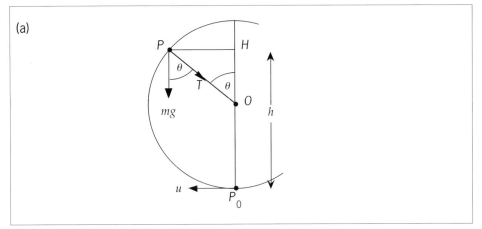

(a)

We'll find our equations from our two sources.

(a) *Conservation of energy*: If we take the zero potential level to be at the initial position, the initial sum of the energies is

$$\tfrac{1}{2}mu^2 + O = \tfrac{1}{2}mu^2 \qquad \qquad \dots ①$$
$$\text{KE} \qquad \quad \text{KE}$$

At the later position, if we call the velocity v, the kinetic energy will be $\tfrac{1}{2}mv^2$ and we need to find its potential energy, *mgh*. From $\triangle OPH$,

$$\cos \theta = \frac{OH}{OP} \implies OH = OP \cos \theta = a \cos \theta$$
$$h = P_0O + OH = a + a \cos \theta = a(1 + \cos \theta)$$

giving a potential energy of $mga\,(1 + \cos \theta)$

This gives the new sum of energies

$$\tfrac{1}{2}mv^2 + mga\,(1 + \cos \theta) \qquad \qquad \dots ②$$

and equating these sums ① and ② by conservation of energy,

$$\tfrac{1}{2}mu^2 = \tfrac{1}{2}mv^2 + mga\,(1 + \cos \theta) \qquad \qquad \dots ③$$

Circular motion: Since the motion is circular, we know the force towards the centre must be $\dfrac{mv^2}{a}$. Resolving the weight along *PO* together with the tension gives

$$mg \cos \theta + T = \frac{mv^2}{a} \qquad \qquad \dots ④$$

Rearranging

$$T = \frac{mv^2}{a} - mg \cos \theta \qquad \qquad \dots ⑤$$

But from ③,

$$\tfrac{1}{2}mv^2 = \tfrac{1}{2}mu^2 - mga\,(1 + \cos \theta)$$

$$\times \frac{2}{a} \qquad \frac{mv^2}{a} = \frac{mu^2}{a} - 2mg\,(1 + \cos \theta)$$

This into ⑤ gives $\quad T = \dfrac{mu^2}{a} - 2mg\,(1 + \cos\theta) - mg\cos\theta$

$$= \dfrac{mu^2}{a} - 2mg - 2\,mg\cos\theta - mg\cos\theta$$

i.e. $\quad T = \dfrac{mu^2}{a} - mg\,(2 + 3\cos\theta)$ $\hspace{2cm}$ ... ⑥

(b) The question is asking for the range of values of u which correspond to the second of the three possible cases, i.e. where the string becomes slack ($T = 0$) and the particle continues as a projectile.

Putting $T = 0$ into ⑥ gives

$$\dfrac{mu^2}{a} = mg\,(2 + 3\cos\theta)$$

$$\Rightarrow \dfrac{u^2}{ga} = 2 + 3\cos\theta \Rightarrow \cos\theta = \dfrac{1}{3}\left(\dfrac{u^2}{ga} - 2\right) \hspace{1.5cm} \text{...⑦}$$

Since the particle is above the level of the centre of the circle, $0 < \theta < \dfrac{\pi}{2}$ and so $0 < \cos\theta < 1$

i.e. $\quad 0 < \dfrac{1}{3}\left(\dfrac{u^2}{ga} - 2\right) < 1 \quad$ from ⑦

$$\Rightarrow \quad 0 < \dfrac{u^2}{ga} - 2 < 3$$

$$\Rightarrow \quad 2 < \dfrac{u^2}{ga} < 5$$

$$\Rightarrow \quad 2ga < u^2 < 5ga$$

It's very important that you are able to derive an expression for the tension T at any point – i.e. to arrive at the equation ⑥ in the previous example. You will find it appears in some form or other in most of the questions you are faced with. In the following example, you are given the general expression and need to deduce a more particular form.

Example

A particle P, of mass m, is attached to a fixed point O by a light inextensible string of length a, and is executing complete circular revolutions in a vertical plane. When OP is inclined at an angle θ to the downward vertical, the tension T in the string is given by

$$T = mg\,(3\cos\theta - 2) + \dfrac{mu^2}{a}$$

where u is the speed of P when it passes through its lowest points. Show that, if $3T_0$ and T_0 are the greatest and least tensions in the string during the motion, then

$$u^2 = 8ag \quad \text{and} \quad T = T_0\,(2 + \cos\theta).$$

Solution

The minimum tension is when $\theta = 180°$, giving

$$T_0 = mg\,(3\cos 180° - 2) + \dfrac{mu^2}{a} = \dfrac{mu^2}{a} - 5mg \hspace{1.5cm} \text{...①}$$

The maximum tension is when $\theta = 0°$, which gives

$$3T_0 = mg (3 \cos 0° - 2) + \frac{mu^2}{a} = \frac{mu^2}{a} + mg \qquad \qquad \text{...②}$$

Putting ① into ②, $3\left(\frac{mu^2}{a} - 5mg\right) = \frac{mu^2}{a} + mg$

$$\frac{3mu^2}{a} - 15mg = \frac{mu^2}{a} + mg$$

$$\frac{2mu^2}{a} = 16mg \quad \Rightarrow u^2 = 8ag$$

This into ① gives $T_0 = \frac{8mag}{a} - 5mg = 3mg \qquad \qquad \text{...③}$

and from the given equation,

$$T = mg (3 \cos \theta - 2) + \frac{8mag}{a}$$

$$= 3mg \cos \theta - 2mg + 8mg$$

$$= 3mg \cos \theta + 6mg = 3mg (2 + \cos \theta)$$

$$= T_0 (2 + \cos \theta) \text{ from ③}$$

Practice questions A

1 An object of mass 20 kg is suspended from a fixed point O by a light inextensible string of length 2 m. The object moves in a vertical plane under gravity, with the string always taut. When the object is directly beneath O, its speed is 3 m s^{-1}. Calculate the tension in the string at this instant.

2 A conker of mass 20 g is attached to one end of a string of length 25 cm and the other end of the string is fixed. The conker describes a vertical circle. The conker is modelled as a particle and the string is assumed to be light and inextensible. It is also assumed that there is no air resistance. Find the minimum speed which the conker must have at the lowest point of the motion in order to complete a vertical circle.

3

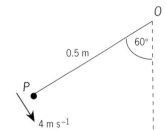

A particle P of mass 0.2 kg moves in a vertical circle of radius 0.5 m. The centre of the circle is the fixed point O, and P is attached to O by a light inextensible string of length 0.5 m. When the angle between the string and the downward

vertical is 60° the speed of P is 4 m s^{-1} (see diagram). Calculate the tension in the string at this instant.

4 One end of a light inextensible string of length a is fixed and to the other end is attached a particle of mass m. When the particle is hanging freely at rest it is given a horizontal velocity u so that it moves in a complete vertical circle. Given that, during the motion, the minimum tension in the string is $3mg$, show that $u = \sqrt{(8ag)}$.

5 A stone of mass m is attached to one end of a rope of length l. The other end of the rope is fixed. The stone is modelled as a particle and the rope as being light and inextensible. It is also assumed that the only forces acting on the stone are its weight and the force due to the tension in the rope. The stone moves in a vertical circle with the rope taut.

The maximum speed of the stone is three times its minimum speed.

(a) Show that the speed of the stone when the rope is horizontal is $\sqrt{\left(\frac{5gl}{2}\right)}$.

(b) Hence show that the tension in the rope when the rope is horizontal is $\frac{5mg}{2}$.

(c) State one physical factor that has been ignored in your model.

6 One end of a light inextensible string of length R is attached to a fixed point O. A particle P of mass m is attached to the other end of the string. The particle is held in a position with the string taut and OP horizontal, and it is then projected vertically downwards with speed $\sqrt{(2gR)}$. When OP makes an angle θ with the downward vertical and the string is still taut, the speed of P is v. Air resistance is to be neglected.

(a) Express v^2 in terms of R, g and θ.

(b) Show that P will not describe a complete vertical circle, and find, to the nearest degree, the value of θ when the string becomes slack for the first time.

7 A mass hangs freely at rest at one end of a light inextensible string of length a, the other end of which is fixed. If the mass is then given a horizontal velocity of $\sqrt{\left(\frac{7ga}{2}\right)}$, show that the string is on the point of becoming slack when it makes an angle of 60° with the upward vertical.

Threaded particle

OCR M3 5.9.4 (b)

When the particle is threaded on something like a smooth hoop which keeps the motion circular, slightly different equations arise. This is because the reaction of the hoop on the particle can act *towards* or *away from* the centre of the motion. Let's look at the case where the particle is moving on the upper half of the vertical circle.

Figure 5.7

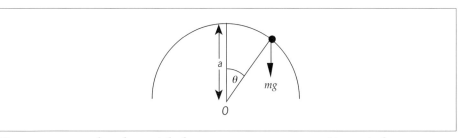

Here we can see that the weight has a component $mg \cos \theta$ *towards* the centre. When the velocity is large, this central component may be insufficient for the force needed inwards, i.e. $\dfrac{mv^2}{a}$. In this case the additional force is supplied by the reaction which then also acts inwards. When the velocity is not so large, the inward component of the weight may be enough, or more than enough, to supply the necessary force inwards and the reaction will act away from the centre. Here is an example of this.

Example

A small bead of mass m slides on a smooth circular hoop, with centre O and radius a, which is fixed in a vertical plane. The bead is projected with speed u, where $2ag < u^2 < 4ag$, from A, the lowest point of the hoop, and at subsequent time t, the bead is at a point P where angle $POA = \theta$. Find in terms of u, a, g and θ, an expression for $\left(\dfrac{d\theta}{dt}\right)^2$ and deduce that R, the magnitude of the force exerted by the hoop on the bead, is given by

$$aR = \left| \, mu^2 - mga\,(2 - 3 \cos \theta) \, \right|.$$

Solution	Fig. 5.8 shows this system.

Figure 5.8

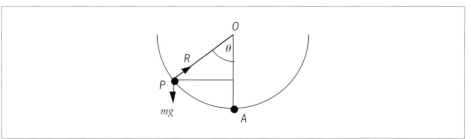

By energy, $\frac{1}{2}mu^2 = \frac{1}{2}mv^2 + mga\,(1 - \cos\theta)$

$\Rightarrow\quad v^2 = u^2 - 2ga\,(1 - \cos\theta)$ ...①

Since $v = a\omega = a\left(\frac{d\theta}{dt}\right)$, $v^2 = a^2\left(\frac{d\theta}{dt}\right)^2$

$\Rightarrow\quad \left(\frac{d\theta}{dt}\right)^2 = \frac{1}{a^2}\left[u^2 - 2ga\,(1 - \cos\theta)\right]$

Inward force $R_1 - mg\cos\theta = ma\left(\frac{d\theta}{dt}\right)^2$

$$= \frac{m}{a}\left[u^2 - 2ga\,(1 - \cos\theta)\right]$$

$$= \frac{mu^2}{a} - 2mg + 2mg\cos\theta$$

$\Rightarrow\quad R_1 = \frac{mu^2}{a} - 2mg + 3mg\cos\theta$

$\Rightarrow\quad aR_1 = mu^2 - mga\,(2 - 3\cos\theta)$

Depending on the initial value of u^2, R_1 can be positive or negative for different values of θ, and we put

$$aR = \left|\,mu^2 - mga\,(2 - 3\cos\theta)\,\right| \quad \text{where } R = |R_1|$$

Here's another example of vertical circles at the end of a string where the conditions also change during the motion – this time the string meets a peg at its mid-point.

Example	The end O of a light inelastic string OP of length a is fixed and a particle of mass m is attached at the other end P. The particle is held with the string taut and horizontal and is given a velocity u vertically downwards. When the string becomes vertical it begins to wrap itself around a small smooth peg, A, at a depth $\frac{a}{2}$ below O. Find the tension in the string when AP subsequently makes an angle θ with the downward vertical and show that if $u = 0$ the string becomes slack when $\cos\theta = -\frac{2}{3}$.

Find the minimum value of u in order that the particle makes complete revolutions about A.

Solution

In Fig. 5.9 the path of the particle is represented as it starts on the right and moves clockwise until the string is vertical. It then begins to wrap itself around the peg and P_1 represents the position when the string makes an angle θ with the downward vertical.

Figure 5.9

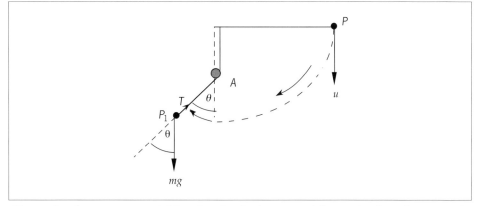

If we take the zero potential level to be the bottom of the circle, then the sum of the kinetic and potential energies in the initial position with the string horizontal will be

$$\frac{1}{2}mu^2 + mga \qquad \qquad \dots \text{①}$$

$$\text{KE} \qquad \text{PE}$$

Looking at the vertical position of P_1 more closely

Figure 5.10

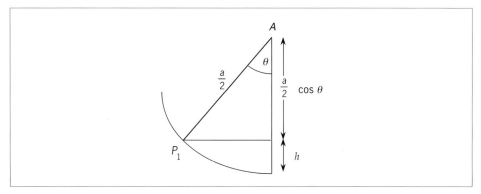

we can see that the height h will be $\frac{a}{2} - \frac{a}{2}\cos\theta$ and if we call the velocity of the particle at this point v, the sum of the energies at P_1 will be

$$\frac{1}{2}mv^2 + mg\left(\frac{a}{2} - \frac{a}{2}\cos\theta\right) \qquad \qquad \dots \text{②}$$

Equating these two expressions for the total energy,

$$\frac{1}{2}mu^2 + mga = \frac{1}{2}mv^2 + mg\left(\frac{a}{2} - \frac{a}{2}\cos\theta\right)$$

$$= \frac{1}{2}mv^2 + \frac{mga}{2} - \frac{mga}{2}\cos\theta$$

i.e. $\quad \frac{1}{2}mv^2 = \frac{1}{2}mu^2 + \frac{1}{2}mga + \frac{1}{2}mga\cos\theta$

$\times \frac{2}{m} \quad v^2 = u^2 + ag(1 + \cos\theta) \qquad \qquad \dots \text{①}$

Now since the motion around the peg is circular with radius $\frac{a}{2}$, the force

towards the centre, i.e. the peg, must be $\dfrac{mv^2}{\left(\frac{a}{2}\right)}$

i.e. $T - mg \cos \theta = \dfrac{2mv^2}{a}$ ... ②

Putting ① into this equation,

$$T = \frac{2m[u^2 + ag(1 + \cos \theta)]}{a} + mg \cos \theta$$

$$= \frac{2mu^2}{a} + 2mg(1 + \cos \theta) + mg \cos \theta$$

$$= \frac{2mu^2}{a} + mg(2 + 3 \cos \theta)   \qquad ... ③$$

If $u = 0$ and $T = 0$ when the string becomes slack

$$0 = mg(2 + 3 \cos \theta) \Rightarrow \cos \theta = -\frac{2}{3}$$

Since we need $T \geq 0$ at the top, where $\theta = 180°$, putting these values into ③, the condition for complete circles becomes

$$\frac{2mu^2}{a} + mg(2 + 3 \cos 180°) \geq 0 \quad \text{and since } \cos 180° = -1$$

$$\frac{2mu^2}{a} + mg(2 - 3) \geq 0 \quad \Rightarrow \frac{2mu^2}{a} \geq mg$$

$$\Rightarrow u^2 \geq \frac{ag}{2} \text{ or } u \geq \sqrt{\left(\frac{ag}{2}\right)}$$

Practice questions B

1

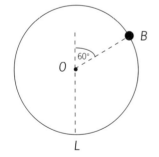

L

A small bead *B*, of mass *m*, is threaded onto a smooth circular wire, with centre *O* and radius *r*. The wire is fixed in a vertical plane and initially *B* is at the position where *OB* makes an angle of 60° with the upward vertical, as shown in the above figure. The lowest point of the wire is *L*. The bead is released from rest. Find:

(a)   the speed of *B* as it passes through *L*

(b)   the magnitude of the force exerted by the wire on *B* when it passes through *L*.

2   A small bead *P* of mass *m* is threaded on a smooth circular wire, with centre *O* and radius *r*, which is fixed in a vertical plane. Initially the bead is at rest at the highest point of the wire. If the bead is slightly displaced from this position, determine an expression for the speed of the bead when the line *OP* has turned through an angle *θ*. Show that the magnitude of the force exerted by the wire on the bead in the direction *OP* is $mg\,(3 \cos \theta - 2)$.

State the direction of this force when *θ* increases beyond the value $\cos^{-1}\frac{2}{3}$.

3   The pilot of a stunt aircraft flies it in a vertical circle of radius 200 m. Near the top of the circle, the aircraft is flying upside down at a constant speed of 40 m s^{-1}. The mass of the pilot is 61 kg. Show that, at the top of the circle, the magnitude of the reaction between the pilot, modelled as a particle, and her aircraft is approximately 110 N.

State whether, at the top of the circle, the pilot feels that she is being pressed into her seat, or is hanging suspended in the safety harness.

4

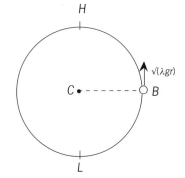

A bead *B*, of mass *m*, is threaded and can move freely on a smooth circular hoop, centre *C* and radius *r*. The hoop is fixed in a vertical plane. The bead *B* is projected vertically upwards with speed $\sqrt{(\lambda gr)}$ from a point level with *C*, as shown in the diagram. The highest point of the loop is *H* and the lowest point is *L*.

(a) Show that, i f the bead *B* passes through *H*, then $\lambda > 2$.

Given that $\lambda = 5$,

(b) find the speed of *B* at the instant when it passes through:

(i)   *H*   (ii) *L*

giving your answer in each case in terms of *g* and *r*,

(c) the magnitude of the force exerted by *B* on the hoop at the instant when *B* passes through:

(i)   *H*   (ii) *L*

giving your answers in terms of *m* and *g*.

5 A thin smooth wire in the form of a circle of radius *a* is fixed in a vertical plane, and a small bead of mass *m* is threaded on the wire. A light inextensible string attached to the bead passes through a small smooth ring fixed at the centre of the wire and supports a particle of mass *M* which hangs freely. The bead is projected from the lowest point of the wire with speed $\sqrt{(kga)}$.

(c) Show that the inward normal force *R* exerted by the wire on the bead is given by

$$R = mg(3 \cos \theta + k - 2) - Mg$$

where θ is the angle between the two parts of the string, and find the least value of *k* for the bead to reach the highest point of the wire.

Given that $k = 6$ and $M = 2m$:

(b) find the value of θ for which $R = 0$

(c) find also the magnitude of the acceleration of the particle at this instant.

Motion inside a smooth sphere

OCR M3 5.9.4 (b)

Here we have a normal reaction taking the place of the tension in the previous case – otherwise the equations are identical.

Example

A particle is at rest at the lowest point inside a smooth sphere of radius *a*. It is projected horizontally with speed $\sqrt{\left(\frac{7ag}{2}\right)}$. If ϕ is the angle the line joining the particle to the centre makes with the upward vertical, find

(a) the value of ϕ at the point where it leaves the sphere

(b) the speed at this point

(c) the greatest height above *O*, the centre of the sphere

Solution

See Fig. 5.11.

From energy, $\frac{1}{2} mv^2 = \frac{1}{2} mu^2 - mga(1 - \cos \theta)$ ... ①

and circles, $R - mg \cos \theta = \frac{mv^2}{a}$ ... ②

Figure 5.11

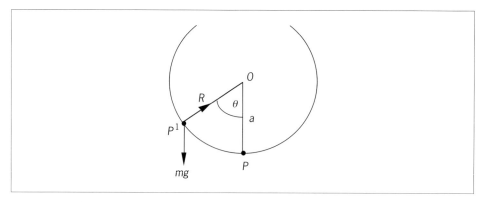

From ① and ② we find:

$$R = \frac{mu^2}{a} + mg(3 \cos \theta - 2) \qquad \dots ③$$

as in previous questions (with T in place of R).

The **minimum** horizontal velocity for complete circles is the same as before, i.e. $\sqrt{5ag}$ and since $u = \sqrt{\left(\frac{7ag}{2}\right)}$ is less than this, the particle will leave the surface of the sphere. To determine this point, we put the value of u and $R = 0$ into ③ to give

$$0 = \frac{m}{a}\left(\frac{7ag}{2}\right) + mg(3 \cos \theta - 2)$$

$$= \frac{7mg}{2} + 3mg \cos \theta - 2mg$$

$$\Rightarrow 3mg \cos \theta = -\frac{3}{2}mg$$

$$\text{i.e. } \cos \theta = -\frac{1}{2} \Rightarrow \theta = 120°$$

and the line joining the particle at this point, i.e. OQ, makes an angle of $180° - 120° = 60°$ with the **upward** vertical.

Figure 5.12

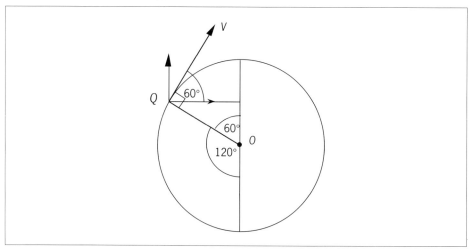

We want to find the velocity at this point – and so we look at the energy equation ①. Multiplying by 2 gives

$$mv^2 = mu^2 - 2mga\,(1 - \cos \theta)$$

Substituting

$$u = \sqrt{\left(\tfrac{7ag}{2}\right)} \text{ and } \cos\theta = -\tfrac{1}{2} \text{ gives}$$

$$mv^2 = m\left(\tfrac{7ag}{2}\right) - 2mga\left(\tfrac{3}{2}\right) = \tfrac{mga}{2}$$

i.e. $v^2 = \tfrac{ag}{2} \Rightarrow v = \sqrt{\left(\tfrac{ag}{2}\right)}$

The **vertical** component of this velocity (see Fig. 5.12) will be $v\sin 60°$,

i.e. $\sqrt{\left(\tfrac{ag}{2}\right)} \times \tfrac{\sqrt{3}}{2} = \tfrac{1}{2}\sqrt{\left(\tfrac{3ag}{2}\right)}$

If H is the greatest height above Q, we have

$$u = \tfrac{1}{2}\sqrt{\left(\tfrac{3ag}{2}\right)},\ v = 0,\ s = H,\ a = -g$$

$$\Rightarrow\quad v^2 = u^2 + 2as$$

$$\Rightarrow\quad 0 = \tfrac{1}{4} \times \tfrac{3ag}{2} - 2gH$$

$$\Rightarrow\quad 2gH = \tfrac{3ag}{8}\quad \Rightarrow H = \tfrac{3a}{16}$$

Since Q is at a height $a + a\cos 60°$ above O, i.e. $\tfrac{3a}{2}$, the greatest height above O reached by the particle is $\tfrac{3a}{2} + \tfrac{3a}{16} = \tfrac{27a}{16}$.

Practice questions C

1

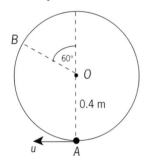

A particle P moves inside a smooth hollow cylinder of internal radius 0.4 m, fixed with its axis horizontal. The point O is on the axis of the cylinder.

The particle is projected with speed u metres per second, horizontally and perpendicular to the axis of the cylinder, from the point A, which is on the inner surface of the cylinder vertically below O. At the point B, where OB makes an angle of 60° with the upward vertical, as shown in the above figure, P loses contact with the inner surface of the cylinder.

(a) Show that the speed of P at B is 1.4 m s^{-1}.

(b) Find the value of u, giving your answer to 1 decimal place.

(c) Find the greatest height above O reached by P.

2 A marble P of mass m moves in a vertical circle, with centre O and radius a, inside a hollow cylinder. The axis of the cylinder is horizontal and perpendicular to the plane of the motion of P.

In a model of the situation, it is assumed that the marble is a particle, the cylinder is smooth, and the only forces acting on the marble are its weight and the force exerted by the cylinder.

Initially P is at a point A on the circle, where OA is horizontal, and is moving with a vertical speed of $\sqrt{(5ga)}$ in a downwards direction. In the subsequent motion, when OP makes an angle θ with OA, the speed of P is v and the force exerted by the cylinder on P has magnitude R.

(a) Find an expression for v^2 in terms of a, g and θ.

(b) Find an expression for R in terms of m, g and θ.

(c) Show that P will make complete revolutions with losing contact with the surface of the cylinder.

(d) Find the minimum value of the speed of P.

(e) State two forces which have been ignored in the above model.

3 (*Hard*). A particle is at rest at the lowest point *A* inside a smooth hollow sphere of radius *a*. It is projected horizontally with velocity $\sqrt{\left(\frac{7}{2}ga\right)}$.

Show that it loses contact with the sphere at a height $\frac{3}{2}a$ above *A* and will next strike the sphere at *A*.

Motion on the outer surface of a sphere

OCR M3 5.9.4 (b)

The two main equations in this case still come from conservation of energy and circular motion, although the last of these takes a slightly different form.

Figure 5.13

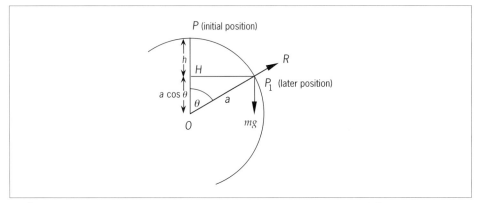

If the particle starts from rest, as it usually does in questions of this kind, and we take the top of the circle to be the zero potential level, then the sum of the energies at P_1 is zero.

When the particle is at P_1, where OP_1 makes an angle θ with OP, if we assume the velocity to be v then the kinetic energy will be $\frac{1}{2}mv^2$.

From the triangle OHP_1, $OH = a \cos \theta$ and so h, the vertical distance fallen, will be $a - a \cos \theta$ and the potential energy $mg(a - a \cos \theta)$.

At P_1 then,

$$\frac{1}{2}mv^2 - mg\,(a - a\cos\theta) = 0$$

$$\Rightarrow \frac{1}{2}mv^2 = mg(a - a\cos\theta)$$

$$v^2 = 2ag(1 - \cos\theta) \qquad \qquad \text{...①}$$

Since the motion is circular, the force towards the centre is $\dfrac{mv^2}{a}$,

i.e. $mg \cos\theta - R = \dfrac{mv^2}{a}$ $\qquad \qquad$ ... ②

Substituting ① into ②,

$$mg \cos\theta - R = \frac{m}{a} \times 2ag(1 - \cos\theta)$$

$$= 2mg - 2mg \cos\theta$$

then $R = 3mg \cos\theta - 2mg$

$$= mg(3 \cos\theta - 2) \qquad \qquad \text{... ③}$$

The condition for the particle to be in contact with the sphere is $R > 0$,

i.e. $mg(3 \cos\theta - 2) > 0$

$\cos\theta > \dfrac{2}{3}$

It loses contact, i.e. $R = 0$, at the point where $\cos \theta = \frac{2}{3}$

Putting these values into ②,

$$mg \times \frac{2}{3} - 0 = \frac{mv^2}{a} \Rightarrow v^2 = \frac{2ag}{3}$$

and $\qquad v = \sqrt{\left(\frac{2ag}{3}\right)}$

If you are asked about the **subsequent** motion of the particle, it will be a projectile whose initial horizontal and vertical components come from the value of v and θ at this point.

Figure 5.14

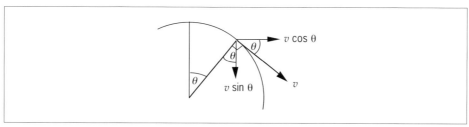

Horizontally $\qquad u_H \qquad = v \cos \theta = \sqrt{\left(\frac{2ag}{3}\right)} \times \frac{2}{3} = \frac{2}{3}\sqrt{\left(\frac{2ag}{3}\right)}$

Vertically $\qquad u_V \qquad = v \sin \theta$

$$= \sqrt{\left(\frac{2ag}{3}\right)} \times \frac{\sqrt{5}}{3}$$

$$= \frac{1}{3}\sqrt{\left(\frac{10ag}{3}\right)}$$

Practice questions D

1 A solid smooth hemisphere has its base, of centre O and radius a, fixed to a horizontal plane. The highest point of the hemisphere is A, and B is a point on the rim of the base. A particle P of mass m is projected from A with speed $\left(\frac{2ag}{5}\right)^{\frac{1}{2}}$ in a direction parallel to OB.

If at any instant in the subsequent motion the line OP makes an angle θ with OA and the particle is still in contact with the hemisphere, find expressions for the speed v of P and for the reaction R of the hemisphere upon it in terms of m, a, g and θ.

Show that the particle leaves the hemisphere when the angle made by OP with OA is α, where $\cos \alpha = \frac{4}{5}$.

2 A solid hemisphere rests with its plane face, centre O, on a horizontal table. A particle of mass m is placed on the hemisphere at its highest point and is slightly disturbed from rest so that it begins to slide down the curved surface, the friction between the hemisphere and the particle being negligible.

If the hemisphere is fixed, show that, when the line OP has turned through an angle θ, the reaction between the hemisphere and the particle is $mg(3 \cos \theta - 2)$. State the value of θ when P leaves the surface of the hemisphere.

3

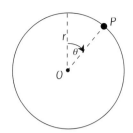

The diagram shows the circular cross-section of a smooth fixed cylinder of radius r, whose horizontal axis of symmetry passes through O. A particle P, of mass m, is free to move on the surface of the cylinder in a plane which is perpendicular to the axis through O. The speed of P is v when OP makes an angle θ with the upward vertical through O. The particle is released from rest after being slightly displaced from its initial position on top of the cylinder. For the motion while the particle is in contact with the cylinder

(a) find v^2 in terms of g, r and θ

(b) show that the magnitude of the force exerted on the particle by the cylinder is $mg\,(3\cos\theta-2)$.

Given that $r = 0.5$ m, find the speed of the particle at the instant when it leaves the surface of the cylinder.

4 A smooth sphere of radius a and centre O is rigidly fixed at its lowest point to a horizontal plane. A particle P, initially at rest at A, the highest point of the sphere, is slightly displaced so that it commences to slide down the outside of the sphere. Show that it leaves the surface of the sphere when the angle AOP is $\cos^{-1}\left(\dfrac{2}{3}\right)$.

Show also that the particle strikes the horizontal plane at a distance $\dfrac{5}{27}(\sqrt{5}+4\sqrt{2})a$ from the point of contact of the sphere with the plane.

5

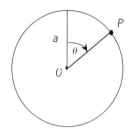

A particle P, of mass m, is placed on the highest point of a smooth fixed sphere, centre O and radius a. The particle is displaced slightly from rest. Show that, as long as the particle remains in contact with the sphere, the magnitude R of the reaction of the sphere on the particle is given by

$$R = mg(3\cos\theta - 2)$$

where θ is the angle which OP makes with the upward vertical.

Deduce that when the particle leaves the sphere its velocity has magnitude $\sqrt{\left(\dfrac{2ag}{3}\right)}$, and show that the time which elapses between the particle leaving the sphere and reaching the horizontal plane through O is

$$\dfrac{\sqrt{3}(\sqrt{46}-\sqrt{10})}{9}\sqrt{\left(\dfrac{a}{g}\right)}$$

SUMMARY EXERCISE

1 One end of a light inextensible string of length a is fixed at a point O and to the other end P is attached a particle of mass m. The string is held taut with OP horizontal and the particle is given a vertical velocity V. Find the least value of V in order that the particle describes complete circles.

If the string breaks when the tension in the string is $\dfrac{15}{2}mg$, find:

(a) the angle OP makes with the vertical when the string breaks if $V = \sqrt{6ag}$

(b) the minimum value of V for the string to break.

2 A particle of mass m is attached to the end A of a light inextensible string OA of length a. The other end O of the string is fixed. Initially A is held vertically above O with the string taut and the particle is projected horizontally with speed V, where $V > \sqrt{ag}$. Show that the speed of A when it is vertically below O is:

$$\sqrt{(V^2 + 4ag)}$$

At the instant when the particle is vertically below O, it collides and coalesces with a stationary particle of mass $2m$. Assuming the string has remained taut, find the tension in the string attached to the composite particle of mass $3m$, when OA makes an angle θ with the downward vertical.

Find also the least value of V for which the composite particle describes complete vertical circles.

3 One end of a light inextensible string of length a is fixed and to the other end is attached a particle of mass m. When the particle is hanging freely at rest, it is given a horizontal velocity u so that it moves in a complete vertical circle. Given that, during the motion, the minimum tension in the string is $3mg$, show that $u = \sqrt{8ag}$.

When the string is at an angle θ to the downward vertical, find, in terms of m, g and θ,

(a) the tension in the string

(b) the horizontal and vertical components of the acceleration of the particle.

4 Show that the velocity with which a particle hanging from a fixed point by a string of length a must be started so as to describe a complete vertical circle, must not be less than $\sqrt{5ag}$. The particle is started with a velocity of $2\sqrt{ag}$, and when the string is horizontal, the string is held at such a point that the particle just completes the circle. Where must the point be situated on the string?

5 A particle, of mass m, is fixed to one end A of a light inextensible string OA of length a. The other end O of the string is attached to a fixed peg. At time $t = 0$, A is vertically below O with the string taut and the particle is projected horizontally with speed V, where $V^2 > 2ag$. Show that, provided the string remains taut, the speed of the particle when it is vertically above O is $\sqrt{(V^2 - 4ag)}$.

Show also that the particle performs complete circular revolutions provided that $V \geq \sqrt{5ag}$.

At the instant when the particle is vertically above O, it collides and coalesces with a stationary particle, also of mass m. Find the least value of V for which the composite particle describes complete vertical circles.

Assuming the composite particle describes a complete vertical circle find, in terms of V a, m, g and θ the tension in the string when OA makes an angle θ with the downward vertical.

6

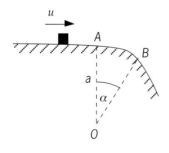

7 A toboggan of mass M, moving with speed u on smooth level ground, suddenly encounters a smooth downward slope, as shown in the above figure. The motion takes place in a vertical plane, and the downward slope is in the shape of an arc of a circle, radius a and centre O. The points A and B on the arc are such that OA is vertical and $\angle AOB = \alpha$, where $\cos \alpha > \frac{2}{3}$.

(a) Show that, for the toboggan to remain in contact with the slope on arc AB,

$$u^2 \leq ag\,(3 \cos \alpha - 2).$$

Given that $\alpha = \arccos\left(\frac{5}{6}\right)$, and that the toboggan loses contact with the slope at the point B

(b) find the sudden decrease, at the point A, in the magnitude of the force exerted by the ground on the toboggan.

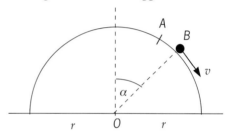

The above figure shows a smooth solid hemisphere H of radius r fixed with its plane surface, centre O, in contact with horizontal ground. A particle is released from rest on the surface of H at a point A such that OA makes an angle $\arccos \frac{7}{8}$ with the upward vertical.

The particle slides freely until it leaves the surface of H at the point B with speed v.

Given that OB makes an angle α with the upward vertical.

(a) show that $\cos \alpha = \frac{7}{12}$

(b) find v^2 in terms of g and r.

Given that the particle strikes the ground with speed U,

(c) find U^2 in terms of g and r.

8

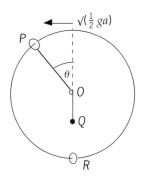

A small ring P, of mass $3m$, is threaded on a fixed smooth vertical hoop of radius a and centre O. The ring is connected by a light inextensible string of length l, where $a < l < 2a$, to a particle Q of mass $3m$. Initially P is at the highest point of the hoop and Q hangs freely. The ring P is given a horizontal speed $\sqrt{\left(\frac{1}{2}ga\right)}$ in the direction which causes the string to wrap around a small smooth fixed peg at O (see diagram). At time t after the start of the motion the radius OP has turned through an angle θ. Show that the outward force N, exerted by the hoop on the ring, is given by

$$N = \frac{9}{2}mg\,(2\cos\theta - 1).$$

A small ring R, of mass m, is at rest at the lowest point of the hoop. The ring P collides with R and after the collision R adheres to P. Find the speed at which the combined ring begins to move just after the collision.

9 A particle of mass m is attached to one end of a light inextensible string of length a. The other end of the string is attached to a fixed point O. The particle hangs at rest vertically below O. The particle is given a horizontal velocity of magnitude $\sqrt{(kag)}$, where $k > 2$, and when the string makes an angle θ with the upward vertical the string goes slack. Show that at this instant $\cos\theta = \dfrac{k-2}{3}$ and the speed of the particle is $\sqrt{\left(\dfrac{(k-2)\,ag}{3}\right)}$.

10

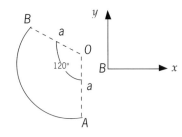

The diagram shows a smooth wire in the form of an arc of a circle, with centre O and radius a,

which is fixed in a vertical plane. The lowest point is A, OA is vertical and the size of angle AOB is $120°$.

A small bead of mass m is threaded on the wire and is projected along the wire from A with speed $\sqrt{(6\,ag)}$. Given that the bead leaves the wire at B and then moves freely under gravity, show that its speed on leaving the wire is $\sqrt{(3\,ag)}$. Show that the equation of the subsequent path of the bead referred to horizontal and vertical axes through B (in the directions indicated in the diagram) is

$$y = x\sqrt{3} - \frac{2x^2}{3a}.$$

Using this equation, or otherwise, determine the greatest height of the bead above the horizontal plane through A and show that the bead meets this plane at the point whose x-coordinate is $\dfrac{3a}{4}(\sqrt{3} + \sqrt{7})$.

11

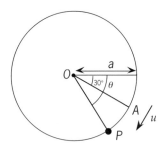

A particle P, of mass m, is attached to one end of a light inextensible string of length a, and the other end of the string is attached to a fixed point O. Initially P is at A, where $OA = a$, and the line OA makes an angle $30°$ below the horizontal through O, and the particle has speed u in a downwards direction perpendicular to OA.
The particle is moving in a vertical circle of radius a (see diagram). The tension in the string is T when OP makes an angle θ below the horizontal.

(a) Show that:

$$T = \frac{mu^2}{a} - mg + 3mg\sin\theta$$

(b) The string will break if the tension exceeds $6mg$. Show that the greatest possible value of u, if the string is not to break at any stage of the circular motion, is $2\sqrt{(ga)}$.

(c) Given that $u = \sqrt{(3ga)}$, find the value of θ when the string goes slack, and find also the speed of P at this instant.

(d) Hence find the greatest height of P above O in the subsequent motion.

SUMMARY

When you have finished, you should:

- know that the two main equations for solving the system come from conservation of energy and circular motion

- know that three different types of motion are possible, dependent on the initial conditions

- be able to derive the conditions necessary for complete circles

- know that maximum speeds and tensions occur at the bottom of the circle, minimum at the top

- be able to derive expressions for the velocity and/or tension at any point

- know that when a particle is threaded on a wire, the reaction can be in either direction, dependent on the speed

- know that motion in or on a sphere has much the same working as with a string, the reaction taking the place of the tension.

ANSWERS

Practice questions A

1   286 N
2   3.5 m s^{-1}
3   7.38 N
5   (c)   Air resistance
6   (a) $2gR(1 + \cos \theta)$
    (b)   132°

Practice questions B

1   (a) $\sqrt{3gr}$ (b) $4mg$

2   $v = [2gr(1 - \cos \theta)]^{\frac{1}{2}}$

    Direction PO.

3   Suspended

4   (b)   (i) $\sqrt{3gr}$ (ii) $\sqrt{7gr}$
    (c)   (i) $2mg$ (ii) $8mg$

5   (a) $k \geq 4$ (b)   131.8°   (c) $\frac{1}{3} g \sqrt{69}$

Practice questions C

1   (b)   3.7   (c)   0.275 m
2   (a) $v^2 = ag(5 + 2 \sin \theta)$
    (b) $R = mg(5 + 3 \sin \theta)$
    (d) $v_{MIN} = \sqrt{3ag}$
    (e)   Friction, Air resistance

Practice questions D

1   $v = \left[\dfrac{12ag}{5} - 2ag \cos \theta \right]^{\frac{1}{2}},$

    $R = 3mg \cos \theta - \dfrac{12mg}{5}$

2   $\cos^{-1}\left(\dfrac{2}{3}\right)$

3   (a) $v^2 = 2gr(1 - \cos \theta)$; $\sqrt{\left(\dfrac{g}{3}\right)}$ m s^{-1}

6

Statics of rigid bodies

INTRODUCTION   We have already seen in Unit M2 how we can find the centres of mass of a number of regular laminas, including cases where pieces are added or removed. In this section we are going to extend the range of shapes and objects for which we can find the centre of mass using the powerful tool of integration: this will allow us to find the centre of mass of regular solid bodies and composites of these. As with the previous work, we shall use these results to analyse situations where the body is suspended or placed on a plane.

Finding the centre of mass by integration   OCR M4 5.10.2 (a)(i)

We can deduce neat formulae which give us the x- and the y-coordinates of the centre of mass in most cases using the same principle that we used in the case of composite figures, i.e.

Sum of the separate moments = Moment of the whole

We find expressions for each side of this relation and equating these

expressions gives us an equation from which we can find $\bar{x}$ or $\bar{y}$. We'll take each side in turn and see how we can find approximate expressions.

Sum of separate moments

Before we start, we have to be familiar with a way of looking at integration as the limit of a sum of small components, so that as $\delta x \to 0$,

$$\sum x \delta x \to \int x \mathrm{d}x, \text{ for example, and } \sum y^2 \delta x \to \int y^2 \mathrm{d}x$$

where the arrow means 'tends towards'.

We can split the method for finding our expression into 4 stages

1   Find the moment of a small strip

2   Find the sum of these moments

3   Express the limit of this sum (as the strips become narrower) as an integral

4   Evaluate the integral

Let's take as an example the thin lamina bounded by the curve $y = 4 - x^2$ and the positive x- and y-axis. To find the position of $\bar{x}$ we need to find moments about the y-axis. The diagram shows the shape together with a small strip of thickness δx taken down from the point (x, y)

Figure 6.1

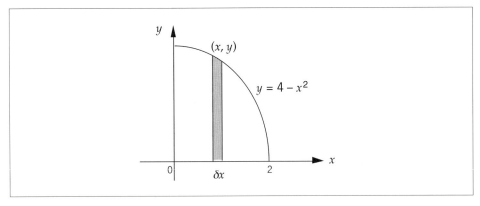

1 Moment of strip:

Since the height is y and the breadth δx, we can take the area to be $y\delta x$. Assuming a constant density of ρ per unit area, this gives a mass of $\rho y \delta x$. Since the strip is at a distance x from the y-axis, the moment about that axis is $\rho x y \delta x$

2 Sum of moments:

Dividing the whole shape into thin strips of equal thickness gives a total sum of

$$\sum \rho x y \delta x$$

3 Limit of sum:

As the strips are taken thinner, i.e. $\delta x \to 0$,

$$\sum_{\text{all}} \rho x y \delta x \quad \to \quad \int_{\text{all}} \rho x y \, dx \qquad \qquad \dots \text{Ⓐ}$$

4 Evaluating the integral:

The integral above is for a general curve: in the case we are looking at, $y = 4 - x^2$ and x lies between 0 and 2.

This gives the sum of the moments as

$$\int_0^2 \rho x (4 - x^2) \, dx \; = \; \rho \int_0^2 (4x - x^3) \, dx$$

$$= \; \rho \left[2x^2 - \frac{x^4}{4} \right]_0^2$$

$$= \; 4\rho \qquad \qquad \dots \text{①}$$

Moment of the whole

This is easier: if we assume the centre of mass is at a point $\bar{x}$ from the y-axis, the moment will be mass $\times \bar{x} =$ density $\times$ area $\times \bar{x}$

$$= \; \rho \bar{x} \int_{\text{all}} y \, dx \qquad \qquad \dots \text{Ⓑ}$$

In our particular case, this becomes

$$\rho \bar{x} \int_0^2 (4 - x^2) \, dx \quad = \; \rho \bar{x} \left[4x - \frac{x^3}{3} \right]_0^2$$

$$= \; \frac{16 \rho \bar{x}}{3} \qquad \qquad \dots \text{②}$$

Equating ① and ② gives $\dfrac{16\rho\bar{x}}{3} = 4\rho$

$\Rightarrow \bar{x} = \dfrac{3}{4}$

Looking at the diagram of the shape, this is a reasonable result. Since there is more mass to the left, we expect $\bar{x}$ to be something less than 1.

Similarly, we would expect $\bar{y}$ to be a little less than 2. The method for calculating $\bar{y}$ is very similar: we use the same strip, only now the distance of the centre of mass of this strip from the *x-axis* will be half-way up, i.e. $\dfrac{y}{2}$.

This gives a moment for the strip about the x-axis as $\rho \times y\delta x \times \dfrac{y}{2} = \dfrac{\rho y^2}{2}\,\delta x$ and a corresponding sum of all these of

$$\sum \rho \dfrac{y^2}{2}\,\delta x$$

In the limit, as $\delta x \to 0$, this tends to $\dfrac{\rho}{2}\displaystyle\int_{\text{all}} y^2\,\mathrm{d}x$ ... ©

In this case, this is $\dfrac{1}{2}\rho\displaystyle\int_0^2 (4 - x^2)^2\,\mathrm{d}x$

$$= \dfrac{1}{2}\rho\int_0^2 (16 - 8x^2 + x^4)\,\mathrm{d}x$$

$$= \dfrac{1}{2}\rho\left[16x - \dfrac{8x^3}{3} + \dfrac{x^5}{5}\right]_0^2 \quad = \dfrac{128\rho}{15} \qquad\qquad \text{... ③}$$

The moment of the whole is as before with $\bar{y}$ instead of $\bar{x}$, i.e.

$$\rho\bar{y}\int y\,\mathrm{d}x \qquad\qquad \text{... ⑩}$$

giving in this case, since $\displaystyle\int_0^2 y\,\mathrm{d}x = \dfrac{16}{3}$, $\dfrac{16\rho\bar{y}}{3}$ ... ④

Equating ③ and ④ gives $\dfrac{16\rho\bar{y}}{3} = \dfrac{128\rho}{15}$

$\Rightarrow \bar{y} = \dfrac{8}{5}$

which is about the prediction.

We can equate the expressions Ⓐ and Ⓑ to give a position for $\bar{x}$ for any (suitable) shape

i.e. $\rho\displaystyle\int xy\,\mathrm{d}x = \rho\bar{x}\int y\,\mathrm{d}x \Rightarrow \bar{x} = \dfrac{\int xy\,\mathrm{d}x}{\int y\,\mathrm{d}x}$

Similarly, equating © and ⑩ gives $\bar{y} = \dfrac{1}{2}\dfrac{\int y^2\,\mathrm{d}x}{\int y\,\mathrm{d}x}$

This is an important general result …

> For (suitable) areas, the position of the centre of mass can be found from
>
> $$\bar{x} = \frac{\int xy\,dx}{\int y\,dx}, \qquad \bar{y} = \frac{\frac{1}{2}\int y^2\,dx}{\int y\,dx}$$

Practice questions A

1 Find the coordinates of the centre of mass of the following uniform laminas

(a) The area enclosed by the curve $y = x^2 + 1$, the x- and y- axes and the line $x = 1$

(b) The finite area enclosed by the curve $y^2 = 4x$ and the line $x = 1$

(c) The finite area enclosed by the curve $y^2 = x^3$ and the line $x = 5$

(d) The area enclosed by the curve $y = \dfrac{1}{x^3}$ and the lines $x = 1$, $x = 2$

(e) The area enclosed by the curve $y = 4 - x^2$ and the positive x- and y-axes.

2 A uniform lamina OPQ has the shape of the region enclosed by the x-axis, the line $x = 9a$ and the part of the curve with equation $y = 4\sqrt{(ax)}$ for which $0 \le x \le 9a$, where a is a positive constant. O is the origin, P is the point $(9a, 0)$ and Q is the third vertex of the lamina. The mass per unit area of the lamina is k. Show that the x-coordinate of the centre of mass of the lamina is $\dfrac{27}{5}a$ and find the y-coordinate of the centre of mass.

Volumes of revolution

OCR M4 5.10.2 (a)(ii)

Very little adjustment is needed to find the centre of mass of a volume formed by rotating a solid about the x-axis. Since the x-axis is an axis of symmetry, we only need to find $\bar{x}$. If we take a strip as before and rotate it around the x-axis, we end up with a thin disc; radius y and thickness δx.

Figure 6.2

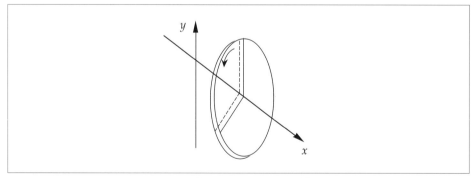

The volume of this cylinder is $\pi y^2 \delta x$, its mass is $\rho \pi y^2 \delta x$ where ρ is the density and its moment about the y-axis is $\rho \pi y^2 \delta x \times x = \rho \pi x y^2 \delta x$.

The sum of these is $\sum \rho \pi x y^2 \delta x$ which tends to $\rho \pi \int x y^2 dx$ as $\delta x \to 0$.

Since the volume is $\pi \int y^2 dx$, the moment of the whole about the y-axis is $\rho \pi \bar{x} \int y^2 dx$ and equating these two expressions,

$$\rho \pi \int x y^2 dx = \rho \pi \bar{x} \int y^2 dx \Rightarrow \bar{x} = \frac{\int x y^2 dx}{\int y^2 dx}$$

For (suitable) volumes formed by rotating an area around the x-axis,
the coordinates of its centre of mass are

$$\bar{x} = \frac{\int xy^2 dx}{\int y^2 dx}, \qquad \bar{y} = 0$$

Practice questions B

1 Find the coordinates of the centre of mass of the following solids of revolution.

(a) $y^2 = 4x$ and the line $x = 1$: about x-axis

(b) $y^2 = x^3$ and the line $x = 5$: about x-axis

(c) $y = 1 - x^2$ and the x- and y-axes
: about y-axis

(d) $y = \frac{1}{x^2}$, the lines $x = 1$ and $x = 2$
: about x-axis

2

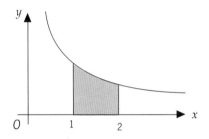

The region R is bounded by the curve with the equation $y = \frac{1}{x}$, the lines $x = 1$, $x = 2$ and the x-axis, as shown in the above figure. The unit of length on both axes is 1 m. A solid plinth is made in the shape of a solid formed by rotating R through 2π about the x-axis.

(a) Show that the volume of the plinth is $\frac{\pi}{2} m^3$.

(b) Find the distance of the centre of mass of the plinth from its larger plane face, giving your answer in cm to the nearest cm.

3 A solid of revolution is formed by rotating about the x-axis the region bounded by the x-axis, the lines $x = 4$, $x = 1$ and the curve $y^2 = x$. Show that the x-coordinate of the centre of mass of the uniform solid so formed is $\frac{14}{5}$.

Standard results

OCR M4 5.10.2 (a)(i)(ii)

The two sets of formulae, one for area and one for volume, allow us to calculate the position of the centre of mass of a number of standard figures without too much trouble.

Right-angled triangle

If we suppose a height is h and the base b we can align it with our axes as in Fig. 6.3.

Figure 6.3

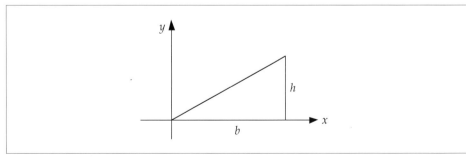

the defining line has equation $y = \frac{h}{b} x$.

$$\text{Using } \bar{x} = \frac{\int xy \, dx}{\int y \, dx} \Rightarrow \bar{x} = \frac{\int_0^b x\left(\frac{h}{b}\right)x \, dx}{\int_0^b \frac{h}{b}x \, dx} = \frac{\int_0^b x^2 dx}{\int_0^b x \, dx} = \frac{2b}{3}$$

This is from the apex: from the base it will be $\frac{b}{3}$. Similarly $\bar{y}$ from the base is $\frac{h}{3}$.

Cone

We can use the same line as in the previous case and rotate it around the x-axis.

Using the formula $\bar{x} = \frac{\int xy^2 dx}{\int y^2 dx}$ gives

$$\bar{x} = \frac{\frac{h^2}{b^2}\int_0^b x^3 dx}{\frac{h^2}{b^2}\int_0^b x^2 dx} = \frac{\frac{b^4}{4}}{\frac{b^3}{3}} = \frac{3b}{4} \text{ from the vertex}$$

i.e. the centre of mass of a cone is a quarter of the way up from the base.

Hemisphere

We can use a quadrant of a circle with radius a: if the centre of the circle is at the origin its equation will be:

$$x^2 + y^2 = a^2$$

Figure 6.4

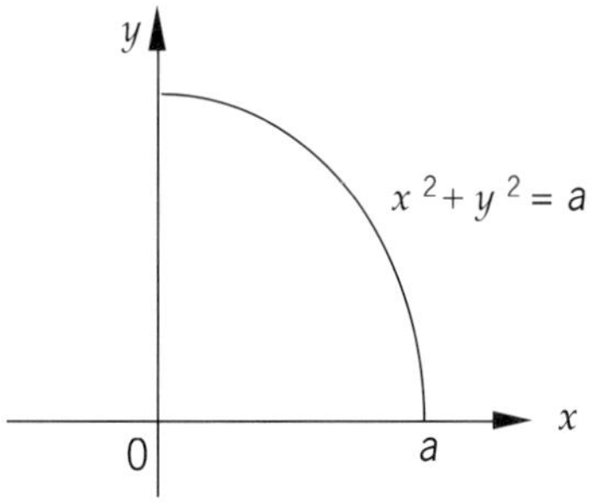

Then we have $\bar{x} = \frac{\int xy^2 dx}{\int y^2 dx} = \frac{\int_0^a x(a^2 - x^2) \, dx}{\int_0^a (a^2 - x^2) \, dx}$

$$= \frac{\left[a^2\frac{x^2}{2} - \frac{x^4}{4}\right]_0^a}{\left[a^2x - \frac{x^3}{3}\right]_0^a} = \frac{\frac{a^2}{4}}{\frac{2a^3}{3}} = \frac{3a}{8}$$

i.e. the centre of mass of a solid hemisphere is $\frac{3a}{8}$ from the centre of the sphere.

As before with the work in M2, we can find the centres of mass of composite bodies or remainders using these standard results.

Example

A uniform solid is formed from a hemisphere of radius r and a cone of base radius r and height h, the base of the cone being coincident with the plane face of the hemisphere, as shown in the diagram.

Figure 6.5

Given that the centre of mass of the solid is at a distance h from the vertex of the cone, find the numerical value of the ratio $h : r$.

Solution

(Taking moments about a diameter of the common face, on which the centre of mass (CoM) lies, of the parts gives

$$\frac{1}{3}\pi r^2 h \quad \times \quad \frac{h}{4} \quad - \quad \frac{2}{3}\pi r^3 \quad \times \quad \frac{3}{8}r \quad = \quad 0$$

Volume cone	CoM	Volume hemisphere	CoM	moment of whole

$$\Rightarrow \quad \frac{\pi r^2 h^2}{12} \quad = \quad \frac{\pi r^4}{4} \quad \Rightarrow \quad \frac{h^2}{r^2} = 3 \quad \Rightarrow \quad h : r \ = \ \sqrt{3} : 1$$

Example

Fig. 6.6 shows a solid truncated cone (i.e. a frustrum) whose plane faces are circles of radii 20 cm and 30 cm at a distance 40 cm apart. Find the position of the centre of mass.

Figure 6.6

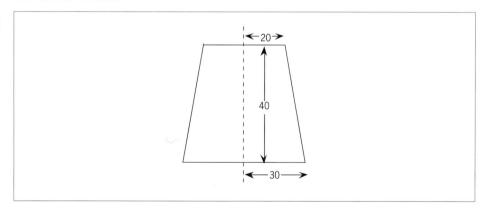

Solution

Before removal of the top two-thirds, the moment of the total cone about the base is $\frac{1}{3}\pi r^2 h\rho \times \frac{h}{4}$, i.e.

$$\left[\frac{1}{3}\pi \times 30^2 \times 120\right]\rho \ \times \ \frac{120}{4} \qquad\qquad \dots ①$$

The moment of the removed portion *about the same base* is

$$\left[\frac{1}{3}\pi \times 20^2 \times 80\right] \ \rho \ \times \ \left[\frac{80}{4}+40\right] \qquad\qquad \dots ②$$

The moment of the remainder about the base is

$$\left[\frac{1}{3}\pi \times 30^2 \times 120 - \frac{1}{3}\pi \times 20^2 \times 80\right]\rho \times \bar{y} \qquad \qquad \dots \; ③$$

Using ③ = ① − ② ,

$$\left[\frac{1}{3}\pi \times 30^2 \times 120 - \frac{1}{3}\pi \times 20^2 \times 80\right]\bar{y} = \left[\frac{1}{3}\pi \times 30^2 \times 120\right]\rho \times \frac{120}{4}$$
$$- \left[\frac{1}{3}\pi \times 20^2 \times 80\right]\rho \times \frac{240}{4}$$

$\div$ by $\frac{1}{3}\pi\rho$, $76\,000\,\bar{y} = 1\,320\,000 \Rightarrow \bar{y} = 17.4$ cm (1 d.p.)

i.e. The centre of mass is on the axis of symmetry, 17.4 cm above the base.

Practice questions C

1 A uniform composite body consists of a solid circular cylinder of radius a and height a and a solid hemisphere of radius a such that the plane face of the hemisphere coincides with the base of the cylinder. Determine the distance of the centre of mass of the composite body from the plane face of the hemisphere.

2 Five circular discs of radii 5 cm, 4 cm, 3 cm, 2 cm and 1 cm are cut from a uniform slab of material of thickness 1 cm. The discs are placed on top of each other on a horizontal table in order of decreasing size. Given that the centres of the discs all lie on the same vertical line, find the height of the centre of mass of the five discs above the table.

3 A uniform solid hemisphere of radius a has mass M. A concentric hemisphere of mass $\frac{1}{8}M$ is removed. Show that the centre of mass of the remainder is at a distance $\frac{45}{112}a$ from the centre O of the plane base.

4 Two uniform spheres of equal density but of radii na and a respectively are in contact. Show that the distance from the centre of the sphere of radius na to the centre of mass of the two spheres regarded as one combined body is $\frac{a(n+1)}{n^3+1}$.

5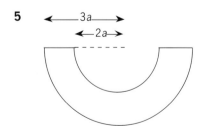

A uniform body is in the form of a thick hemispherical shell having internal and external radii $2a$ and $3a$. Show that the distance of the centre of mass from the centre of the plane face is $\frac{195}{152}a$.

6 A uniform solid cone of mass m, height $4a$ and base radius a and a uniform solid cylinder of mass $3m$ height $2a$ and base radius a are joined at their bases to form a composite body B. Find the distance of the centre of mass of B from the vertex of the cone.

7 The base of a uniform solid hemisphere has radius $2a$ and its centre is at O. A uniform solid S is formed by removing, from the hemisphere, the solid hemisphere of radius a and centre O. Determine the position of the centre of mass of S.

8 A uniform solid right circular cylinder of radius a and height $3a$ is fixed with its axis vertical, and has a uniform solid sphere of radius r attached to its upper face. The sphere and the cylinder have the same density and the centre of the sphere is vertically above the centre of the cylinder. Given that the centre of mass of the resulting composite body is at the point of contact of the sphere with the cylinder, find r in terms of a.

9 A composite body B is formed by joining, at the rims of their circular bases, a uniform solid right circular cylinder of radius a and height $2a$ and a uniform right circular cone of radius a and height $2a$. Given that the cylinder and the cone have masses M and λM respectively, find:

(a) the distance of the centre of mass of B from the common plane face when $\lambda = 1$,

(b) the value of λ such that the centre of mass of B lies in the common plane face.

10 The figure below represents a solid formed by the removal of a sphere of radius $\frac{a}{2}$ from a uniform solid hemisphere of base-radius a. The point O denotes the centre of the plane base of the hemisphere and C is that point on the hemisphere which is farthest from the base. Show that the centre of mass of the solid is on OC at a distance of $\frac{a}{3}$ from O.

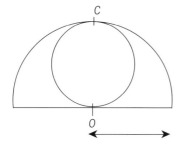

11 The figure below shows a plane section through the axis of a uniform solid cone of height h and base radius $2h$ from which a coaxial cone of height a and base radius h has been removed.

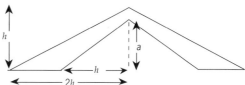

Given that the centre of mass of the resulting solid S is at a distance $\frac{4h}{15}$ from its plane base, find the possible values of a.

12 A uniform hollow hemisphere has inner and outer radii b and a respectively. Show that the distance of the centre of mass from the common centre of the hemispherical surfaces is

$$\frac{3(a^4 - b^4)}{8(a^3 - b^3)}$$

Objects suspended from strings or pivoted

OCR M2 5.8.2 (c)

This again is an extension of the work in M2: remember that the centre of mass is vertically below the point of suspension.

Example

The diagram shows a uniform lamina of mass M, which has the shape of the region enclosed by the x-axis and the curve with equation $ay = ax - x^2$, where a is a positive constant. The centre of mass of the lamina is at G.

Figure 6.7

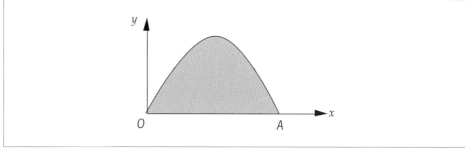

Find the coordinates of G, and prove that if the lamina were freely suspended from O, the line OA would make an angle θ with the vertical where $\tan \theta = \frac{1}{5}$.

Solution

$$ay = ax - x^2 \implies \text{when } y = 0, \quad ax - x^2 = 0$$
$$x(a - x) = 0$$
$$x = 0 \text{ or } x = a$$

Since a parabola is symmetrical about its turning point, the centre of mass will lie along this axis of symmetry, i.e. $\overline{x} = \frac{a}{2}$

Now we have $\bar{y} = \dfrac{\frac{1}{2}\int y^2 \, dx}{\int y \, dx} = \dfrac{\frac{1}{2}\int_0^a \frac{1}{a^2}\left(ax - x^2\right)^2 \, dx}{\int_0^a \frac{1}{a}\left(ax - x^2\right) \, dx}$

$= \dfrac{\frac{1}{2a^2}\int_0^a \left(a^2x^2 - 2ax^3 + x^4\right) \, dx}{\frac{1}{a}\int_0^a \left(ax - x^2\right) \, dx}$

$= \dfrac{\frac{1}{2a^2}\left[\frac{a^2x^3}{3} - \frac{2ax^4}{4} + \frac{x^5}{5}\right]_0^a}{\frac{1}{a}\left[\frac{ax^2}{2} - \frac{x^3}{3}\right]_0^a} = \dfrac{\frac{1}{2a^2} \times \frac{a^5}{30}}{\frac{1}{a} \times \frac{a^3}{6}} = \dfrac{a}{10}$

i.e. the coordinates of G are $\left(\dfrac{a}{2}, \dfrac{a}{10}\right)$

Figure 6.8

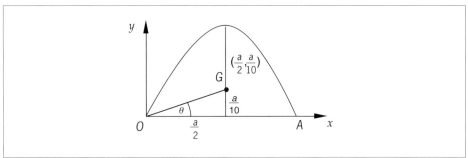

Suspended from O, OG would be vertical. $\operatorname{Tan} \theta = \dfrac{a}{10} \div \dfrac{a}{2} = \dfrac{1}{5}$ as required.

Practice questions D

(For the first two questions, you need to know that the centre of mass of a semicircular uniform wire is at a distance $\dfrac{2r}{\pi}$ from the centre, where r is the radius.)

1 A uniform wire of length $(2 + \pi)a$ is bent into the form of a semicircular arc together with the diameter AB joining the ends of the arc, and hangs in equilibrium from the point A. Show that AB makes an angle θ with the vertical, where

$$\tan \theta = \dfrac{2}{2 + \pi}$$

2 A uniform wire of weight W, bent into a semicircular arc, has a particle of weight W attached to one end and is suspended freely from the other end. Show that when the system is in equilibrium the straight line through the ends of the wire makes an angle $\tan^{-1}\left(\dfrac{3\pi}{2}\right)$

with the horizontal.

3 A composite body B is constructed by joining, at their rims, the bases of a uniform solid hemisphere of base radius a and a solid cylinder, constructed from different uniform material, and whose base is also of radius a. The mass of the cylinder is twice that of the hemisphere. When B is suspended from a point on the rim of the base of the hemisphere the axis of the cylinder is inclined at an angle $\sin^{-1}\left(\dfrac{1}{\sqrt{5}}\right)$ to the vertical. Show that the centre of mass of B is at a distance $2a$ from the base of the hemisphere and find the height of the cylinder.

4 A right circular uniform cone is of height h and base radius h. Show, by integration, that the centre of mass of the cone is at a distance $\frac{3h}{4}$ from the vertex.

The cone is then joined at its base to the circular base of a circular cylinder of the same material with radius h and height $3h$. Show that the centre of mass of this composite body is at a distance $\frac{93h}{40}$ from the vertex of the cone.

The composite body is freely suspended in equilibrium from a point on the rim of the common base of the cone and cylinder. Find the tangent of the angle which the axis of the cone makes with the vertical.

5 A uniform solid hemispherical bowl has internal radius $\frac{a}{2}$ and external radius a and the axes of the inner and outer surfaces coincide. The point O is the centre of a diameter AB of the outer rim of the bowl. Show that the centre of mass of the bowl is at a distance $\frac{45a}{112}$ from O.

The bowl is suspended by a light inextensible string, one end of which is attached at the point A, the other end of which is attached to a fixed point C. Find the tangent of the angle which AB makes with the vertical when the bowl hangs in equilibrium.

Toppling

If we place an object on a plane which is initially horizontal and then start to tilt the plane at an increasing angle, eventually one of two things will happen. Either the object will start to **slip** down the plane or, if the plane and/or solid are sufficiently rough, the object will **topple**. The condition for toppling, assuming that there is no slipping, is that the vertical line through the centre of mass passes outside the point about which the object is liable to topple.

Figure 6.9

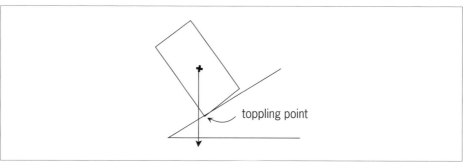

This object will topple, since the vertical lies outside the toppling point.

Figure 6.10

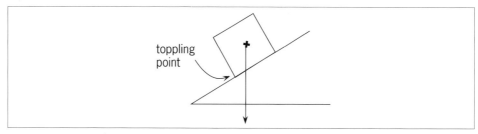

Vertical inside the toppling point, so body will not topple.

Let's try a couple of examples which use this principle.

A cuboid has a square base of side 6 cm and a height of 10 cm. It is placed on an inclined plane making an angle of α to the horizontal. Find the size of α if the cuboid is on the point of toppling. (Assume the plane to be sufficiently rough to prevent slipping.)

Again, we start with a diagram.

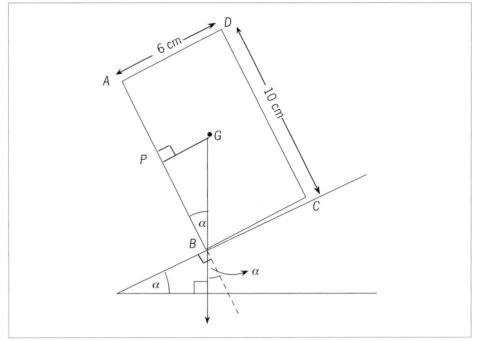

Since the cuboid is on the point of toppling, the vertical through G passes exactly through B. G is the position of the centre of mass, so that $PG = 3$ cm and $PB = 5$ cm. The angle PBG is α, the same as the angle made by the plane to the horizontal, and so

$$\tan \alpha = \frac{PG}{PB} = \frac{3}{5} \Rightarrow \alpha = 31.0° \text{ (1 d.p.)}$$

The same principle applies for a case where the object is on a horizontal plane: the vertical through the centre of mass has to pass through the base of the object and not outside it.

Fig. 6.12 shows the cross-section $ACDEF$ of a body consisting of a uniform cube of side a from which an isosceles right-angled prism of length a and section ABC, where $AB = BC = x$, has been removed.

The body rests with one of its surfaces, of area $a(a - x)$, in contact with a smooth horizontal plane. Determine the perpendicular distance of the centre of mass of the body from the face containing AF and show that the body will not topple provided that

$$2x^3 - 6a^2x + 3a^3 > 0.$$

Figure 6.12

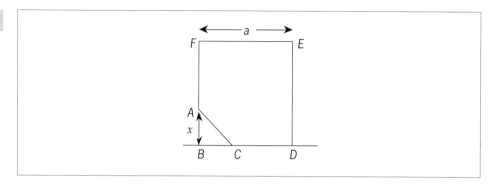

Solution

The centre of mass of the prism section ABC is $\dfrac{x}{3}$ from AB (standard result).

Moments about AF

Whole:

$$a^3 \times \rho \times \frac{a}{2} \quad = \frac{1}{2}a^4\rho$$

Triangular prism:

$$\frac{1}{2}x^2 a \times \rho \times \frac{x}{3} \quad = \frac{1}{6}x^3 a\rho$$

Remainder:

$$\left(a^3 - \frac{1}{2}x^2 a\right)\rho \times \bar{x}$$

Equating these:

$$\frac{1}{2}a^4\rho - \frac{1}{6}x^3 a\rho = \left(a^3 - \frac{1}{2}x^2 a\right)\rho\bar{x}$$

$$\Rightarrow \bar{x} = \frac{\frac{1}{2}a^4\rho - \frac{1}{6}x^3 a\rho}{\left(a^3 - \frac{1}{2}x^2 a\right)\rho} = \frac{3a^3 - x^3}{3(2a^2 - x^2)}$$

It will not topple provided that C is to the left of the vertical through the centre of mass, i.e. $\bar{x} > x$

$$\frac{3a^3 - x^3}{3(2a^2 - x^2)} > x \quad \Rightarrow 3a^3 - x^3 > 6a^2 x - 3x^3$$

i.e. $2x^3 - 6a^2 x + 3a^3 > 0$.

Practice questions E

1 Show that the centre of mass of a uniform solid hemisphere of radius a is at a distance $\dfrac{3a}{8}$ from its plane face.

A solid S is formed by joining the hemisphere to a uniform solid cylinder of the same material and of radius a and height $\dfrac{3a}{2}$ so that the plane face of the hemisphere coincides with one end of the cylinder. Find the distance of the centre of mass of S from its plane face.

Show that S could rest with its plane face on a sufficiently rough plane inclined to the horizontal at an angle β provided that

$$\tan \beta < \frac{52}{57}.$$

2 Show, by integration, that the centre of mass of a uniform solid right circular cone of height h is situated at a distance of $\dfrac{3h}{4}$ from its vertex V.

A frustrum of this cone is formed by cutting away a right circular cone of height $\dfrac{h}{2}$ and vertex V. Show that the centre of mass of the frustrum divides its axis in the ratio $11 : 17$.

When the frustrum is placed with part of its curved surface in contact with a horizontal plane, equilibrium is on the point of being broken by the frustrum toppling over. Find the base radius of the original cone in terms of h.

3 A cylindrical can of circular cross-section is made of thin material. The can is open at the top. The can's height is $2a$ and the radius of its plane base is a. The material used for the base is different from that used for the curved surface, but it is known that the centre of mass of the can is on the axis of the can and is $\frac{2}{3}a$ from the base.

(a) The can is placed with its base on a plane inclined at an angle θ to the horizontal. The plane is sufficiently rough to prevent sliding. Prove that the can will topple if $2\tan\theta > 3$.

(b) The can is suspended by a string attached to a point on the rim of its open end and hangs freely under gravity. Calculate the angle which the plane base of the can makes with the horizontal.

4

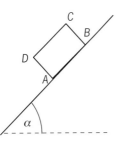

A uniform rectangular block, one of whose faces has corners labelled A, B, C and D, can rest in equilibrium with the edge AB along a line of greatest slope of a rough plane inclined at an angle α to the horizontal (see diagram).
$AB = 25$ cm and $BC = 15$ cm. Show that $\tan\alpha \le \frac{5}{3}$.

The block cannot rest in equilibrium with the face $ABCD$ vertical and the edge BC along a line of greatest slope of the plane. Given that the plane is rough enough to prevent sliding, show that $\tan\theta > \frac{3}{5}$.

5 A uniform cube rests in equilibrium with one face in contact with a rough horizontal plane. The plane is gradually tilted so that one pair of opposite faces of the cube remains vertical. The coefficient of friction between the cube and the plane is $\frac{3}{4}$. Prove that the block will will slide down the plane before it topples.

6 *(Hard)*

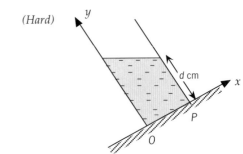

A water tank made of thin material of negligible mass consists of a square base of side 40 cm and four rectangular sides 40 cm wide by 1 m high. The base is placed on an inclined plane of slope $\tan^{-1}\left(\frac{1}{2}\right)$, sufficiently rough to prevent slipping, and the tank is partly filled with water. The diagram shows a section through the tank: O and P are the mid-points of opposite sides of the base, and OP lies along a line of greatest slope of the plane. The depth of water on the upper side of the tank is $d$cm (where $0 < d < 80$), as indicated. The centre of mass of the water has coordinates $(\bar{x}, \bar{y})$ referred to the axes Ox, Oy shown in the diagram. Show that

$$\bar{y} = \frac{3d^2 + 60d + 400}{6(10 + d)}$$

and find an expression for $\bar{x}$.

Find the set of values for d for which the tank can rest in equilibrium without toppling.

[Hint: Divide the water into a triangular and a rectangular prism.]

Particles

OCR M2 5.8.2 (b)

Once we have found the position of the centre of mass of a body, we may find that the system involves some additional force to maintain equilibrium.
The basic principle is that we then take moments about a suitable axis and solve the subsequent equation to determine the unknown quantity.

(a) A composite body B is formed by joining, at the rims of their circular bases, a uniform solid hemisphere of base radius a and a uniform right circular cone of base radius a and height a. The mass of the hemisphere is m. Given that the centre of mass of B lies within the cone and at a perpendicular distance $\frac{a}{8}$ from its base, find the mass of the cone in terms of m.

(b) The body B, when suspended from a point on the rim of the base of the cone, is in equilibrium with the axis of the cone inclined at an angle α to the vertical. Find $\tan \alpha$.

(c) Find also the least mass that has to be attached to the surface of the hemisphere so that when B is suspended from a point on the rim of the base of the cone, the axis of the cone is horizontal.

See Fig. 6.13.

Figure 6.13

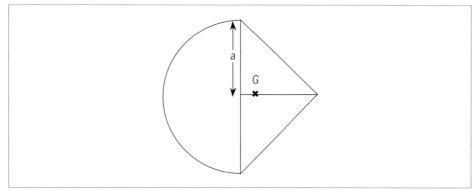

(a) Moments about common face:

$$\text{Hemisphere:} \quad m \times \rho \times \frac{-3a}{8} \quad = \quad \frac{-3ma\rho}{8}$$

$$\text{Cone :} \quad M \times \rho \times \frac{a}{4} \quad = \quad \frac{Ma\rho}{4}$$

$$\text{Total:} \quad (M + m) \times \rho \times \frac{a}{8} \quad = \quad \frac{(M + m)a\rho}{8}$$

Equating these:

$$\frac{-3ma\rho}{8} + \frac{Ma\rho}{4} = \frac{(M + m)a\rho}{8}$$

$$\times \frac{8}{a\rho} \qquad -3m + 2M = M + m$$

$$\Rightarrow \qquad M = 4m$$

Figure 6.14

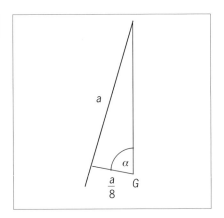

(b) $\tan \alpha = \dfrac{a}{\frac{a}{8}} = 8$

Figure 6.15

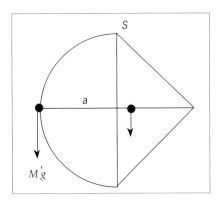

(c) The total mass of the body is
$m + M = m + 4m = 5m$

If we take moments about the vertical axis passing through the point of suspension S,

$$M'g \times a = 5\,mg \times \frac{a}{8}$$

$$\Rightarrow M' = \frac{5m}{8}$$

Two strings

When the object is suspended by two strings, we take moments about the axis through one string and then the axis through the other to determine the tensions.

Figure 6.16

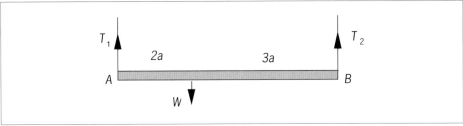

The diagram shows a non-uniform plank AB of length $5a$ with its centre of mass $2a$ from one end.

Moments about the vertical through A : $2aW = 5aT_2 \Rightarrow T_2 = \frac{2}{5}W$ ... ①

Moments about the vertical through B : $3aW = 5aT_1 \Rightarrow T_1 = \frac{3}{5}W$ ... ②

Note that the forces on the plank are in equilibrium, i.e. $T_1 + T_2 = W$, which we could have used instead of ② to find T_1. Here's an example of this idea.

| Example | From a uniform solid right circular cone of height H is removed a cone with the same base and of height h, the two axes coinciding. Show that the centre of mass of the remaining solid S is a distance |

$$\frac{1}{4}(3H - h)$$

from the vertex of the original cone.

The solid S is suspended by two vertical strings, one attached to the vertex and the other attached to a point on the bounding circular base. Given that S is in equilibrium, with its axis of symmetry horizontal, find, in terms of H and h, the ratio of the magnitude of the tension in the string attached to the vertex to that in the other string.

| Solution | See Fig. 6.17. |

Figure 6.17

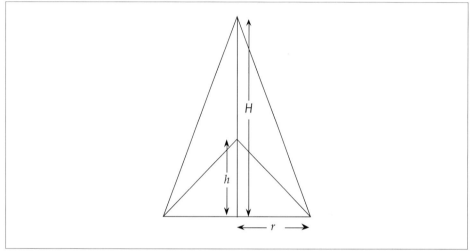

The centre of mass of a right circular cone is a quarter of the height above the base:

Large cone :   Vol is $\frac{1}{3}\pi r^2 H$ $\Rightarrow$ moment is $\frac{1}{3}\pi r^2 H\rho \times \dfrac{H}{4}$

Small cone :   Vol is $\frac{1}{3}\pi r^2 h$ $\Rightarrow$ moment is $\frac{1}{3}\pi r^2 h\rho \times \dfrac{h}{4}$

Remainder :   Vol is $\frac{1}{3}\pi r^2 (H - h)$ $\Rightarrow$ moment is $\frac{1}{3}\pi r^2 (H - h)\rho \times \bar{y}$

Moment of large = moment of small + moment of remainder

$$\frac{1}{3}\pi r^2 H\rho \times \frac{H}{4} = \frac{1}{3}\pi r^2 h\rho \times \frac{h}{4} + \frac{1}{3}\pi r^2 (H - h)\rho\bar{y}$$

$$\Rightarrow (H - h)\bar{y} = \frac{H^2}{4} - \frac{h^2}{4} = \frac{1}{4}(H^2 - h^2)$$

$$\Rightarrow \bar{y} = \frac{1}{4}\frac{H^2 - h^2}{H - h} = \frac{1}{4}(H + h)$$

So from the vertex of the original cone, the centre of mass will be

$$H - \bar{y} = H - \frac{1}{4}(H + h) = H - \frac{1}{4}H - \frac{1}{4}h = \frac{3}{4}H - \frac{1}{4}h$$

$$= \frac{1}{4}(3H - h)$$

Figure 6.18

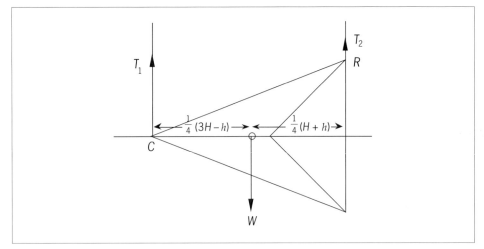

Taking moments about the **vertical axis** through C,

$$W \times \frac{1}{4}(3H - h) = T_2 H \qquad \qquad \dots ①$$

Moments about **vertical axis** through R,

$$W \times \frac{1}{4}(H + h) = T_1 H \qquad \qquad \dots ②$$

Dividing ② by ① $\quad \dfrac{T_1 H}{T_2 H} = \dfrac{W \times \frac{1}{4}(H + h)}{W \times \frac{1}{4}(3H - h)} \Rightarrow \dfrac{T_1}{T_2} = \dfrac{H + h}{3H - h}$

Practice questions F

1 A uniform solid concrete pillar used in a motorway bridge construction is a frustrum of a right circular cone. The radii of its circular ends are 3 m and 1 m, the centres of these ends being A and B respectively, and AB is of length 26 m. Calculate the distance of the centre of mass of the pillar from A.

The pillar is lifted by two vertical cables, one attached at each end, and held at rest with AB horizontal. Find the ratio of the tensions in the two cables.

2 (*Hard*) A right circular cone of height h and radius a and a hemisphere of radius a are joined so that their bases coincide. The density of the hemisphere is ρ and the density of the cone is 4ρ. Find the distance of the centre of mass of the combined body from the vertex of the cone.

Given that the centre of mass of the combined body lies in the cone, show that $2h > a\sqrt{3}$.

The combined body has mass M and is placed on a plane which is inclined at an angle of 30° to the horizontal so that the hemisphere is in contact with the plane. A particle of mass m is attached to the point which lies on the rim of the common plane face and is furthest away from the foot of the slope. The system rests in equilibrium with the axis of the cone at right angles to the line of greatest slope of the plane. Given that $h = 2a$, show that

$$m = \frac{53}{80} M (1 + \sqrt{3}).$$

SUMMARY EXERCISE

1 A uniform lamina has the shape of the region enclosed by the x-axis and the part of the curve $y = x(2-x)$ for which $0 \le x \le 2$. Find the coordinates of the centre of mass of the lamina.

2 The diagram shows part of the curve $y = x^2 + 1$ between $x = 0$ and $x = 1$. Find the coordinates of the centre of mass of the solid obtained when this area is rotated 360° around the x-axis.

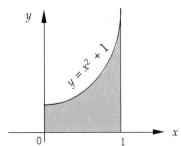

3

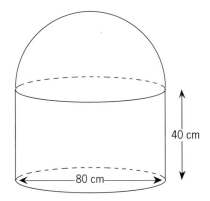

The above figure shows a uniform solid standing on horizontal ground. The solid consists of a uniform solid right circular cylinder, of diameter 80 cm and height 40 cm, joined to a uniform solid hemisphere of the same density. The circular base of the hemisphere coincides with the upper circular end of the cylinder and has the same diameter as that of the cylinder.

Find the distance of the centre of mass of the solid from the ground.

4 Show that the centre of mass of a uniform hemisphere is at a distance $\frac{3}{8}r$ from the centre of the plane face, where r is the radius.

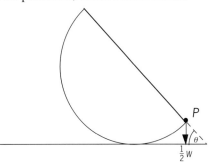

A uniform solid hemisphere of weight W is placed with its spherical surface on a smooth horizontal plane. A particle P of weight $\frac{1}{2}W$ is attached to its rim. In the position of equilibrium the plane face of the hemisphere is inclined at an angle θ to the horizontal, as shown in the diagram. Find $\tan \theta$.

5

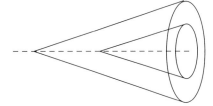

Show that the centre of mass of a uniform solid right circular cone of height h and base-radius a is at a distance $\frac{3}{4}h$ from the vertex.

A hole in the shape of a right circular cone of base-radius $\frac{1}{2}a$ and height $\frac{2}{3}h$ is bored out of this cone; the axis of the hole coincides with that of the cone. The resulting solid is shown in the diagram. Find the distance of the centre of mass of this solid from the vertex of the original cone.

6

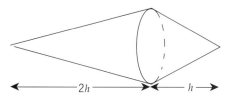

A spindle is formed by joining two right solid circular cones so that their circular bases coincide. The cones have the same base radius and have the same uniform density. The heights of the two cones are h and $2h$, as shown in the above figure.

(a)   Find the distance of the centre of mass of the spindle from the vertex of the larger cone.

The spindle is placed on horizontal ground with the sloping surface of the smaller cone in contact with the ground. It rests in equilibrium but is on the point of toppling.

(b)   Show that the radius of the common base of the two cones is $\frac{1}{2}h$.

7   The diagram shows a vertical section through the centres of three uniform cubical blocks which are glued together. The cubes all have the same density. The lowest cube, cross-section $ABCD$, has edge $3a$, the middle one has edge $2a$ and the uppermost one has edge a. Referred to AB and AD, as axes of x and y respectively, the centre of mass has coordinates $(\bar{x}, \bar{y})$.

Show that $\bar{x} = \frac{29}{18}a$ and find $\bar{y}$ in terms of a.

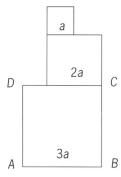

The composite solid is placed, with AB along a line of greatest slope and with B above A, on a rough plane inclined at an angle α to the horizontal. Find $\tan\alpha$, given that the solid is on the point of toppling.

(Note that they are *cubes* and not just squares!)

8   (a)   Prove, by integration, that the centre of mass of a uniform solid right circular cone of height h is at a distance $\frac{3}{4}h$ from the vertex V of the cone.

(b)   From this cone, which has base radius $4r$, a smaller cone, of height $\frac{1}{4}h$ and vertex V, is removed by cutting along a plane parallel to the base of the cone. Find the height above the base of the centre of mass of the frustum remaining.

(c)   This frustum, which has weight W, is placed with its smaller plane face in contact with a rough horizontal table. A horizontal force of magnitude P is applied to a point on the curved surface of the frustum, the line of action of P passing through the centre of mass of the frustum. The value of P is gradually increased from zero. Given that $h = 6r$ and that the table is sufficiently rough for equilibrium to be broken by the overturning of the frustum, find, in terms of W, the value of P for which this occurs.

9   A uniform circular cylinder has height h and radius r. From the cylinder, a cone C, with vertex O at the centre of one plane end of the cylinder and with the other plane end as base, is removed. Show that the distance of the centre of mass of the remaining solid R from O is $\frac{3}{8}h$.

(The position of the centre of mass of a cone may be quoted without proof.)

The plane circular faces of C and R are now glued together, with their circumferences coincident, and the resulting body is suspended in equilibrium from a point on the circumference of their common plane face. Given that $h = 2r$, find the tangent of the angle between the axis of symmetry of the body and the horizontal.

10

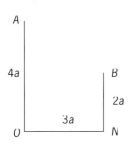

A uniform straight wire AB, of length $9a$, is bent through $90°$ at the point O, where $OA = 4a$, and also at N, where $NB = 2a$, as shown in the diagram. The four points A, O, N and B are coplanar. Show that the distance, $\bar{x}$, of the centre of mass of the bent wire from OA is given by $\bar{x} = \frac{7}{6}a$ and find $\bar{y}$, the distance of the centre of mass from ON.

The bent wire is freely suspended from B and hangs in equilibrium. Find the tangent of the angle of inclination of BN to the vertical.

11 Show by integration that the centre of mass of a uniform solid right circular cone of height h is at a distance $\frac{3}{4}h$ from the vertex.

Two uniform solid right circular cones, each with the same base radius a and the same density, have heights h and λh, where $\lambda > 1$. These cones are joined together, with their circular bases coinciding, to form a spindle. Show that the centre of mass of this spindle is at a distance $\frac{1}{4}h\,(3\lambda + 1)$ from the vertex of the larger cone.

Given that $a = h$, show that the spindle can rest in equilibrium with the curved surface of the smaller cone in contact with a horizontal plane provided that $\lambda \leq 5$.

12

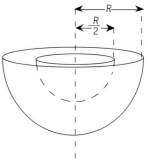

A solid S is formed by removing from a hemisphere of radius R a smaller hemisphere of radius $\frac{R}{2}$ having the same axis of symmetry and the same plane face, as shown in the above figure.

(a) Show that the distance of the centre of mass of the solid S from the plane face is $\frac{45R}{112}$.

(It may be assumed without proof that the centre of mass of a uniform solid hemisphere of radius R is on the axis of symmetry at a distance $\frac{3}{8}R$ from the plane face.)

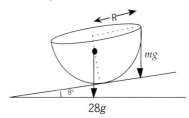

A flower tub which is hemispherical is placed on a sloping pavement. A mass m kg is attached to its rim and the tub is in equilibrium with its rim parallel to the pavement as shown in the above figure.

The tub, which has mass 28 kg, is modelled as the solid S. The added mass is modelled as a particle of mass m kg and the sloping pavement as a rough plane inclined at an angle $8°$ to the horizontal. All the forces acting on the tub are in a vertical plane through a line of greatest slope of the inclined plane.

(b) Find the value of m, giving your answer to 2 significant figures.

13

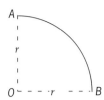

A uniform arc AB is part of a circle, centre O and radius r, with $\angle AOB = \frac{\pi}{2}$, as shown in the above figure. By using the standard result for the centre of mass of a circular arc,

(a)   show that the perpendicular distance of the centre of mass of AB from OA is $\frac{2r}{\pi}$.

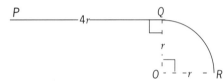

A walking stick is modelled as a uniform rod PQ of length $4r$ joined to a uniform arc QR of a circle, centre O and radius r, with $\angle QOR = \frac{\pi}{2}$.

O, P, Q and R are coplanar and the radius OQ is perpendicular to PQ, as shown in the above figure. The rod PQ and the arc QR have the same mass per unit length.

(b)   Show that the perpendicular distance of the centre of mass of the walking stick from OQ is $\frac{14r}{(8 + \pi)}$.

(c)   Show that the perpendicular distance of the centre of mass of the walking stick from OR is $\frac{10r}{(8 + \pi)}$.

The walking stick has a small loop, of negligible size and mass, at its end R and the stick is stored by hanging it on a hook using this loop. When the walking stick is hanging freely in equilibrium from the loop at R, the angle between OR and the downward vertical is α.

(d)   Find, in terms of ρ, the value of $\tan \alpha$.

14   A solid body consists of a solid hemisphere joined to a cylinder of the same radius whose height is three times the radius of its base. It is placed with its plane face in contact with a rough plane, and the inclination of the plane to the horizontal is gradually increased. Prove that it will slide down the plane without toppling over, provided that the coefficient of friction between the body and the plane is less than $\frac{44}{81}$.

SUMMARY

This section has dealt with the use of integration in finding the centre of mass of plane laminas and solids, as well as using the knowledge of the position of the centre of mass to solve problems involving systems in equilibrium. You should now:

● be able to derive the position of the centre of mass of standard laminas and solids

● know that the centre of mass lies along any axis of symmetry of a lamina or solid

● be able to take moments about a suitable axis to solve problems involving additional forces acting on a figure

● know the condition for toppling to occur.

ANSWERS

Practice questions A

1. (a) $\left(\frac{9}{16}, \frac{7}{10}\right)$ (b) $\left(\frac{3}{5}, 0\right)$

    (c) $\left(\frac{25}{7}, 0\right)$ (d) $\left(\frac{4}{3}, \frac{31}{120}\right)$

    (e) $\left(\frac{3}{4}, \frac{8}{5}\right)$

2. $\bar{y} = \frac{9a}{2}$

Practice questions B

1. (a) $\left(\frac{2}{3}, 0\right)$ (b) $(4, 0)$

    (c) $\left(0, \frac{1}{3}\right)$ (d) $\left(\frac{9}{7}, 0\right)$

2. (b) 39 cm

Practice questions C

1. $\frac{3a}{20}$

2. $\frac{31}{22}$ cm

6. $\frac{9a}{2}$

7. $\frac{45a}{56}$ from O

8. $\left(\frac{3}{2}\right)^{\frac{3}{4}} a$

9. (a) $\frac{a}{4}$ (b) 2

11. $\frac{2h}{5}, \frac{2h}{3}$

Practice questions D

3. $\frac{51a}{8}$

4. $\tan \theta = \frac{40}{53}$

5. $\tan \theta = \frac{45}{112}$

Practice questions E

1. $\frac{57}{52} a$

2. $h \sqrt{\left(\frac{17}{28}\right)}$

3. (b) 36.9°

5. 4 m; $\tan \alpha = 8$; $\frac{5m}{8}$

6. $\bar{x} = \frac{20(3d + 20)}{3(d + 10)}$; $0 \le d \le 10 (3 + \sqrt{13})$

Practice questions F

1. 9 m, 17 : 9

2. $\frac{12h^2 + 8ha + 3a^2}{8(2h + a)}$

M3
Practice examination paper

1

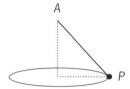

The conical pendulum shown in the diagram consists of a light inextensible string which has one end attached to a fixed point A. A particle P, of mass m, is attached to the other end of the string. The particle P moves with constant speed completing two orbits of its circular path every second and the tension in the string is $2mg$.

Find, to the nearest cm:

(a)   the radius of the circular path of P

(b)   the length of the string.

2   A particle P, of mass m, lies inside a fixed smooth hollow sphere of internal radius a and centre O. When P is at rest at the lowest point A of the sphere, it is given a horizontal impulse of magnitude mu.

The particle P loses contact with the inner surface of the sphere at the point B, where $\angle AOB = 120°$.

(a)   Show that $u^2 = \dfrac{7}{2}ga$.

(b)   Find the greatest height above B reached by P.

3   Show by integration that the centre of mass of a uniform solid hemisphere of radius r is situated at a distance $\dfrac{3r}{8}$ from the centre of its plane face.

A solid composite uniform body consists of a right circular cylinder, of radius r and height $2r$, and a hemisphere of radius r, the plane face of the hemisphere coinciding with a circular end of the cylinder. Find the distance of the centre of mass of the composite body from its plane face.

The plane face of this body is placed on a perfectly rough plane which is inclined at an angle θ to the horizontal. If the body is on the point of toppling, find the value of $\tan\theta$.

4   A cyclist and her bicycle have a total mass of 60 kg. The cyclist rides her bicycle up a straight slope inclined at 7° to the horizontal, starting from rest. At time t seconds after starting, she is moving with velocity v m s^{-1} up a line of greatest slope. In a mathematical model for the motion, the cyclist creates a force of magnitude $150e^{-\frac{t}{30}}$ N in the direction of motion, and all resisting forces are ignored. The cyclist with her bicycle is treated as a particle.

(a)   Show that $\dfrac{dv}{dt} = \dfrac{5}{2}e^{-\frac{t}{30}} - 1.2$, approximately.

(b)   Find v when $t = 12$.

Explain how the mathematical model corresponds to the fact that the cyclist tires as she rides up the slope.

5   A particle P, of mass 0.01 kg, moves along a straight line with simple harmonic motion. The centre of the motion is the point O. At the points L and M, which are on opposite sides of O, the particle P has speeds of 0.09 m s^{-1} and 0.06 m s^{-1} respectively and $2OL = OM = 0.02$ m.

(a)   Show that the period of this motion is $2\pi\sqrt{\left(\dfrac{1}{15}\right)}$ seconds.

Find:

(b)   the greatest value of the magnitude of the force acting on P, giving your answer to 2 significant figures

(c)   the time for P to move directly from L through O to M, giving your answer to 2 significant figures.

6

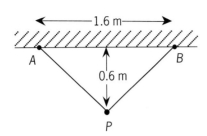

Two light elastic strings each have natural length 0.8 m and modulus λ N. One end of each string is fastened to a particle P, of mass 0.2 kg, and the other ends are attached to fixed points A and B on a horizontal ceiling, where $AB = 1.6$ m. Initially, P is held on the ceiling at the mid-point of AB. After being released from rest in this position, P falls vertically and comes instantaneously to rest at a point 0.6 m below the level of the ceiling, as shown in the diagram.

Using the principle of conservation of energy,

(a) show that $\lambda = 23.52$

(b) find the speed of P at the instant when the length of each string is 0.9 m, giving your answer to 2 significant figures.

7 One end of a light elastic spring of natural length l is fixed to a point O. A particle P, of mass m, is attached at the other end of the spring and hangs in equilibrium at a distance $\dfrac{7l}{5}$ below O.

(a) Find, in terms of m and g, the modulus of elasticity of the spring.

The particle P is pulled down a further distance $\dfrac{l}{5}$ from its equilibrium position and released from rest. At time t after P is released, the length of the spring is $x + \dfrac{7l}{5}$.

(b) Find a differential equation for the motion of P relating x and t, and deduce that P is moving with simple harmonic motion.

Giving your answers in terms of l and g, find:

(c) the period of the motion of P

(d) the greatest speed of P.

M3

Solutions

Section 1

1 $a = 2 - 2t \Rightarrow \dfrac{dv}{dt} = 2 - 2t$ $\int dv = \int 2 - 2t \, . \, dt$

$$v = 2t - t^2 + C$$

$v = 3$ when $t = 0 \Rightarrow C = 3$ $v = 2t - t^2 + 3$

When $t = 3$, $v = 6 - 9 + 3 = 0$ as required

$$\dfrac{ds}{dt} = 2t - t^2 + 3 \quad \Rightarrow \quad \int ds = \int 2t - t^2 + 3 \; dt$$

$$s = t^2 - \dfrac{t^3}{3} + 3t + d$$

When $t = 0$, $s = 0 \Rightarrow d = 0 \Rightarrow s = t^2 - \dfrac{t^3}{3} + 3t$

When $t = 3$, $s = 9 - 9 + 9 = 9$ m

2 $\dfrac{dv}{dt} = e^{2t}$ $\Rightarrow \int dv = \int e^{2t} \, dt, v = \dfrac{1}{2} e^{2t} + C$

when

$t = 0, v = 0 \Rightarrow O = \dfrac{1}{2} + C, C = \dfrac{-1}{2}, v = \dfrac{1}{2}(e^{2t} - 1)$

3 (a) Force is positive, $F = 8x \Rightarrow mv \dfrac{dv}{dx} = 8x, m = 2$

$$v \dfrac{dv}{dx} = 4x$$

(b) $\int v \, dv = \int 4x \, dx$

$$\dfrac{v^2}{2} = 2x^2 + C$$

$v = 0$ when $x = 2$ $0 = 8 + C \Rightarrow C = -8$

$\dfrac{v^2}{2} = 2x^2 - 8 \Rightarrow v^2 = 4(x^2 - 4)$

$$v = 2\sqrt{x^2 - 4} \;\; (> 0)$$

4 (a) Force is negative, $F = -mkx^2$

$$\Rightarrow \quad mv \dfrac{dv}{dx} = -mkx^2$$

$$\dfrac{v \, dv}{dx} = -kx^2$$

$$\int v \, dv = \int -kx^2 \, dx$$

$$\dfrac{v^2}{2} = \dfrac{-kx^3}{3} + C$$

$v = 0$ when $x = c$, $0 = \dfrac{-kc^3}{3} + C \Rightarrow C = \dfrac{kc^3}{3}$

$$\dfrac{v^2}{2} = \dfrac{k}{3}(c^3 - x^3)$$

$x = 0, \quad \dfrac{v^2}{2} = \dfrac{k}{3} c^3 \Rightarrow v^2 = \dfrac{2kc^3}{3},$

$$v = \sqrt{\left(\dfrac{2kc^3}{3} \right)}$$

(b) Work done is increase of KE,

i.e. $\dfrac{1}{2} m \left(-\sqrt{\left(\dfrac{2kc^3}{3} \right)} \right)^2 = \dfrac{mkc^3}{3}$

5 $v \dfrac{dv}{dx} = k \left[\dfrac{3a^2}{x^2} - 1 \right]$

$$\int v \, dv = k \int \left(\dfrac{3a^2}{x^2} - 1 \right) dx$$

$$\dfrac{v^2}{2} = k \left[\dfrac{-3a^2}{x} - x \right] + C$$

$x = 2a, v = \sqrt{ka}$ $\dfrac{ka}{2} = k \left[\dfrac{-3a^2}{2a} - 2a \right] + C \Rightarrow C = 4ka$

$$\dfrac{v^2}{2} = 4ka - k \left[\dfrac{3a^2}{x} + x \right]$$

$$v^2 = 8ka - 2k \left[\dfrac{3a^2}{x} + x \right] = \dfrac{2k}{x} \left[4ax - 3a^2 - x^2 \right]$$

$$= \dfrac{2k}{x}(x - 3a)(a - x)$$

Max. and min. values of x when $v = 0$, i.e.

$x = 3a$ and $x = a$, $a \le x \le 3a$.

6 F is negative (towards 0) so work *against* is

$$\int_a^b + F \, dx = \int_a^b \dfrac{km}{x^2} \, dx = \left[\dfrac{-km}{x} \right]_a^b = km \left(-\dfrac{1}{b} + \dfrac{1}{a} \right)$$

$$= \dfrac{km(b - a)}{ab}$$

Difference in KE is $\dfrac{m}{2}(4u^2 - u^2) = \dfrac{3mu^2}{2} = km \dfrac{(b - a)}{ab}$

$$\Rightarrow u^2 = \dfrac{2k(b - a)}{3ab} \Rightarrow u = \left[\dfrac{2k(b - a)}{3ab} \right]^{\frac{1}{2}}$$

If speed O, diff KE is $\dfrac{4mu^2}{2} = \dfrac{km(c - a)}{ac}$

$$\Rightarrow \dfrac{b - a}{3ab} = \dfrac{c - a}{4ac}$$

$4cb - 4ac = 3bc - 3ab$

$$\Rightarrow 3ab = 4ac - bc$$

$$\Rightarrow c = \dfrac{3ab}{4a - b}$$

7

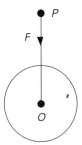

There's a temptation when thinking about forces acting on the particle in a case like this to assume that gravity is acting in the normal way, i.e. that there is an additional force of mg acting 'downwards'. In fact, there is only the given force acting – this would reduce to mg in the particular case that $x = R$, i.e. the particle is on the surface of the earth.

Since this is given as a **force** and not an acceleration, we use $F = ma$ and as we are taking the direction $\overrightarrow{OP}$, i.e. **away** from the centre of the earth, to be positive, this force, which is **towards** the centre of the earth, will be negative. We can now put down our preliminary equation

$$F = ma = -\frac{mg\,R^2}{x^2} \qquad \dots ①$$

Looking at the question, we see it asks for the distance travelled, so for a we use the form $v\frac{dv}{dx}$ and our equation becomes

$$mv\frac{dv}{dx} = \frac{-mg\,R^2}{x^2} \qquad \dots ②$$

Dividing through by m and rearranging our differential equation

$$\int v\,dv = \int \frac{-gR^2}{x^2}\,dx$$

$$= gR^2 \int \left(-\frac{1}{x^2}\right)dx$$

since g, R are constants

$$= gR^2 \int (-x^{-2})\,dx$$

$$\Rightarrow \quad \frac{v^2}{2} = gR^2(x^{-1}) + C$$

$$= \frac{gR^2}{x} + C \qquad \dots ③$$

We have to be a bit careful here – since it is projected from the surface of the earth and the distance is measured from O, the centre of the earth, the initial distance

$$x = R \text{ when } v = \sqrt{gR}.$$

Putting these into ③ gives

$$\frac{gR}{2} = \frac{gR^2}{R} + C \Rightarrow C = -\frac{gR}{2}$$

giving our particular solution as

$$\frac{v^2}{2} = \frac{gR^2}{x} - \frac{gR}{2} \qquad \dots ④$$

We want to find x when $v = \frac{1}{2}\sqrt{gR}$. Substituting this value for v gives

$$\frac{1}{2}\left(\frac{gR}{4}\right) = \frac{gR^2}{x} - \frac{gR}{2}$$

$$\Rightarrow \frac{gR^2}{x} = \frac{gR}{2} + \frac{gR}{8} = \frac{5gR}{8}$$

$$\Rightarrow x = \frac{8R}{5}$$

The final hurdle is to note that the question asks for the **distance travelled** and not distance from the centre. Since x was R initially, the distance travelled is

$$\frac{8R}{5} - R = \frac{3R}{5}$$

8 Since the distance is measured in the positive x-direction from O, we have to take this as our positive direction for the velocity and the acceleration. The initial direction of the velocity is **towards** O, so this will be negative; the acceleration is initially **away** from O and so this will be positive.

$$a = \frac{k}{2x^2} + \frac{k}{4a^2} \qquad \dots ①$$

We want to connect v and x, so we use

$$a = v\frac{dv}{dx}$$

$$v\frac{dv}{dx} = \frac{k}{2x^2} + \frac{k}{4a^2}$$

$$\int v\,dv = \int \left(\frac{k}{2x^2} + \frac{k}{4a^2}\right)dx$$

$$\frac{v^2}{2} = -\frac{k}{2x} + \frac{kx}{4a^2} + C \qquad \dots ②$$

The particle passes through A, $x = 2a$, with a speed of $\sqrt{\left(\frac{k}{a}\right)}$ towards O, i.e. $v = -\sqrt{\left(\frac{k}{a}\right)}$.

Putting these into ②

$$\frac{k}{2a} = -\frac{k}{4a} + \frac{k \times 2a}{4a^2} + C$$

$$\Rightarrow \quad C = \frac{k}{4a} \text{ and this back in ② gives}$$

$$\frac{v^2}{2} = -\frac{k}{2x} + \frac{kx}{4a^2} + \frac{k}{4a}$$

Now when the particle is at B, where $x = a$,

$$\frac{v^2}{2} = -\frac{k}{2a} + \frac{ka}{4a^2} + \frac{k}{4a} = 0$$

Now the acceleration changes and our new equation is

$$v\frac{dv}{dx} = \frac{k}{2x^2} - \frac{k}{4a^2}$$

$$\int v\,dv = \int \left(\frac{k}{2x^2} - \frac{k}{4a^2}\right)\,dx$$

$$\frac{v^2}{2} = -\frac{k}{2x} - \frac{kx}{4a^2} + C \qquad \dots ③$$

But at B, where $x = a$, the particle was at rest, $v = 0$

$$0 = \frac{-k}{2a} - \frac{ka}{4a^2} + C \Rightarrow C = \frac{3k}{4a}$$

and ③ becomes

$$\frac{v^2}{2} = \frac{-k}{2x} - \frac{kx}{4a^2} + \frac{3k}{4a} \qquad \dots ④$$

$$= -\frac{k}{4a^2x}\left[2a^2 + x^2 - 3ax\right]$$

$$= \frac{-k}{4a^2x}\left[(x-a)(x-2a)\right]$$

So when $v = 0$, either

$x - a = 0$ or $x - 2a = 0$

$x = a$ (which is where it starts at B)

or $x = 2a$, i.e. at A, the next point where it comes instantaneously to rest.

9 (a) $v\dfrac{dv}{dx} = 6x - 4x^3 \, dx$

$\Rightarrow \displaystyle\int v \, dv = \int (6x - 4x^3) \, dx$

$\dfrac{v^2}{2} = 3x^2 - x^4 + C$

$x = 1, v = 0$

$\Rightarrow 0 = 3 - 1 + C \Rightarrow C = -2$

$\dfrac{v^2}{2} = 3x^2 - x^4 - 2$

When $x = \sqrt{2}$,

$\dfrac{v^2}{2} = 3 \times 2 - 4 - 2 = 0 \Rightarrow v = 0$

(b) $\dfrac{dv}{dt} = -v^4 \Rightarrow \displaystyle\int \dfrac{-1}{v^4} \, dv = \int dt$

$\dfrac{1}{3v^3} = t + C$

$v = 2$ when $t = 0$

$\Rightarrow \dfrac{1}{24} = C \quad \Rightarrow \quad t = \dfrac{1}{3v^3} - \dfrac{1}{24}$

$v\dfrac{dv}{dx} = -v^4 \Rightarrow \displaystyle\int \dfrac{-1}{v^3} \, dv = \int dx$

$\dfrac{1}{2v^2} = x + C$

$v = 2$ when $x = 0$

$\Rightarrow \dfrac{1}{8} = C \quad \Rightarrow x = \dfrac{1}{2v^2} - \dfrac{1}{8}$

When $v = 1$, $t = \dfrac{1}{3} - \dfrac{1}{24} = \dfrac{7}{24}$

and $x = \dfrac{1}{2} - \dfrac{1}{8} = \dfrac{3}{8}$

$\Rightarrow$ Average speed is $\dfrac{\frac{3}{8}}{\frac{7}{24}} = \dfrac{3}{8} \times \dfrac{24}{7} = \dfrac{9}{7}$

10 $mv\dfrac{dv}{dx} = \dfrac{-k}{x^2} \Rightarrow \displaystyle\int v \, dv = \int -\dfrac{2k}{x^2} \, dx$

$\dfrac{v^2}{2} = \dfrac{2k}{x} + C$

$v = 0$ when $x = 5$ $0 = \dfrac{2k}{5} + C \Rightarrow C = \dfrac{-2k}{5}$

$\dfrac{v^2}{2} = \dfrac{2k}{x} - \dfrac{2k}{5}$ and when $x = 2, v = 12$

$72 = \dfrac{2k}{2} - \dfrac{2k}{5} \Rightarrow k = 120$

Section 2

1 In equilibrium $T = mg$ and also, for an elastic string, $T = \dfrac{\lambda x}{l}$. Equating these with $m = 2$, $l = 3$ and $\lambda = 12g$ gives

$mg = \dfrac{\lambda x}{l} \Rightarrow 2g = \dfrac{12gx}{3}$

$\Rightarrow x = 0.5$ m

2 As before, $mg = \dfrac{\lambda x}{l}$ with $m = 0.5$ (in kg)

$l = 0.5 \qquad x = 0.05$

$\Rightarrow 0.5g = \dfrac{\lambda \, 0.05}{0.5} \Rightarrow \lambda = 5g$

3

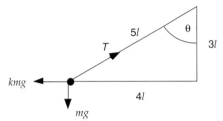

Marking in the angle θ and noting that the triangle is $3 - 4 - 5$ so that

$\sin \theta = \dfrac{4}{5}, \ \cos \theta = \dfrac{3}{5}, \ \tan \theta = \dfrac{4}{3}$

Resolving vertically, $T \cos \theta = mg$ ... ①

horizontally, $T \sin \theta = kmg$ ... ②

But the string is elastic with the extension $x = 5l - 4l = l$, and so

$T = \dfrac{\lambda \, (\text{extension})}{\text{natural length}} = \dfrac{\lambda l}{4l} = \dfrac{\lambda}{4}$

Putting this into ① with $\cos \theta = \dfrac{3}{5}$ gives

$\dfrac{\lambda}{4} \times \dfrac{3}{5} = mg \quad \Rightarrow \lambda = \dfrac{20mg}{3}$

Hence $T = \dfrac{\lambda}{4} = \dfrac{\frac{20mg}{3}}{4} = \dfrac{5mg}{3}$

Dividing equation ② by ① gives

$\dfrac{T \sin \theta}{T \cos \theta} = \dfrac{kmg}{mg} \Rightarrow k = \tan \theta = \dfrac{4}{3}$

4 The tension throughout the joined string will be the same and since the suspended particle has mass M, this tension will be Mg.

For AB: $T = \dfrac{\lambda_1 x_1}{c} \Rightarrow Mg = \dfrac{9Mg \, x_1}{c}$

$\Rightarrow x_1 = \dfrac{c}{9}$ ... ①

For CD: $T = \dfrac{\lambda_2 x_2}{c} \Rightarrow Mg = \dfrac{12Mg \, x_2}{c}$

$\Rightarrow x_2 = \dfrac{c}{12}$ ... ②

The length of AD will be:

natural lengths + total extension

i.e. $c + c + \dfrac{c}{9} + \dfrac{c}{12} = \dfrac{79c}{36}$

5

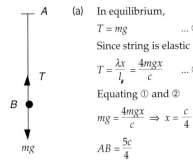

(a) In equilibrium,

$T = mg$ ... ①

Since string is elastic

$T = \dfrac{\lambda x}{l_{\bullet}} = \dfrac{4mgx}{c}$ ... ②

Equating ① and ②

$mg = \dfrac{4mgx}{c} \Rightarrow x = \dfrac{c}{4}$

$AB = \dfrac{5c}{4}$

(b) At A, KE is zero

PE is zero (taking level of A as zero level)

EE is zero

At D, the point of maximum distance between A and B, which we can call d,

KE is zero (since at rest before going up again)

PE is $-mgd$ (negative since a loss)

EE is $\dfrac{\lambda(d-c)^2}{2c}$ since $d = c + x$, when x is the extension

$\Rightarrow x = d - c$

i.e. $\dfrac{\lambda(d-c)^2}{2c} = mgd \Rightarrow \dfrac{4mg(d-c)^2}{2c} = mgd$

$4(d-c)^2 = 2cd \Rightarrow 2d^2 - 4cd + 2c^2 = cd$

$2d^2 - 5cd + 2c^2 = 0$

$(2d - c)(d - 2c) = 0$

Since $d > c$, we ignore $d = \dfrac{c}{2}$,

and then $d = 2c$

6 $T = mg = \dfrac{\lambda x}{l} = \dfrac{\lambda \times \frac{l}{12}}{l} \Rightarrow \lambda = 12mg$

At top, PE $= 0 =$ EE

At greatest depth, PE $= -mgd$

EE $= \dfrac{1}{2}\dfrac{\lambda x^2}{l} = \dfrac{1}{2} \times \dfrac{12mg \times (d-l)^2}{l}$

$\Rightarrow -mgd + \dfrac{6mg(d-l)^2}{l} = 0$

$\Rightarrow -dl + 6d^2 - 12dl + 6l^2 = 0$

$\Rightarrow 6d^2 - 13dl + 6l^2 = 0$

$\Rightarrow (3d - 2l)(2d - 3l) = 0$

$\Rightarrow d = \dfrac{2l}{3}$, not possible, or $d = \dfrac{3l}{2}$

$\Rightarrow$ extension is $\dfrac{l}{2}$

When it has fallen a distance h,

PE $= -mgh$ KE $= \dfrac{1}{2}mv^2$

EE $= \dfrac{1}{2} \times \dfrac{12mg \times (h-l)^2}{l}$

These add up to zero, so

$K = \dfrac{1}{2}mv^2 = mgh - \dfrac{6mg(h-l)^2}{l}$

To find maximum, differentiate both sides with respect to the variable h and put

$\dfrac{dK}{dh} = 0$

i.e. $mg - \dfrac{12mg(h-l)}{l} = 0$

$\Rightarrow 12(h-l) = l$

$12h - 12l = l$

$h = \dfrac{13l}{12}$, i.e. equilibrium position

7 The acceleration will be zero when no force is acting, i.e. at the static equilibrium position.

$T = \dfrac{\lambda x}{l} \Rightarrow mg = \dfrac{3mgx}{a} \Rightarrow x = \dfrac{a}{3}$

Distance AP is $a + \dfrac{a}{3} = \dfrac{4a}{3}$

Maximum speed is when acceleration is zero, i.e. when $x = \dfrac{a}{3}$

At top, PE $= 0$ (zero level)

KE $= \dfrac{1}{2}m(\sqrt{3ga})^2 = \dfrac{3mga}{2}$

EE $= 0$

When $x = \dfrac{a}{3}$ PE $= -\dfrac{4mga}{3}$

KE $= \dfrac{1}{2}mv^2$

EE $= \dfrac{1}{2} \times \dfrac{3mg\left(\frac{a}{3}\right)^2}{a} = \dfrac{mga}{6}$

Equating the two sums,

$\dfrac{3mga}{2} = -\dfrac{4mga}{3} + \dfrac{1}{2}mv^2 + \dfrac{mga}{6}$

$\dfrac{3mga}{2} + \dfrac{4mga}{3} - \dfrac{mga}{6} = \dfrac{1}{2}mv^2$

$\dfrac{1}{2}v^2 = \dfrac{16ga}{6} \Rightarrow v = 4\sqrt{\left(\dfrac{ga}{3}\right)}$ (maximum)

8

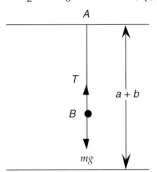

(a) In equilibrium, $T = mg$ ... ①

but $T = \dfrac{\lambda x}{l} = \dfrac{mga}{b} \times \dfrac{x}{a}$ ... ②

Equating ① and ②, $mg = \dfrac{mgx}{b} \Rightarrow x = b$

and so AB is $a + b$, the ball is just in contact with the floor.

(b) The sum of the energies at A will be $mg(a + b)$, the potential energy (taking the floor to be the zero level). Just before striking the floor, the kinetic energy will be $\frac{1}{2}mv^2$ and the elastic energy

$$\frac{1}{2}\lambda\frac{x^2}{l} = \frac{1}{2}\times\frac{mga}{b}\times\frac{b^2}{a} = \frac{mgb}{2}$$

with sum $\frac{1}{2}mv^2 + \frac{mgb}{2}$

Equating these two sums,

$$mg(a + b) = \frac{1}{2}mv^2 + \frac{mgb}{2}$$

$$mga + mgb = \frac{1}{2}mv^2 + \frac{mgb}{2}$$

$$\Rightarrow \frac{1}{2}mv^2 = mga + \frac{mgb}{2}$$

$$v^2 = 2ga + gb = g(2a + b)$$

(c) If the coefficient of restitution is e, the velocity after bouncing will be $ev = e\sqrt{g(2a + b)}$.

This represents a kinetic energy of

$$\frac{1}{2}mv^2 = \frac{1}{2}me^2\left[g(2a + b)\right]$$

The potential energy at the maximum height a after rebound is mga.

Equating these two energies,

$$\frac{1}{2}me^2\left[g(2a + b)\right] = mga$$

$$e^2(2a + b) = 2a$$

$$\Rightarrow e^2 = \frac{2a}{2a + b}$$

$$\Rightarrow e = \sqrt{\left(\frac{2a}{2a + b}\right)}$$

9

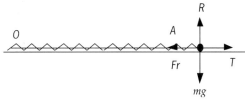

(a) The friction opposes the thrust, which is away from O.

$$R = mg \text{ and } Fr = T = \frac{\lambda x}{l} = \frac{2mg\left(\frac{a}{8}\right)}{a} = \frac{mg}{4}$$

Since $Fr \le \mu R$, $\quad \frac{mg}{4} \le \mu\, mg \Rightarrow \mu \ge \frac{1}{4}$

(b) The particle will accelerate until the spring reaches its natural length and will then slow down as the tension in the spring, directed back toward O, increases. The difference in EPE at the two points P_1 and P_2 where the velocity is zero is equal to the work done against friction.

i.e.

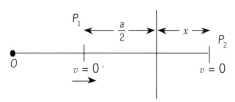

Natural length

EPE at P_1 is $\dfrac{2\,mg\left(\frac{a}{2}\right)^2}{2a}$ EPE at P_2 is $\dfrac{2\,mgx^2}{2a}$

Distance against friction of $\mu R = \frac{3}{8}mg$ is $\left(\frac{a}{2} + x\right)$,

so work done is $\frac{3}{8}mg\left(\frac{a}{2} + x\right)$

i.e. $\quad \dfrac{2\,mg\left(\frac{a}{2}\right)^2}{2a} = \dfrac{2\,mg\,x^2}{2a} + \dfrac{3}{8}mg\left(\frac{a}{2} + x\right)$

$\div mg \quad \dfrac{a}{4} = \dfrac{x^2}{a} + \dfrac{3a}{16} + \dfrac{3x}{8} \Rightarrow \dfrac{x^2}{a} + \dfrac{3x}{8} - \dfrac{a}{16} = 0$

$16x^2 + 6ax - a^2 = 0$

$(8x - a)(x + 2a) = 0$

$x = \dfrac{a}{8}$ (or $x = -2a$, but $x > 0$ so ignored)

So P moves $\dfrac{a}{2} + \dfrac{a}{8} = \dfrac{5a}{8}$

10 (a) At 0,

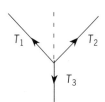

Horizontally, $T_1\sin 60° = T_2\sin 60°$

$\Rightarrow T_1 = T_2$

Vertically, $T_1\cos 60° + T_2\cos 60° = T_3$

$T_1 = T_2$ and $\cos 60° = \frac{1}{2} \Rightarrow 2\times T_1\left(\frac{1}{2}\right) = T_3$

$\Rightarrow T_1 = T_3$

i.e. $T_1 = T_2 = T_3$

(b)

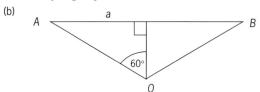

$OA = \dfrac{a}{\sin 60°} = \dfrac{2a}{\sqrt{3}}$

(c) Extension in OA is $\dfrac{2a}{\sqrt{3}} - a$

$\Rightarrow$ tension is $\dfrac{\lambda\left(\frac{2a}{\sqrt{3}} - a\right)}{a} = \lambda\left(\frac{2}{\sqrt{3}} - 1\right) = \lambda\left(\frac{2 - \sqrt{3}}{\sqrt{3}}\right)$

since all tensions equal

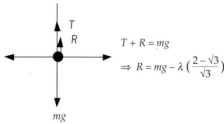

$$T + R = mg$$

$$\Rightarrow R = mg - \lambda \left(\frac{2 - \sqrt{3}}{\sqrt{3}} \right)$$

Since resting on table, $R \geq 0$

$$\Rightarrow mg - \lambda \left(\frac{2 - \sqrt{3}}{\sqrt{3}} \right) \geq 0$$

$$\lambda \left(\frac{2 - \sqrt{3}}{\sqrt{3}} \right) \leq mg \Rightarrow \lambda \leq \frac{\sqrt{3} mg}{2 - \sqrt{3}}$$

11 (a) If he falls d metres, loss in GPE is Mgd

Gain in EPE is $\dfrac{\lambda x^2}{2l} = \dfrac{12 \, Mg \, (d - 4)^2}{2 \times 4}$

Equating, $\qquad Mgd = \dfrac{12 \, Mg \, (d - 4)^2}{8}$

$$\Rightarrow \qquad 8d = 12 \, (d - 4)^2$$

$$2d = 3d^2 - 24d + 48$$

$$3d^2 - 26d + 48 = 0$$

$$(3d - 8)(d - 6) = 0 \Rightarrow d = \frac{8}{3} \text{ or } d = 6$$

Since $\dfrac{8}{3}$ m is less than natural length, fall is 6 m

(b) $T = \dfrac{\lambda x}{l} \Rightarrow Mg = \dfrac{12Mgx}{4} \Rightarrow x = \dfrac{1}{3}$ m

(c) At this point, fall is $4\dfrac{1}{3}$ m $\Rightarrow$ loss in GPE is $\dfrac{13Mg}{3}$

Gain in KE is $\dfrac{1}{2} mv^2 = \dfrac{1}{2} Mv^2$

Gain in EPE is $\dfrac{\lambda x^2}{2l} = \dfrac{12Mg \left(\frac{1}{3} \right)^2}{8} = \dfrac{Mg}{6}$

$$\Rightarrow \dfrac{12Mg}{3} = \dfrac{1}{2} Mv^2 + \dfrac{Mg}{6} \Rightarrow \dfrac{25Mg}{6} = \dfrac{1}{2} Mv^2$$

$$\Rightarrow v^2 = \dfrac{25g}{6} \Rightarrow v = 5\sqrt{\left(\dfrac{g}{6} \right)}$$

(d) Air resistance

12 (a) Using $T = \dfrac{\lambda x}{l}$, $150 = \dfrac{\lambda \times 0.1}{0.2} \Rightarrow \lambda = 300$ N

(b) By Pythagoras, $AP = 25$ cm $\Rightarrow$ total length is
50 cm, an extension of 30 cm $\Rightarrow T = \dfrac{300 \times 0.3}{0.2}$

$$= 450 \text{ N}$$

$F = 2T \cos \theta :$

$\cos \theta = \dfrac{20}{25}$

$\Rightarrow F = 900 \times \dfrac{20}{25} = 720$ N

(c) EPE in string is initially $\dfrac{1}{2} \times \dfrac{300}{0.2} (0.3)^2 = 67.5$ J

When between A and B, $\dfrac{1}{2} \times \dfrac{300}{0.2} (0.1)^2 = 7.5$ J

$\Rightarrow$ loss is 60 J, gain in KE is $\dfrac{1}{2} mv^2 = \dfrac{1}{2} \times 0.1 \times v^2$

$\Rightarrow v^2 = \dfrac{120}{0.1} \Rightarrow v = 34.6$ m s^{-1} (1 d.p.)

13 Basically, the inital KE is converted to stored elastic energy.

KE initial is $\dfrac{1}{2} mv^2 = \dfrac{1}{2} m \, (2ga) = mga$

If x is the subsequent compression, stored energy is

$$\dfrac{1}{2} \dfrac{\lambda x^2}{l} = \dfrac{1}{2} \times \dfrac{6mg \times x^2}{3a}$$

Equating these, $mga = \dfrac{mgx^2}{a} \Rightarrow x = a$

Section 3

1 $a = 7$

$T = 4 \Rightarrow \dfrac{2\pi}{\omega} = 4 \Rightarrow \omega = \dfrac{2\pi}{4} = \dfrac{\pi}{2}$

$v_{\text{MAX}} = \omega a = \dfrac{7\pi}{2} \text{ cm s}^{-1}$

$v^2 = \omega^2(a^2 - x^2)$ and when $x = 3$

$v^2 = \left(\dfrac{\pi}{2}\right)^2 [49 - 9] = \left(\dfrac{\pi}{2}\right)^2 (40)$

$\Rightarrow v = \dfrac{\pi}{2}\sqrt{40} = \pi\sqrt{10} \text{ cm s}^{-1}$

2   (a)   Since acceleration is $-\omega^2 x$ and we're told that it is positive $\dfrac{9}{4}$, the distance x must be negative, i.e.

$x = -9$

$\Rightarrow \dfrac{9}{4} = -\omega^2 \times (-9) \Rightarrow -\omega^2 = \dfrac{1}{4}, \ \omega = \dfrac{1}{2}$

The period $T = \dfrac{2\pi}{\omega} = \dfrac{2\pi}{\frac{1}{2}} = 4\pi$ seconds

   (b) $v^2 = \omega^2(a^2 - x^2) \Rightarrow 36 = \dfrac{1}{4}(a^2 - 81)$

$\Rightarrow 144 = a^2 - 81$

$a^2 = 225 \Rightarrow a = 15 \text{ m}$

   (c) $v_{\text{MAX}} = \omega a = \dfrac{15}{2} \text{ m s}^{-1}$

3   (a)   5 complete oscillations per second means that time for one oscillation, T, is $\dfrac{1}{5}$ sec

$\Rightarrow T = \dfrac{2\pi}{\omega} = \dfrac{1}{5} \Rightarrow \omega = 10\pi$

Distance between extremes is twice the amplitude, so

$2a = 0.1 \Rightarrow a = 0.05 \text{ m}.$

$v_{\text{MAX}} = \omega a = 10\pi \times 0.05 = \dfrac{\pi}{2} \text{ m s}^{-1}.$

Maximum force $\Rightarrow$ acceleration is a maximum $\Rightarrow x = a$ and magnitude is

$\omega^2 a = 100\pi^2 \times 0.05 = 5\pi^2.$

$F = ma$, so maximum force is

$0.2 \times 5\pi^2 = \pi^2 \text{ N}$

   (b)   Frequency is unaltered $\Rightarrow \omega = 10\pi$ still, a is now 0.1 and we want speed when $x = 0.05$

$v^2 = \omega^2(a^2 - x^2) = 100\pi^2(0.1^2 - 0.05^2)$

$= 100\pi^2(0.0075)$

$\Rightarrow v = 2.72 \approx 2.7 \text{ m s}^{-1}$

4

```
      A          O          B
      ●──────────┼──────────●
      ◄──────────a─────────►
```

If a is the amplitude, we connect the distance and velocity by the formula

$v^2 = \omega^2(a^2 - x^2)$

Putting the two pairs of values for v and x into this gives

$4^2 = \omega^2(a^2 - 4^2)$ ... ①

and $8^2 = \omega^2(a^2 - 2^2)$ ... ②

Dividing ② by ① to eliminate the ω^2,

$\dfrac{8^2}{4^2} = \dfrac{a^2 - 2^2}{a^2 - 4^2} \Rightarrow 4 = \dfrac{a^2 - 4}{a^2 - 16}$

$4a^2 - 64 = a^2 - 4$

$3a^2 = 60$

$a^2 = 20$

$a = 2\sqrt{5} \text{ m}$ ... ③

Since a is *half* the distance between A and B, distance AB is $4\sqrt{5}$ m.

Substituting $a = 2\sqrt{5}$ back into ① gives

$16 = \omega^2(20 - 16)$

$\Rightarrow \quad \omega^2 = 4, \ \omega = 2$

Since the *period* of the oscillation is given by $\dfrac{2\pi}{\omega}$, this will be $\dfrac{2\pi}{2} = \pi$ seconds.

When 2 m from A, it will be $(2\sqrt{5} - 2)$ m from O and its speed is given by

$v^2 = \omega^2(a^2 - x^2)$

$= 4[(2\sqrt{5})^2 - (2\sqrt{5} - 2)^2]$ since $\omega = 2$

$= 4(2)(4\sqrt{5} - 2)$ using $a^2 - b^2 = (a - b)(a + b)$

Since kinetic energy is $\dfrac{1}{2}mv^2$, this will be

$\dfrac{1}{2} \times 2 \times 4 \times 2(4\sqrt{5} - 2) = 16(2\sqrt{5} - 1) \text{ J}$

If M is the mid-point of OB, OM is $\dfrac{a}{2}$,

i.e. $x = \dfrac{a}{2}.$

Using the formula $t = \dfrac{1}{\omega}\sin^{-1}\dfrac{x}{a}$

where the time t is measured from the point when the particle is at O,

$t = \dfrac{1}{2}\sin^{-1}\dfrac{\frac{a}{2}}{a} = \dfrac{1}{2}\sin^{-1}\dfrac{1}{2} = \dfrac{1}{2} \times \dfrac{\pi}{6} = \dfrac{\pi}{12}$

This is the time from O to M. For A to O, which is $\dfrac{1}{4}$ of an oscillation, the time is

$\dfrac{1}{4} \times \pi = \dfrac{\pi}{4}$

Total time from A to M is $\dfrac{\pi}{4} + \dfrac{\pi}{12} = \dfrac{\pi}{3}$

5   The maximum speed is $\omega a = 0.5$ ... ①

The maximum acceleration is when $x = a$,

i.e. $\omega^2 a = 0.1$ ... ②

②$\div$① $\Rightarrow \omega = 0.2,$

so the period $T = \dfrac{2\pi}{\omega} = \dfrac{2\pi}{0.2} = 10\pi \text{ s}$

The amplitude a, from ① is

$a = \dfrac{0.5}{\omega} = \dfrac{0.5}{0.2} = 2.5 \text{ m}$

6

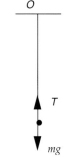

Resolving vertically

$T - mg = 0$

$\Rightarrow T = mg$ ... ①

But $T = \dfrac{\lambda x}{l} = \dfrac{\lambda a}{l}$ ... ②

From ① and ②,

$\dfrac{\lambda a}{l} = mg \Rightarrow \lambda = \dfrac{mgl}{a}$

Natural length l

Equilibrium $l + a$

Subsequent position $l + a + x$

$F = mf \Rightarrow T - mg = -mf$ ... ①

using f for acceleration(minus since against the direction of x increasing)

$T = \dfrac{\lambda(\text{Ext})}{l} = \dfrac{\lambda(a + x)}{l}$

But $\lambda = \dfrac{mgl}{a}$

$\Rightarrow T = \dfrac{mgl(a + x)}{al} = \dfrac{mg(a + x)}{a}$ ... ②

② into ① $\Rightarrow \dfrac{mg(a + x)}{a} - mg = -mf$

$\times$ by a $mg(a + x) - mga = -maf$

$mga + mgx - mga = -maf$

$\Rightarrow -maf = mgx \Rightarrow f = -\dfrac{g}{a}x$

i.e. we have simple harmonic motion, since it is proportional to distance,

with $\omega^2 = \dfrac{g}{a}$

$\Rightarrow \omega = \sqrt{\left(\dfrac{g}{a}\right)}$

Using $T = \dfrac{2\pi}{\omega} \Rightarrow$ period is $\dfrac{2\pi}{\sqrt{\left(\dfrac{g}{a}\right)}} = 2\pi \sqrt{\left(\dfrac{a}{g}\right)}$

7 In eqilibrium, $T = mg \Rightarrow \dfrac{\lambda\left(\frac{3}{4}l\right)}{l} = mg \Rightarrow \lambda = \dfrac{4\,mg}{3}$

If x is distance from equilibrium point m,

$\dfrac{md^2x}{dt^2} = -\dfrac{\lambda x}{l} \Rightarrow \dfrac{md^2x}{dt^2} = -\dfrac{4mgx}{3l}$

i.e. SHM with $\omega^2 = \dfrac{4g}{3l} \Rightarrow$ period is $\dfrac{2\pi}{\omega}$

$= 2\pi \times \sqrt{\left(\dfrac{3l}{4g}\right)}$

$= \pi\sqrt{\left(\dfrac{3l}{g}\right)}$

(a) The amplitude is

$|\text{ original position} - \text{equilibrium position }|$

i.e. $\left|\dfrac{3}{2}l - \dfrac{7}{4}l\right| = \dfrac{l}{4}$. Lowest is equilibrium

position + amplitude, i.e. $\dfrac{7}{4}l + \dfrac{l}{4} = 2l$.

(b) This is half a cycle, $\dfrac{1}{2} \times \pi\sqrt{\left(\dfrac{3l}{g}\right)} = \dfrac{\pi}{2}\sqrt{\left(\dfrac{3l}{g}\right)}$

(c) Taking upwards as positive, $x = \dfrac{l}{4}$ when $t = 0 \Rightarrow$

$x = \dfrac{l}{4}\cos \omega t = \dfrac{l}{4}\cos \sqrt{\left(\dfrac{4g}{3l}\right)}\, t$

When $t = \dfrac{\pi}{3}\sqrt{\left(\dfrac{3l}{g}\right)}$, $x = \dfrac{l}{4}\cos\left[\dfrac{\pi}{3}\sqrt{\left(\dfrac{4g}{3l}\right)}\sqrt{\left(\dfrac{3l}{g}\right)}\right]$

$= \dfrac{l}{4}\cos\dfrac{2\pi}{3} = -\dfrac{l}{8}$

i.e. $\dfrac{l}{8}$ below centre, $\dfrac{7l}{4} + \dfrac{l}{8} = \dfrac{15}{8}l$ below 0.

8 (a) The average of the depths of water is 7 m, and so the amplitude $a = 3$ m. Time for half a cycle is $6\frac{1}{3}$

hours $= \dfrac{19}{3}$ hours.

$\Rightarrow \dfrac{1}{2}T = \dfrac{\pi}{\omega} = \dfrac{19}{3} \Rightarrow \omega = \dfrac{3\pi}{19}$.

We want $x = -3$ when $t = 0$ and $x = 3$ when $t = \dfrac{19}{3}$

where x is height above 7 m and t is time after 1100 hours.

Using $x = a\sin(\omega t + c)$ and substituting

$x = -3$ when $t = 0, a = 3$

$-3 = 3\sin c \Rightarrow \sin c = -1 \Rightarrow c = \dfrac{3\pi}{2}$

i.e. $x = 3\sin\left(\dfrac{3\pi t}{19} + \dfrac{3\pi}{2}\right)$ ... ①

$\Rightarrow v = \dfrac{dx}{dt} = \dfrac{9\pi}{19}\cos\left(\dfrac{3\pi t}{19} + \dfrac{3\pi}{2}\right)$ ... ②

At 1235, i.e. $t = 1\dfrac{7}{12} = \dfrac{19}{12}$

$\Rightarrow v = \dfrac{9\pi}{19}\cos\left(\dfrac{\pi}{4} + \dfrac{3\pi}{2}\right) = \dfrac{9\pi}{19\sqrt{2}}$ m h^{-1}

(b) From ①, $x = 3\sin\left(\dfrac{3\pi t}{19} + \dfrac{3\pi}{2}\right)$

when $x = \dfrac{3}{2}$ (above 7 m)

$\dfrac{3}{2} = 3\sin\left(\dfrac{3\pi t}{19} + \dfrac{3\pi}{2}\right)$

$\dfrac{1}{2} = \sin\left(\dfrac{3\pi t}{19} + \dfrac{3\pi}{2}\right)$

$\Rightarrow \dfrac{3\pi t}{19} + \dfrac{3\pi}{2} = \dfrac{\pi}{6}$ or $\dfrac{5\pi}{6}$ or $\dfrac{13\pi}{6}$ or ...

The first of these to give a positive answer is $\frac{13\pi}{6}$,

i.e.

$$\frac{3\pi t}{19} + \frac{3\pi}{2} = \frac{13\pi}{6} \Rightarrow \frac{3\pi t}{19} = \frac{2\pi}{3}$$

$$\Rightarrow t = \frac{38}{9} = 4 \text{ hours } 13 \text{ minutes}$$

$\therefore$ The time will be 1513 hours.

9   (a)   We can use the same argument as in question 6 to show that the period is

$$2\pi \sqrt{\left(\frac{a}{g}\right)} \Rightarrow \omega = \sqrt{\left(\frac{g}{a}\right)}$$

Since a is the extension produced by the weight, in this case Mg, and we are given that $a = 0.2$

$$\Rightarrow \omega = \sqrt{\left(\frac{9.8}{0.2}\right)} = \sqrt{49} = 7$$

and the period is $\frac{2\pi}{7}$

(b)   (i)   When at a distance x from 0, acceleration is $-\omega^2 x$ and the speed is $\omega\sqrt{a^2 - x^2}$.

When $x = 3$, $\omega^2 x = \omega\sqrt{a^2 - x^2}$

$$\Rightarrow 3\omega = \sqrt{a^2 - 9} \qquad \dots ①$$

Also the maximum speed, $\omega a = 2$ $\dots②$

$$\omega = \frac{2}{a} \text{ into } ① \text{ gives } \frac{6}{a} = \sqrt{a^2 - 9}$$

$$\Rightarrow \frac{36}{a^2} = a^2 - 9 \qquad \text{by squaring}$$

$$36 = a^4 - 9a^2 \Rightarrow a^4 - 9a^2 - 36 = 0$$

$$(a^2 - 12)(a^2 + 3) = 0$$

$$\Rightarrow a^2 = 12 \ (a^2 + 3 = 0 \text{ not possible})$$

$$\Rightarrow a = \sqrt{12} = 2\sqrt{3} \quad \text{(since } a > 0)$$

Putting this into $②$, $\omega \times 2\sqrt{3} = 2 \Rightarrow \omega = \frac{1}{\sqrt{3}}$

Period, $t = \frac{2\pi}{\omega} = 2\sqrt{3}\,\pi$

(ii)   Denoting x_A the distance of A from O

$$x_A = a \sin(\omega t + c)$$

Putting $x_A = 2\sqrt{3}$ when $t = 0$, and $\omega = \frac{1}{\sqrt{3}}$

$$\Rightarrow 2\sqrt{3} = 2\sqrt{3} \sin c$$
$$\Rightarrow \sin c = 1$$
$$c = \frac{\pi}{2}$$

$$\Rightarrow x_A = 2\sqrt{3} \sin\left(\frac{t}{\sqrt{3}} + \frac{\pi}{2}\right) \qquad \dots ③$$

$$x_B = a \sin(\omega t + c)$$

$$x_B = 2\sqrt{3} \text{ when } t = \frac{\sqrt{3}}{2}\pi$$

$$\Rightarrow 2\sqrt{3} = 2\sqrt{3} \sin\left(\frac{\pi}{2} + c\right)$$

$$\Rightarrow \sin\left(\frac{\pi}{2} + c\right) = 1 \Rightarrow c = 0$$

$$\Rightarrow x_B = 2\sqrt{3} \sin\left(\frac{t}{\sqrt{3}}\right) \qquad \dots ④$$

Putting $x_A = x_B$ gives

$$2\sqrt{3} \sin\left(\frac{t}{\sqrt{3}} + \frac{\pi}{2}\right) = 2\sqrt{3} \sin\left(\frac{t}{\sqrt{3}}\right)$$

$$\sin\left(\frac{t}{\sqrt{3}} + \frac{\pi}{2}\right) = \sin\left(\frac{t}{\sqrt{3}}\right)$$

But $\sin\left(\frac{t}{\sqrt{3}}\right) = \sin\left(\pi - \frac{t}{\sqrt{3}}\right)$ or $\sin\left(3\pi - \frac{t}{\sqrt{3}}\right)$

$$\Rightarrow \frac{t}{\sqrt{3}} + \frac{\pi}{2} = \pi - \frac{t}{\sqrt{3}} \quad \text{or} \quad \frac{t}{\sqrt{3}} + \frac{\pi}{2} = 3\pi - \frac{t}{\sqrt{3}}$$

$$t = \frac{\sqrt{3}}{4}\pi \qquad \text{or} \quad t = \frac{5\sqrt{3}}{4}\pi$$

The first solution is before B is released, so we discard.

The second solution is

$$\frac{5\sqrt{3}}{4}\pi - \frac{\sqrt{3}}{2}\pi = \frac{3\sqrt{3}}{4}\pi \text{ after release of } B.$$

The distance from O is given by

$$\left| 2\sqrt{3} \sin\left(\frac{5\sqrt{3}}{4}\pi \times \frac{1}{\sqrt{3}}\right)\right|$$

$$= \left| 2\sqrt{3} \sin\frac{5\pi}{4}\right| = \left|\frac{-2\sqrt{3}}{\sqrt{2}}\right| = 2\sqrt{\left(\frac{3}{2}\right)}$$

since distance > 0

10

Suppose distance OP is x, extension in spring AP is $l - x$, in spring BP is $l + x$.

$$\Rightarrow T_1 = \frac{\lambda\,(l-x)}{l} = \frac{4\,mg\,(l-x)}{l}, \ T_2 = \frac{4\,mg\,(l+x)}{l}$$

$$\Rightarrow \frac{m d^2 x}{dt^2} = T_1 - T_2 = \frac{4\,mg}{l}[(l-x) - (l+x)]$$

$$= \frac{4\,mg}{l} \times -2x = \left(\frac{-8\,mg}{l}\right) x$$

$$\Rightarrow \frac{d^2 x}{dt^2} = -\left(\frac{8g}{l}\right) x$$

i.e.   SHM with $\omega^2 = \frac{8g}{l} \Rightarrow \omega = 2\sqrt{2}\sqrt{\left(\frac{g}{l}\right)}$

$$\Rightarrow \text{period is } \frac{2\pi}{2\sqrt{2}\sqrt{\left(\frac{g}{l}\right)}} = \pi\sqrt{\left(\frac{l}{2g}\right)}$$

(a)   Released when $x = \frac{l}{3}$, i.e. $a = \frac{l}{3}$, the amplitude.

Max. speed is $\omega a = \sqrt{8} \times \sqrt{\left(\frac{g}{l}\right)} \times \frac{l}{3} = \frac{1}{3}\sqrt{8gl}$

(b)   Using $v^2 = \omega^2(a^2 - x^2)$ with $x = \frac{l}{5}$

$$\Rightarrow v^2 = \frac{8g}{l}\left(\frac{l^2}{9} - \frac{l^2}{25}\right) = \frac{8g}{l} \times l^2\left(\frac{16}{9 \times 25}\right)$$

$$\Rightarrow v = \frac{4}{15}\sqrt{8gl}$$

(c) For time, $x = a \cos \omega t = \dfrac{l}{3} \cos \sqrt{\left(\dfrac{8g}{l}\right)} t$

when $x = \dfrac{l}{5}, \dfrac{l}{5} = \dfrac{l}{3} \cos \sqrt{\left(\dfrac{8g}{l}\right)} t$

$\Rightarrow \cos \sqrt{\left(\dfrac{8g}{l}\right)} t = \dfrac{3}{5}$

$\Rightarrow t = \sqrt{\left(\dfrac{l}{8g}\right)} \cos^{-1} \dfrac{3}{5} = 0.328 \sqrt{\left(\dfrac{l}{g}\right)}$

Section 4

1

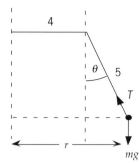

Vertical forces: $\qquad T \cos \theta = mg \qquad \dots \text{①}$

Horizontal forces: $\qquad T \sin \theta = mr\omega^2 \qquad \dots \text{②}$

The radius: $\qquad r = 4 + 5 \sin \theta \qquad \dots \text{③}$

$\text{②} \div \text{①} \Rightarrow \quad \dfrac{T \sin \theta}{T \sin \theta} = \dfrac{mr\omega^2}{mg} \Rightarrow \tan \theta = \dfrac{r\omega^2}{g}$

Put in ③, $\quad \omega^2 = \dfrac{g \tan \theta}{4 + 5 \sin \theta}$

(If we differentiate this, we end up with a gradient of

$\dfrac{4 + 5 \sin^3 \theta}{[\cos \theta (4 + 5 \sin \theta)]^2}$ and this is positive for acute

angles, i.e. it is an increasing function in the range we're interested in.)

Max. value of $\omega^2 = \dfrac{g \times \dfrac{3}{4}}{4 + 5 \times \dfrac{3}{5}} = \dfrac{3g}{28}$

$\Rightarrow \omega_{\text{MAX}} = 1.02 \text{ (3 s.f.)}$

2

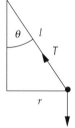

$\tan \theta = \dfrac{5}{12}$

$\Rightarrow \sin \theta = \dfrac{5}{13}$ and $\cos \theta = \dfrac{12}{13}$

Vertically: $\qquad T \cos \theta = mg \qquad \dots \text{①}$

Horizontally: $\qquad T \sin \theta = m\dfrac{v^2}{r} \qquad \dots \text{②}$

$\Delta : \qquad \sin \theta = \dfrac{r}{l} \qquad \dots \text{③}$

Dividing ② by ①, $\dfrac{T \sin \theta}{T \cos \theta} = \dfrac{m\dfrac{v^2}{r}}{mg}$

$\Rightarrow \tan \theta = \dfrac{v^2}{rg} = \dfrac{5}{12} \text{ (given)}$

i.e. $r = \dfrac{12v^2}{5g} = \dfrac{12(2)^2}{5g} = \dfrac{48}{5g} \qquad \dots \text{④}$

Also from Δ, $\sin \theta = \dfrac{r}{l}$ but $\sin \theta = \dfrac{5}{13}$

$\Rightarrow r = \dfrac{5l}{13} \qquad \dots \text{⑤}$

Equating ④ and ⑤, $\dfrac{48}{5g} = \dfrac{5l}{13}$

$\Rightarrow l = \dfrac{48 \times 13}{25g} \approx 2.5 \text{ m if } g \text{ is } 10 \text{ m s}^{-2}$

3

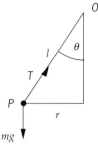

Suppose the mass of the particle is m.

Vertically: $\quad\quad\quad T\cos\theta - mg = 0 \quad\quad\quad$ ... ①

Horizontally: $\quad\quad T\sin\theta = mr\omega^2 \quad\quad\quad$ ... ②

Δ: $\quad\quad\quad\quad\quad \sin\theta = \dfrac{r}{l} \quad\quad\quad\quad\quad$ ... ③

Rearrange ① to get $T\cos\theta = mg$ and divide ② by this

$$\frac{T\sin\theta}{T\cos\theta} = \frac{mr\omega^2}{mg}$$

i.e. $\sin\theta = \dfrac{r\omega^2\cos\theta}{g} \quad\quad\quad\quad$ ... ④

Putting ③ and ④ together

$$\frac{r}{l} = \frac{r\omega^2\cos\theta}{g}$$

$$\Rightarrow \cos\theta = \frac{g}{l\omega^2} \quad\quad\quad\quad\quad \text{... ⑤}$$

Now we're told that the particle makes 2 revolutions in one second, i.e. $2 \times 2\pi = 4\pi$ rad s^{-1} or $\omega = 4\pi$.

Substituting this into ⑤,

$$\cos\theta = \frac{g}{l \times 16\pi^2} \text{ and since } l = 0.125 = \frac{1}{8},$$

$$\cos\theta = \frac{8g}{16\pi^2} = \frac{g}{2\pi^2}$$

4

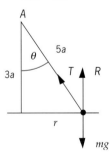

Vertically: $\quad\quad\quad R + T\cos\theta = mg \quad\quad$ ... ①

Horizontally: $\quad\quad T\sin\theta = mr\omega^2 \quad\quad$ ... ②

Δ: $\quad\quad\quad\quad\quad \cos\theta = \dfrac{3}{5} \Rightarrow r = 4a$

(a) $R = 0$, from ①, $T_1\cos\theta = mg$

$$\Rightarrow T_1 = \frac{mg}{\cos\theta} = \frac{5mg}{3}$$

(b) $R = \dfrac{3mg}{4}$, from ①,

$$T_2\cos\theta = mg - \frac{3mg}{4} = \frac{mg}{4}$$

$$T_2 = \frac{5mg}{12}$$

Since from ②, $\omega^2 = \dfrac{T\sin\theta}{mr} = kT$

where $k = \dfrac{\sin\theta}{mr}$, constant

When T_1, $\quad\quad \omega_1^2 = k\dfrac{5mg}{3}$

When T_2, $\quad\quad \omega_2^2 = k\dfrac{5mg}{12}$

then $\dfrac{\omega_1^2}{\omega_2^2} = 4 \Rightarrow \dfrac{\omega_1}{\omega_2} = 2$

ω_1 is twice as fast as ω_2, so the times for one revolution will be 1: 2.

5

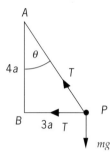

Vertically: $\quad\quad T\cos\theta = mg \quad\quad\quad\quad$ ... ①

Δ: $\quad\quad\quad \tan\theta = \dfrac{3}{4} \Rightarrow \cos\theta = \dfrac{4}{5} \quad$ ... ②

$\sin\theta = \dfrac{3}{5}$

Then from ① and ②, $T \times \dfrac{4}{5} = mg$

$$\Rightarrow T = \frac{5mg}{4}$$

Horizontally: $T + T\sin\theta = \dfrac{mv^2}{r}$

$$\frac{5mg}{4} + \frac{5mg}{4} \times \frac{3}{5} = \frac{mv^2}{3a}$$

$$2mg = \frac{mv^2}{3a} \quad\Rightarrow\quad v^2 = 6ga$$

6

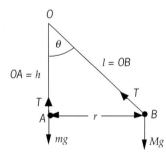

For A, at rest, $T = mg \quad\quad\quad\quad\quad$ ... ①

For B, vertically, $T\cos\theta = Mg \quad\quad$ ... ②

② ÷ ① $\Rightarrow \dfrac{T\cos\theta}{T} = \dfrac{Mg}{mg} \Rightarrow \cos\theta = \dfrac{M}{m} \quad$ ... ③

Since $\cos\theta < 1$, $\dfrac{M}{m} < 1 \Rightarrow m > M$

(a) From ③, $\cos\theta = \dfrac{M}{m} = \dfrac{M}{3M} = \dfrac{1}{3}$.

But $h = l \cos \theta = \dfrac{l}{3}$

and $h + l = 4a \Rightarrow l = 3a$ and $h = OA = a$

(b) For B, horizontally, $T \sin \theta = \dfrac{Mu^2}{r}$ $\qquad$ ... ④

and $\qquad r = l \sin \theta$ $\qquad$ ... ⑤

Eliminating r,

$$Mu^2 = T \sin \theta \,(l \sin \theta) = 3\,Mgl \sin^2\theta$$
$$u^2 = 3\,gl \sin^2\theta = 3\,gl\,(1 - \cos^2\theta)$$
$$= 3\,gl \left(\dfrac{8}{9}\right)$$
$$= 3g\,(3a) \times \dfrac{8}{9} = 8\,ag$$

When the string breaks the vertical component of each particle is zero, so they reach the horizontal plane at the same time.

Particle A has to move $2a - a = a$ vertically, $u = 0$, $a = g$

$$s = ut + \tfrac{1}{2}at^2 \Rightarrow a = \tfrac{1}{2}gt^2 \Rightarrow t = \sqrt{\left(\dfrac{2a}{g}\right)} \;(>0)$$

7

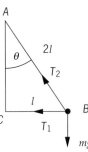

Vertically: $\qquad T_2 \cos \theta = mg$ $\qquad$ ... ①

$\Delta:\;\; \sin \theta = \dfrac{l}{2l} = \dfrac{1}{2} \Rightarrow \theta = 30°$ $\qquad$ ... ②

This into ① gives $T_2 \cos 30° = mg$

$$\Rightarrow T_2 = \dfrac{2mg}{\sqrt{3}} \;\; \left(= \dfrac{2mg\sqrt{3}}{3}\right)$$

Horizontally: $T_1 + T_2 \sin \theta = \dfrac{mu^2}{l}$ $\qquad$ ... ③

$$T_1 + T_2 \times \dfrac{1}{2} = \dfrac{mu^2}{l}$$

$$T_1 = \dfrac{mu^2}{l} - \dfrac{T_2}{2} = \dfrac{mu^2}{l} - \dfrac{mg}{\sqrt{3}}$$

Motion is only possible when $T_1 \geq 0$, i.e.

$$\dfrac{mu^2}{l} - \dfrac{mg}{\sqrt{3}} \geq 0 \qquad\qquad \dfrac{mu^2}{l} \geq \dfrac{mg}{\sqrt{3}}$$

$$u^2 \geq \dfrac{gl}{\sqrt{3}} = \dfrac{gl\sqrt{3}}{3}$$

8 Since in equilibrium,

$$T = mg \text{ and } T = \dfrac{\lambda x}{l} \text{ where } \lambda = 3mg,$$

$$mg = \dfrac{3mgx}{l} \Rightarrow x = \dfrac{l}{3}$$

and the stretched length of the string is $\dfrac{4l}{3}$

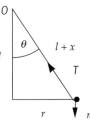

Vertically: $\qquad T \cos \theta = mg$ $\qquad$ ... ①

Horizontally: $\qquad T \sin \theta = mr\omega^2$ $\qquad$ ... ②

Elasticity: $\qquad T = \dfrac{3mgx}{l}$ $\qquad$ ... ③

(a) ③ into ① $\Rightarrow \dfrac{3mgx}{l} \cos \theta = mg$

but $\cos \theta = \dfrac{l}{l+x}$

$$\dfrac{3x}{l} \times \dfrac{l}{l+x} = 1 \Rightarrow 3x = l + x \Rightarrow x = \dfrac{l}{2}$$

and so stretched length is $\dfrac{3l}{2}$.

(b) ③ into ② $\Rightarrow \dfrac{3mgx}{l} \sin \theta = mr\omega^2$

and $\sin \theta = \dfrac{r}{l+x} = \dfrac{2r}{3l}$

$$\dfrac{3gx}{l} \times \dfrac{2r}{3l} = r\omega^2 \text{ and } x = \dfrac{l}{2}$$

$$\dfrac{gl}{2} \times \dfrac{2}{l} = \omega^2 \Rightarrow \omega^2 l = g$$

9 In equilibrium, $\qquad T = mg = \dfrac{\lambda x}{l}$

$$\Rightarrow 5g = \dfrac{\lambda\,0.025}{0.2}$$

$$\Rightarrow \lambda = \dfrac{g}{0.025} = 392 \text{ N}$$

(a)

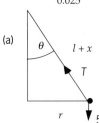

Vertically: $\qquad T \cos \theta = 5g$

and since $\qquad T = 98$ and $g = 9.8$

$$\cos \theta = \dfrac{5 \times 9.8}{98} = \dfrac{1}{2} \Rightarrow \theta = 60°$$

Elasticity: $\qquad T = \dfrac{\lambda x}{l} = \dfrac{392x}{0.2} = 98 \text{ (given)}$

$$\Rightarrow x = \dfrac{0.2}{4} = 0.05$$

Horizontally: $T \sin \theta = mr\omega^2$

and Δ, $\qquad \sin \theta = \dfrac{r}{l+x}$

Combining $\quad 98 \times \dfrac{r}{0.25} = 5r\omega^2$

$$\Rightarrow \omega^2 = \dfrac{4 \times 98}{5} \Rightarrow \omega = \sqrt{\left(\dfrac{392}{5}\right)} \text{ rad s}^{-1}$$

$$= 8.9 \text{ (1 d.p.)}$$

(b) On limit, $T = 196 = \dfrac{392x}{0.2}$

$\Rightarrow x$ would be 0.1

As before, $T \sin \theta = mr\omega^2$ and $\sin \theta = \dfrac{r}{l + x}$

$\Rightarrow T \left(\dfrac{r}{l + x} \right) = mr\omega^2$

and since $T = 196$, $m = 5$ and $l + x = 0.3$

$\dfrac{196}{0.3 \times 5} = \omega^2 \Rightarrow \omega = 11.4$ rad s^{-1} (1 d.p.)

10

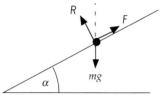

Minimum speed, friction acts upwards

Resolving vertically, $R \cos \alpha + F \sin \alpha = mg$ ... ①

Horizontally: $R \sin \alpha - F \cos \alpha = \dfrac{mv^2}{r}$ ... ②

Limiting: $F = \mu R = \dfrac{1}{2} R$ ... ③

Since $\tan \alpha = \dfrac{3}{4}$, $\sin \alpha = \dfrac{3}{5}$, $\cos \alpha = \dfrac{4}{5}$

① becomes $R \times \dfrac{4}{5} + \dfrac{1}{2} R \times \dfrac{3}{5} = mg \Rightarrow R = \dfrac{10mg}{11}$

② becomes $R \times \dfrac{3}{5} - \dfrac{1}{2} R \times \dfrac{4}{5} = mv^2 \Rightarrow mv^2 = \dfrac{rR}{5}$

$\Rightarrow v^2 = \dfrac{2gr}{11}$

i.e. $v_{\text{MIN}} = \sqrt{\left(\dfrac{2gr}{11} \right)}$

Maximum speed, friction down and the equations are

$R \cos \alpha - F \sin \alpha = mg$ and $R \sin \alpha + F \cos \alpha = \dfrac{mv^2}{r}$

giving $R \times \dfrac{4}{5} - \dfrac{1}{2} R \times \dfrac{3}{5} = mg \Rightarrow R = 2mg$

$R \times \dfrac{3}{5} + \dfrac{1}{2} R \times \dfrac{4}{5} = \dfrac{mv^2}{r} \Rightarrow mv^2 = rR$

$\Rightarrow v^2 = 2gr$

i.e. $v_{\text{MAX}} = \sqrt{2gr} = \sqrt{11} \times v_{\text{MIN}}$.

11 (a)

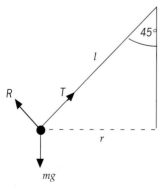

Vertically: $R \sin 45° + T \cos 45° = mg$

$\Rightarrow R + T = \sqrt{2} mg$ ... ①

Horizontally: $T \sin 45° - R \cos 45° = \dfrac{mv^2}{r}$

$\Rightarrow T - R = \dfrac{\sqrt{2} mv^2}{r}$ ... ②

$\Delta: r = l \sin 45° = \dfrac{l}{\sqrt{2}}$ ... ③

① + ② $\Rightarrow 2T = \sqrt{2} m \left[g + \dfrac{v^2}{r} \right] = \sqrt{2} m \left[g + \dfrac{\sqrt{2} v^2}{l} \right]$

from ③

$\Rightarrow T = \dfrac{1}{\sqrt{2}} m \left[g + \dfrac{\sqrt{2} v^2}{l} \right] = m \left(\dfrac{v^2}{l} + \dfrac{g}{\sqrt{2}} \right)$

(b) From ①, $R = \sqrt{2} mg - T = \sqrt{2} mg - \dfrac{mg}{\sqrt{2}} - \dfrac{mv^2}{l}$

$= mg \left(\dfrac{\sqrt{2}}{2} \right) - \dfrac{mv^2}{l} = m \left[\dfrac{g}{\sqrt{2}} - \dfrac{v^2}{l} \right]$

(c) If $v^2 > \dfrac{gl}{\sqrt{2}} \Rightarrow \dfrac{v^2}{l} > \dfrac{g}{\sqrt{2}} \Rightarrow \dfrac{g}{\sqrt{2}} - \dfrac{v^2}{l} < 0$

i.e. $R < 0$ and the particle leaves the surface of the cone.

12

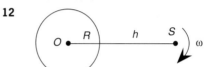

We're given an acceleration (rather than a force) which is $\dfrac{k}{r^2}$.

On the surface of the earth, i.e. when $r = R$, this is g,

i.e. $\dfrac{k}{R^2} = g \Rightarrow k = gR^2$

and so the acceleration is $\dfrac{gR^2}{r^2}$ ... ①

This acceleration is the acceleration of the satellite towards the centre of the earth, i.e. $r\omega^2$ and so

$\dfrac{gR^2}{r^2} = r\omega^2 \Rightarrow \omega^2 = \dfrac{gR^2}{r^3}$ ... ②

But at a height h above the surface of the earth, $r = R + h$ and ② becomes

$\omega^2 = \dfrac{gR^2}{(R + h)^3}$

i.e. $\omega = \left(\dfrac{gR^2}{(R + h)^3} \right)^{\frac{1}{2}}$

For the next part, we need to take care with the units!
When $R = 6400$ km

$= 6.4 \times 10^6$ m and $h = 1.6 \times 10^6$ m,

$\omega = \left(\dfrac{g \times 6.4^2 \times 10^{12}}{8^3 \times 10^{18}} \right)^{\frac{1}{2}}$

$= 0.885 \times 10^{-3}$ rad s^{-1}

$= 5.313 \times 10^{-2}$ rad min^{-1}.

For a complete revolution,

$T = \dfrac{2\pi}{\omega} = 118$ mins

This is approximately 2 hours

13   Force towards centre is $mr\omega^2 = 3r \times 2^2 = 12r$

Tension is $\dfrac{\lambda x}{l} = \dfrac{180\,(r-3)}{3}$

Equating these, $60\,(r-3) = 12r \Rightarrow 48r = 180$

$$r = 3.75 \text{ m}$$

$\Rightarrow$ extension is 75 cm

If tension is 120, $120 = \dfrac{180\,(r-3)}{3} \Rightarrow r = 5$

$\Rightarrow 120 = mr\omega^2 = 3 \times 5 \times \omega^2 \Rightarrow \omega = \sqrt{8} \text{ rad s}^{-1}$

14   (a)   Extension is $(0.6 - l) \qquad \Rightarrow T = \dfrac{\lambda\,(0.6 - l)}{l} = 3$

$$\Rightarrow 3l = \lambda\,(0.6 - l) \qquad \dots \text{①}$$

(b)   Extension is $(0.7 - l) \Rightarrow 0.6 = \dfrac{1}{2}\dfrac{\lambda}{l}(0.7 - l)^2$

$$1.2\,l = \lambda\,(0.7 - l)^2 \qquad \dots \text{②}$$

$\text{②} \div \text{①} \Rightarrow 0.4 = \dfrac{(0.7 - l)^2}{0.6 - l}\ \ 0.24 - 0.4\,l = 0.49 - 1.4\,l + l^2$

$$l^2 - l + 0.25 = 0 \qquad \Rightarrow (l - 0.5)^2 = 0, \ l = 0.5$$

into ①, $1.5 = \lambda\,(0.6 - 0.5) \qquad \Rightarrow \lambda = 15$

(c)

$T\cos\theta = 0.2\,g$

$\Rightarrow 3.92\cos\theta$

$\quad = 0.2 \times 9.8$

$\cos\theta = 0.5 \Rightarrow \theta = 60°$

(d) $3.92 = \dfrac{15(x)}{0.5} \Rightarrow x = 0.13 \ (2 \text{ d.p.})$

$\Rightarrow$ length is 0.63 m (2 d.p.)

(e) $T\sin\theta = \dfrac{mv^2}{r} \qquad \Rightarrow v^2 = \dfrac{Tr\sin\theta}{m}$

$$= 3.92 \times \dfrac{(0.63\sin\theta)}{0.2} \times \sin\theta$$

$$= 9.261 \Rightarrow v = 3.04 \text{ m s}^{-1}$$

$$(2 \text{ d.p.})$$

Section 5

1

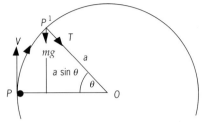

We have a different starting point and so our two equations are not quite the same.

Taking the zero potential level to be the horizontal through O,

Conservation of energy:

$$\frac{1}{2}mV^2 = \frac{1}{2}mv^2 + mga\sin\theta \qquad \dots \text{①}$$

where v is the velocity at P^1.

Circular motion: $T + mg\sin\theta = \dfrac{mv^2}{a} \qquad \dots \text{②}$

From ①, $mv^2 = mV^2 - 2mga\sin\theta$

and putting this into ②

$$T + mg\sin\theta = \frac{mV^2}{a} - 2mg\sin\theta$$

i.e. $T = \dfrac{mV^2}{a} - 3mg\sin\theta \qquad \dots \text{③}$

We need $T \ge 0$ for complete circles, i.e.

$$\frac{mv^2}{a} \ge 3mg\sin\theta$$

$$v^2 \ge 3ag\sin\theta$$

The tension will be least at the top of the circle, i.e. $\theta = 90°$.

so we need $v^2 \ge 3ag\sin 90°$

$$\ge 3ag \Rightarrow v \ge \sqrt{3ag}$$

(a)   Putting $T = \dfrac{15mg}{2}$ and $V = \sqrt{6ag}$ into ③,

$$\frac{15mg}{2} = \frac{m \times 6ag}{a} - 3mg\sin\theta$$

i.e. $3mg\sin\theta = 6mg - \dfrac{15mg}{2} = -\dfrac{3mg}{2}$

$$\Rightarrow \sin\theta = -\frac{1}{2}$$

The string will break when the particle has passed the horizontal on the other side, i.e. when $\theta = 210°$

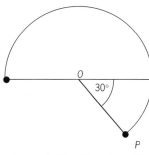

so the angle that OP makes with the *vertical* is 60°

(b)   The greatest tension is at the bottom of the circle, when $\theta = 270°$ and $\sin \theta = -1$.

Putting $T = \dfrac{15mg}{2}$ and $\sin \theta = -1$ into ③,

$$\frac{15mg}{2} = \frac{mV^2}{a} + 3mg$$

$$\frac{9mg}{2} = \frac{mV^2}{a} \Rightarrow V^2 = \frac{9ag}{2}$$

and $V = \sqrt{\left(\dfrac{9ag}{2}\right)}$

2   By conservation of energy, taking the zero potential energy level to be the bottom of the circle

At the top: KE is $\frac{1}{2}mV^2$ PE is $mg\,2a$

At the bottom: KE is $\frac{1}{2}mv^2$ PE is 0

Equating the sums of these

$$\frac{1}{2}mv^2 = \frac{1}{2}mV^2 + 2mga$$

$$v^2 = V^2 + 4ag \Rightarrow v = \sqrt{V^2 + 4ag}$$

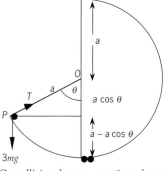

On collision, by conservation of momentum,

$$mv = 3mv' \Rightarrow v' = \frac{v}{3} = \frac{1}{3}\sqrt{V^2 + 4ag}$$

where v' is the speed after the collision.
Now the kinetic energy at bottom is

$$\frac{1}{2} \times 3m \times (v')^2 = \frac{1}{2} \times 3m \times \frac{1}{9}(V^2 + 4ag)$$

Potential energy at P is $3m \times g \times a(1 - \cos \theta)$

and if we call the speed U, the kinetic energy will be

$$\frac{1}{2} \times 3m \times U^2.$$

Equating the sums of the energies at these two points,

$$\frac{1}{2} \times 3m \times \frac{1}{9}(V^2 + 4ag)$$

$$= 3m \times g \times a(1 - \cos \theta) + \frac{1}{2} \times 3m \times U^2$$

$$\Rightarrow \frac{1}{2}U^2 = \frac{1}{18}(V^2 + 4ag) - ag(1 - \cos \theta) \;\dots\; ①$$

The force inwards at P is $T - 3mg \cos \theta$, and since the motion is circular, this must be $\dfrac{3m \times U^2}{a}$

$$T - 3mg \cos \theta = \frac{3m}{a} U^2$$

$$= \frac{3m}{a} \times 2\left[\frac{1}{18}(V^2 + 4ag) - ag(1 - \cos \theta)\right]$$

$$= \frac{m}{3a}(V^2 + 4ag) - 6mg + 6mg \cos \theta$$

$$\Rightarrow \quad T = \frac{mV^2}{3a} + \frac{4mg}{3} - 6mg + 6mg \cos \theta$$
$$+ 3mg \cos \theta$$

$$= \frac{mV^2}{3a} - \frac{14mg}{3} + 9mg \cos \theta$$

For complete circles, we need $T \geq 0$ when $\theta = 180°$, i.e. at the top of the circle. This condition is

$$\frac{mV^2}{3a} - \frac{14mg}{3} + 9mg \cos \theta \geq 0$$

$$\cos 180° = -1$$

$$\frac{V^2}{3a} - \frac{14g}{3} - 9g \geq 0 \Rightarrow \frac{V^2}{3a} > \frac{41g}{3}$$

$$\Rightarrow V^2 \geq 41ag$$

$$\Rightarrow V \geq \sqrt{41ag}$$

3   The minimum tension occurs when the particle is at the highest point of the vertical circle.

At this point, the force towards the centre is

$$T + mg = 3mg + mg = 4mg \qquad \dots ①$$

Initially the KE was $\frac{1}{2}mu^2$

At the top, the PE is $mg \times 2a$,

and the KE is $\frac{1}{2}mv^2$

By conservation of energy,

$$\frac{1}{2}mu^2 = \frac{1}{2}mv^2 + 2mga \Rightarrow v^2 = u^2 - 4ga$$

But force towards centre is

$$\frac{mv^2}{a} = \frac{m(u^2 - 4ga)}{a} \qquad \dots ②$$

Equating ① and ②, $4mg = \dfrac{m(u^2 - 4ga)}{a}$

$$4mga = mu^2 - 4mga$$

$$\Rightarrow u^2 = 8ga \Rightarrow u = \sqrt{8ga}$$

(a)

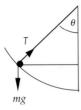

We have from energy,

$$\frac{1}{2}mu^2 = \frac{1}{2}mv^2 + mga\,(1 - \cos\theta)$$

i.e. $8ga = v^2 + 2ga\,(1 - \cos\theta)$

$$\Rightarrow \quad v^2 = 6ga + 2ga\cos\theta \qquad \dots ③$$

Force inwards,

$$T - mg\cos\theta = \frac{mv^2}{a}$$

$$= \frac{6mga + 2mga\cos\theta}{a}$$

$$\Rightarrow \quad T = 6mg + 3mg\cos\theta \qquad \dots ④$$

(b) Horizontal force is :

$$T\sin\theta = 6mg\sin\theta + 3mg\sin\theta\cos\theta$$

since opposes motion, horizontal component is
$-3g\sin\theta\,(2 + \cos\theta)$

Vertical force is :

$$T\cos\theta - mg = 6mg\cos\theta + 3mg\cos^2\theta - mg$$

i.e. vertical component of acceleration is
$6g\cos\theta + 3g\cos^2\theta - g$

4 The first part is covered in the text.

If $V = 2\sqrt{ag}$ at the bottom, the KE is $\frac{1}{2}m(4ag)$

When the string is horizontal, the PE is mga.

The KE is then $\frac{1}{2}m(4ag) - mga = \frac{1}{2}mv^2$

$$\Rightarrow v^2 = 2ag.$$

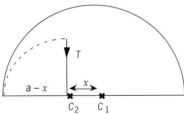

At the top of the circle, gain in PE is $mg(a - x)$.

If velocity is v', KE is $\frac{1}{2}m(v')^2$ and we have

$$\frac{1}{2}m(2ag) = mg(a - x) + \frac{1}{2}m(v')^2 \qquad \dots ①$$

Also, $T + mg = \dfrac{mv'^2}{(a - x)}$

Minimum when $T = 0$

$$\Rightarrow \quad (v')^2 = (a - x)g$$

Into ① gives

$$mag = mag - mgx + \frac{1}{2}mag - \frac{1}{2}mxg$$

$$\Rightarrow \quad \frac{3}{2}mgx = \frac{1}{2}mga \quad \Rightarrow \quad x = \frac{1}{3}a \text{ from the centre}$$

5

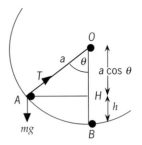

Energies: If the initial position is taken as the zero potential level, the initial sum of energies is:

$$\frac{1}{2}mV^2 \quad (+\,0)$$

when OA makes an angle θ with the downwards vertical, the vertical height h of A above B is $a - a\cos\theta$ $= a\,(1 - \cos\theta)$.

If the velocity is taken to be v, the new sum of energies is:

$$\frac{1}{2}mv^2 = mga\,(1 - \cos\theta)$$

Equating these two sums gives

$$\frac{1}{2}mV^2 = \frac{1}{2}mv^2 + mga\,(1 - \cos\theta) \qquad \dots ①$$

When the particle is vertically above O,

$$\theta = 180° \Rightarrow \cos\theta = -1 \text{ and } ① \text{ becomes}$$

$$\frac{1}{2}mV^2 = \frac{1}{2}mv^2 + 2mga$$

$$\Rightarrow v^2 = V^2 - 4ag$$

$$\Rightarrow v = \sqrt{V^2 - 4ag} \qquad \dots ②$$

Circular motion: Resolving towards the centre gives:

$$T - mg\cos\theta = \frac{mv^2}{a} \qquad \dots ③$$

and combining ② and ③

$$T = m\frac{(V^2 - 4ag)}{a} + mg\cos\theta$$

We need $T > 0$ when $\theta = 180°$,
i.e. $\cos\theta = -1$ for complete circles,

$$\Rightarrow \frac{m(V^2 - 4ag)}{a} - mg > 0$$

$$V^2 - 4ag > ag$$

$$V^2 > 5ag$$

$$V > \sqrt{5ag}$$

For the collision, by conservation of momentum $mv = 2mv'$ where v' is the velocity of the composite particle and so:

$$v' = \frac{1}{2}v = \frac{1}{2}\sqrt{V^2 - 4ag}$$

i.e. the speed of the particle is halved when it picks up the second particle.

At the instant of collision, the tension, which will be a minimum, is given by the circular motion equation for the composite particle.

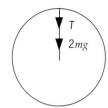

$$T + 2mg = \frac{2mv^2}{a} \qquad \ldots ④$$

(noting that the mass is now doubled)

i.e. $T = \dfrac{2\,mv^2}{a} - 2mg$

$$= \frac{2m}{a}\left[\frac{1}{2}\sqrt{V^2 - 4ag}\,\right]^2 - 2mg$$

$$= \frac{2m}{a} \times \frac{1}{4} \times (V^2 - 4ag) - 2mg$$

$$= \frac{mV^2}{2a} - 2mg - 2mg$$

$$= \frac{mV^2}{2a} - 4mg \qquad \ldots ⑤$$

Since we require $T \geq 0$, $\dfrac{mV^2}{2a} - 4mg \geq 0$

$$\Rightarrow \quad \frac{mV^2}{2a} \geq 4mg \;\Rightarrow\; V^2 \geq 8ag$$

and least value of V is $\sqrt{8ag}$

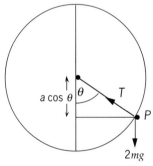

Relative to the top, the composite particle has lost $2mg$ $(a + a\cos\theta)$ in potential energy. If we call the new velocity V', it has gained

$$\frac{1}{2} \times 2m \times v^2 - \frac{1}{2} \times 2m \times V'^2$$

i.e. $m[v^2 - V'^2]$ in kinetic energy.

Then $\qquad m[v^2 - V'^2] = 2mga(1 + \cos\theta)$

and since $\qquad V'^2 = \dfrac{1}{4}(V^2 - 4ag),$

$$v^2 - \frac{1}{4}V^2 + ag = 2ag + 2ag\cos\theta$$

$$\Rightarrow \quad v^2 = \frac{1}{4}V^2 + ag(1 + 2\cos\theta) \qquad \ldots ⑥$$

Our circular motion equation is

$$T - 2mg\cos\theta = \frac{2mv^2}{a} \qquad \ldots ⑦$$

Combining these,

$$T - 2mg\cos\theta = \frac{2m}{a}\left[\frac{1}{4}V^2 + ag(1 + 2\cos\theta)\right]$$

$$T - 2mg\cos\theta = \frac{mV^2}{2a} + 2mg + 4mg\cos\theta$$

$$T = \frac{mV^2}{2a} + 2mg + 6mg\cos\theta$$

(As a check for this, note that if $T = 0$ and $\cos\theta = -1$, $V^2 = 8ag$ which is the result we showed previously.)

6

(a) Loss in PE from A to B is $Mga\,(1 - \cos\alpha)$

If v is velocity at B, by energy

$$\frac{1}{2}Mv^2 = \frac{1}{2}Mu^2 + Mga\,(1 - \cos\alpha) \qquad \ldots ①$$

Circular motion,

$$Mg\cos\alpha - R = \frac{mv^2}{a} \qquad \ldots ②$$

Combining these two,

$$Mg\cos\alpha - R \;=\; \frac{1}{a}\left[Mu^2 + 2Mga\,(1 - \cos\alpha)\right]$$

$$= \frac{Mu^2}{a} + 2Mg - 2Mg\cos\alpha$$

$$\Rightarrow \quad R \;=\; 3Mg\cos\alpha - \frac{Mu^2}{a} - 2Mg$$

For continued contact, $R \geq 0$

$$\Rightarrow \quad 3Mg\cos\alpha - \frac{Mu^2}{a} - 2Mg > 0$$

$$\frac{Mu^2}{a} \leq 3Mg\cos\alpha - 2Mg$$

$$\Rightarrow \quad u^2 \leq ag\,(3\cos\alpha - 2)$$

(b) When loses contact, $u^2 = ag\,(3\cos\alpha - 2)$

$$\Rightarrow \quad u^2 = ag\left(3 \times \frac{5}{6} - 2\right) = \frac{ag}{2} \qquad \ldots ③$$

Initially when travelling horizontally, $R = mg$.

At A, in circular motion,

$$Mg - R \;=\; \frac{Mu^2}{a} = \frac{Mg}{2} \text{ from } ③$$

$$\Rightarrow \quad R \;=\; Mg - \frac{Mg}{2} = \frac{Mg}{2}$$

Decrease in magnitude of R is $\dfrac{Mg}{2}$

7 (a) Loss in PE from A to B is

$$mgr\left[\frac{7}{8} - \cos\alpha\right] \text{ where } m \text{ is mass of particle}$$

Energy: $\quad \frac{1}{2}mv^2 = mgr\left[\frac{7}{8} - \cos\alpha\right] \quad \dots \text{①}$

Circle: $\quad mg\cos\alpha - R = \dfrac{mv^2}{r} \quad \dots \text{②}$

Combining: $\quad R = mg\cos\alpha - \dfrac{2mgr}{r}\left[\frac{7}{8} - \cos\alpha\right]$

$$= 3\,mg\cos\alpha - \frac{7\,mg}{4}$$

When $R = 0$, $\cos\alpha = \dfrac{7mg}{4} \times \dfrac{1}{3\,mg} = \dfrac{7}{12}$

(b) Putting this into ①, $\quad \dfrac{1}{2}v^2 = gr\left[\frac{7}{8} - \frac{7}{12}\right]$

$$= \frac{7gr}{24}$$

$$\Rightarrow \quad v^2 = \frac{7gr}{12}$$

(c) By energy, since B is $\dfrac{7r}{12}$ above ground,

$$\frac{1}{2}mu^2 = \frac{1}{2}mv^2 + mg\left(\frac{7r}{12}\right)$$

$$= \frac{1}{2}m \times \frac{7\,gr}{12} + \frac{7mgr}{12}$$

$$= \frac{7mgr}{8}$$

$$\Rightarrow \quad u^2 = \frac{7gr}{4}$$

8 Tension in string is $3mg$

Loss in PE is $3mga\,(1 - \cos\theta)$

Energy: $\dfrac{1}{2}(3m)\,v^2 = \dfrac{1}{2}\,3mu^2 + 3mga\,(1 - \cos\theta)$

i.e. $\quad v^2 = u^2 + 2ga\,(1 - \cos\theta)$ $\quad \dots \text{①}$

Circles: $\quad T + 3mg\cos\theta - N = \dfrac{3mv^2}{a} \quad \dots \text{②}$

$$\Rightarrow \quad N = 3mg + 3mg\cos\theta - \frac{3m}{a}\left[u^2 + 2ga\,(1 - \cos\theta)\right]$$

$u^2 = \dfrac{1}{2}ga \quad = 3mg + 3mg\cos\theta - \dfrac{3mg}{2} - 6mg$

$$+ 6\,mg\cos\theta$$

$$= 9\,mg\cos\theta - \frac{9mg}{2} = \frac{9}{2}mg\,(2\cos\theta - 1)$$

From ①, when $\quad \theta = 180°$ and $u^2 = \dfrac{1}{2}ga$,

$$v^2 = \frac{1}{2}ga + 4ga = \frac{9ga}{2}$$

$$\Rightarrow \quad v = 3\sqrt{\left(\frac{ga}{2}\right)}$$

At bottom, linear momentum is $3m\left(3\sqrt{\left(\frac{ga}{2}\right)}\right)$ before

after, it is $4\,mv \Rightarrow v = \dfrac{3}{4}\left(3\sqrt{\left(\frac{ga}{2}\right)}\right) = \dfrac{9}{4}\sqrt{\left(\frac{ga}{2}\right)}$

9

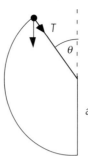

Gain in PE is $mga\,(1 + \cos\theta)$

Energy: $\dfrac{1}{2}\,mv^2$

$$= \frac{1}{2}\,mu^2 - mga\,(1 + \cos\theta)$$

$$= \frac{1}{2}\,m\,kag - mga\,(1 + \cos\theta)$$

$$\Rightarrow v^2 = kag - 2\,ga - 2ga\cos\theta$$

$$= ag\,[k - 2 - 2\cos\theta]$$

Circle: $\quad T + mg\cos\theta = \dfrac{mv^2}{a}$

If $T = 0$, $\quad mg\cos\theta = mg\,[k - 2 - 2\cos\theta]$

$$\Rightarrow 3mg\cos\theta = mg\,[k - 2]$$

$$\Rightarrow \cos\theta = \frac{k-2}{3}$$

and $v^2 = ag\left[k - 2 - \dfrac{2(k-2)}{3}\right] = ag\left(\dfrac{k-2}{3}\right)$

$$\Rightarrow v = \sqrt{\left(\frac{(k-2)\,ag}{3}\right)}$$

10 Gain in PE at B is $mga\,(1 + \cos 60°) = \dfrac{3mga}{2}$

Energy: $\dfrac{1}{2}\,mv^2 = \dfrac{1}{2}\,mu^2 - \dfrac{3mga}{2}$

$$= \frac{1}{2}\,m \times 6ag - \frac{3mga}{2}$$

$$\Rightarrow v^2 = 6ag - 3\,ag = 3ag$$

$$v = \sqrt{3ag}$$

Using cartesian equation, $y = x\tan\theta - \dfrac{gx^2}{2v^2\cos^2\theta}$

with $\theta = 60°$, $v = \sqrt{3ag}$ gives

$$y = x\sqrt{3} - \frac{gx^2}{2 \times 3\,ag \times \frac{1}{4}}$$

$$\Rightarrow y = x\sqrt{3} - \frac{2x^2}{3a}$$

$$\frac{dy}{dx} = \sqrt{3} - \frac{4x}{3a} = 0 \text{ for max} \Rightarrow x = \frac{3\sqrt{3}a}{4}$$

$$\Rightarrow y = \frac{3\sqrt{3}a}{4} \times \sqrt{3} - \frac{2}{3a}\left[\frac{3\sqrt{3}a}{4}\right]^2$$

$$= \frac{9a}{4} - \frac{2}{3a} \times \frac{27a^2}{16} = \frac{9a}{4} - \frac{9a}{8} = \frac{9a}{8}$$

$$\Rightarrow \text{above plane,} \quad \frac{3a}{2} + \frac{9a}{8} = \frac{21a}{8}$$

When reaches plane, $y = -\dfrac{3a}{2}$

$$\Rightarrow -\frac{3a}{2} = x\sqrt{3} - \frac{2x^2}{3a}$$

$$\Rightarrow \frac{2x^2}{3a} - x\sqrt{3} - \frac{3a}{2} = 0$$

$$x = \frac{\sqrt{3} \pm \sqrt{3+4}}{\frac{4}{3a}} = \frac{3a}{4}\,(\sqrt{3} + \sqrt{7})\ (x > 0)$$

11 (a) Loss in PE is $mga\,(\sin\theta - \sin 30°)$

$\Rightarrow$ Energy: $\frac{1}{2}mv^2 = \frac{1}{2}mu^2 + mga\,(\sin\theta$
$- \sin 30°)$

Circle: $T - mg\sin\theta = \dfrac{mv^2}{a}$ ... ①

$\Rightarrow$ $T = mg\sin\theta + \dfrac{mu^2}{a} + 2mg\,(\sin\theta - \sin 30°)$

$= mg\sin\theta + \dfrac{mu^2}{a} + 2mg\sin\theta - mg$

$= \dfrac{mu^2}{a} - mg + 3mg\sin\theta$

(b) Greatest tension is when $\theta = 90°$, and then

$T = \dfrac{mu^2}{a} - mg + 3mg = \dfrac{nu^2}{a} + 2mg$

If $T \le 6\,mg$, $\dfrac{mu^2}{a} + 2mg \le 6mg$

$\dfrac{mu^2}{a} \le 4mg$

$u^2 \le 4ag \Rightarrow u \le 2\sqrt{ag}$

(c) If $u^2 = 3ga$, $T = 3mg - mg + 3mg\sin\theta$
$= 2mg + 3mg\sin\theta$

If $T = 0$, $3mg\sin\theta = -2mg \Rightarrow \sin\theta = -\dfrac{2}{3}$

First position solution for this is $221.8°$

From equation ① , $\dfrac{mv^2}{a} = -mg\left(-\dfrac{2}{3}\right) \Rightarrow mv^2$

$= \dfrac{2mga}{3}$

$v^2 = \dfrac{2ga}{3}$ and $v = \sqrt{\left(\dfrac{2ga}{3}\right)}$

(d) Vertical component is $v\cos\theta$

where $v = \sqrt{\left(\dfrac{2ga}{3}\right)}$ and $\cos\theta = \sqrt{\left(1 - \sin^2\theta\right)}$

$= \sqrt{\left(1 - \dfrac{4}{9}\right)}$

$= \sqrt{\left(\dfrac{5}{9}\right)}$ (positive, since upwards)

$u = v\cos\theta$, $v = 0$, $a = -g$, $s = H$

$v^2 = u^2 + 2as \Rightarrow 0 = v^2\cos^2\theta - 2gH$

$2gH = \dfrac{2ga}{3} \times \dfrac{5}{9} \Rightarrow H = \dfrac{5a}{27}$

Height above O is $\dfrac{2}{3}a + \dfrac{5a}{27} = \dfrac{23a}{27}$

Section 6

1

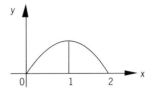

The shape is symmetrical about the maximum point,
i.e. $x = 1$, and so $\bar{x} = 1$.

The y-coordinate of the centre of mass is given by

$\bar{y} = \dfrac{\dfrac{1}{2}\displaystyle\int y^2\,dx}{\displaystyle\int y\,dx} = \dfrac{\dfrac{1}{2}\displaystyle\int_0^2 \left(2x - x^2\right)^2 dx}{\displaystyle\int_0^2 \left(2x - x^2\right) dx}$

$= \dfrac{\dfrac{1}{2}\displaystyle\int_0^2 \left(4x^2 - 4x^3 + x^4\right) dx}{\displaystyle\int_0^2 \left(2x - x^2\right) dx}$

$= \dfrac{\dfrac{1}{2}\left[\dfrac{4x^3}{3} - x^4 + \dfrac{x^5}{5}\right]_0^2}{\left[x^2 - \dfrac{x^3}{3}\right]_0^2}$

$= \dfrac{\dfrac{1}{2}\left(\dfrac{32}{3} - 16 + \dfrac{32}{5}\right)}{\dfrac{4}{3}} = \dfrac{\dfrac{8}{15}}{\dfrac{4}{3}} = \dfrac{2}{5}$

The required coordinates are $\left(1, \dfrac{2}{5}\right)$.

2 Since the x-axis is an axis of symmetry, $\bar{y} = 0$

$\bar{x} = \dfrac{\displaystyle\int xy^2\,dx}{\displaystyle\int y^2\,dx} = \dfrac{\displaystyle\int_0^1 x\left(x^2 + 1\right)^2 dx}{\displaystyle\int_0^1 \left(x^2 + 1\right)^2 dx}$

$= \dfrac{\displaystyle\int_0^1 \left(x^5 + 2x^3 + x\right) dx}{\displaystyle\int_0^1 \left(x^4 + 2x^2 + 1\right) dx}$

$= \dfrac{\left[\dfrac{x^6}{6} + \dfrac{x^4}{2} + \dfrac{x^2}{2}\right]_0^1}{\left[\dfrac{x^5}{5} + \dfrac{2x^3}{3} + x\right]_0^1}$

$= \dfrac{\dfrac{7}{6}}{\dfrac{28}{15}} = \dfrac{5}{8}$, i.e. coordinates are $\left(\dfrac{5}{8}, 0\right)$

3   Taking moments about the base,

Cylinder: $(\pi \times 40^2 \times 40) \times \rho \times 20$

Hemisphere: $(\frac{2}{3}\pi \times 40^3) \times \rho \times [40 + \frac{3 \times 40}{8}]$

Total: $(\pi \times 40^3 \times \frac{5}{3}) \times \rho \times \bar{y}$

Equating, $\pi \times 40^3 \times 20\rho + \frac{2}{3}\pi \times 40^3 \times 55\rho = \frac{5}{3}\pi \times 40^3 \times \bar{y}\,\rho$

$\Rightarrow \bar{y} = \dfrac{20 + \frac{2}{3} \times 55}{\frac{5}{3}} = \dfrac{170}{5} = 34$ cm

4   The first part is standard proof (see p. 110)

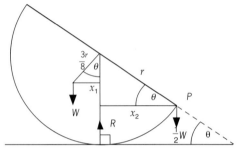

Taking moments about the vertical axis through the point of contact,

$Wx_1 = \frac{1}{2}Wx_2$ ...①

from small Δ, $x_1 = \frac{3r}{8}\sin\theta$ ...②

from large Δ, $x_2 = r\cos\theta$ ...③

② and ③ into ①, $\frac{3r}{8}\sin\theta = \frac{r}{2}\cos\theta$

$\Rightarrow \tan\theta = \frac{4}{3}$

5   The first part is a standard proof (see p. 110).

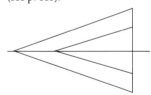

Moments about vertical axis through vertex

$\frac{1}{3}\pi a^2 h\rho \times \frac{3h}{4} - \frac{1}{3}\pi(\frac{a}{2})^2(\frac{2}{3}h)\rho \times \frac{5h}{6}$

$= [\frac{1}{3}\pi a^2 h\rho - \frac{1}{3}\pi(\frac{a}{2})^2(\frac{2h}{3})\rho]\bar{x}$

$\Rightarrow \pi a^2 h^2 \rho [\frac{1}{4} - \frac{5}{108}]$

$= \pi a^2 h\rho [\frac{1}{3} - \frac{1}{18}] \times \bar{x}$

$\Rightarrow \bar{x} = \frac{11}{15}h$

6   (a)   Call the radius r

Taking moments about vertex of larger cone,

Larger: $(\frac{1}{3}\pi r^2 \times 2h) \times \rho \times (\frac{3}{4} \times 2h)$

Smaller: $(\frac{1}{3}\pi r^2 \times h) \times \rho \times (2h + \frac{h}{4})$

Total: $(\frac{1}{3}\pi r^2 \times 3h) \times \rho \times \bar{x}$

$\Rightarrow \bar{x} = \dfrac{2h \times \frac{3h}{2} + h \times \frac{9h}{4}}{3h} = h + \frac{3h}{4} = \frac{7h}{4}$

(b)

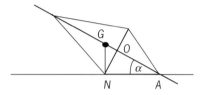

From Δ *OAN*, $\tan\alpha = \frac{r}{h}$

From Δ *OGN*, $\tan\alpha = \dfrac{\frac{h}{4}}{r}$

Equating these, $\frac{r}{h} = \frac{h}{4r} \Rightarrow 4r^2 = h^2$

$r = \frac{h}{2}\ (>0)$

7   Moments about *AD*, assuming ρ is the mass per unit, are:

	Vol	Mass	COM	Moment
Big cube	$27a^3$	$27a^3\rho$	$\frac{3a}{2}$	$\frac{81a^4\rho}{2}$
Medium cube	$8a^3$	$8a^3\rho$	$2a$	$16a^4\rho$
Little cube	a^3	$a^3\rho$	$\frac{3a}{2}$	$\frac{3a^4\rho}{2}$
Whole	$36a^3$	$36a^3\rho$	$\bar{x}$	$36a^3\rho\bar{x}$

Equating, $36a^3\rho\bar{x} = \frac{81a^4\rho}{2} + 16a^4\rho + \frac{3a^4\rho}{2}$

$= (\frac{81+32+3}{2})a^4\rho = \frac{116a^4\rho}{2}$

$\bar{x} = \frac{116a^4\rho}{2} \times \frac{1}{36a^3\rho} = \frac{29a}{18}$

Moments about *AB*:

	Mass	COM	Moment
Big	$27a^3\rho$	$\frac{3a}{2}$	$\frac{81a^4\rho}{2}$
Medium	$8a^3\rho$	$4a$	$32a^4\rho$
Little	$a^3\rho$	$\frac{11a}{2}$	$\frac{11a^4\rho}{2}$
Whole	$36a^3\rho$	$\bar{y}$	$36a^3\rho\bar{y}$

Equating, $36a^3\rho\bar{y} = \frac{a^4\rho}{2}[81 + 64 + 11]$

$\Rightarrow \bar{y} = \frac{39a}{18}$

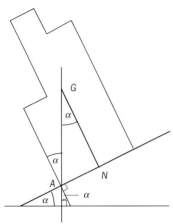

If G is the position of the centre of mass and N the foot of the perpendicular from G on to AB, then $GN = \dfrac{39a}{18}$

and $AN = \dfrac{29a}{18}$

$\Rightarrow \tan \alpha = \dfrac{AN}{GN} = \dfrac{\frac{29a}{18}}{\frac{39a}{18}} = \dfrac{29}{39}$

8 (a) The first part is a standard proof which is covered at the beginning of this section.

(b)

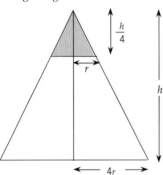

By similar triangles, the radius of the cone removed is going to be r.

Moment whole = Moment remainder + Moment part

Taking moments about the base

$\left(\dfrac{1}{3}\pi\,(4r)^2 h\right) \times \dfrac{h}{4}$

$= \left[\dfrac{1}{3}\pi\,(4r)^2 h - \dfrac{1}{3}\pi\,(r)^2 \left(\dfrac{h}{4}\right)\right]\bar{y} + \dfrac{1}{3}\pi r^2 \dfrac{h}{4}$

$\qquad \times \left(\dfrac{3h}{4} + \dfrac{h}{16}\right)$

$\dfrac{4\pi r^2 h^2}{3} = \dfrac{1}{3}\pi r^2 h \left(\dfrac{63}{4}\right)\bar{y} + \dfrac{13\pi r^2 h^2}{192}$

$\Rightarrow \dfrac{1}{3}\pi r^2 h \left(\dfrac{63}{4}\right)\bar{y} = \dfrac{4\pi r^2 h^2}{3} - \dfrac{13\pi r^2 h^2}{192}$

$= \dfrac{81\pi r^2 h^2}{64}$

$\Rightarrow \bar{y} = \dfrac{4}{21} \times \dfrac{81}{64} h = \dfrac{27h}{112}$

(c)

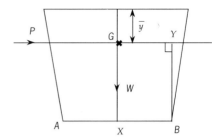

If the force is pushing towards the right, the frustum is going to tip about the point B. This will happen basically when the force overcomes the weight: more precisely when the moment of the force about B is greater than the moment of the weight about B, i.e. when

$P \times BY > W \times BX$ ... ①

Since the height of the frustum is $\dfrac{3}{4}h$ and $\bar{y}$ is $\dfrac{27h}{112}$,

$BY = \dfrac{3}{4}h - \dfrac{27h}{112} = \dfrac{57h}{112} = \dfrac{57(6r)}{112}$ (given)

$BX = r$, which means ① becomes

$P \times \dfrac{57(6r)}{112} > Wr$

i.e. $P > \dfrac{56W}{171}$

9 Moments about axis through O,

$\pi r^2 h\rho \times \dfrac{h}{2} - \dfrac{1}{3}\pi r^2 h\rho \times \dfrac{3h}{4} = \dfrac{2}{3}\pi r^2 h\rho\bar{y}$

$\Rightarrow \dfrac{\pi r^2 h^2}{4} = \dfrac{2}{3}\pi r^2 h\bar{y}$

$\Rightarrow \bar{y} = \dfrac{3h}{8}$

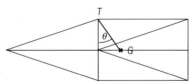

Moments about diameter of common face, right being positive

$-\dfrac{1}{3}\pi r^2 h\rho \times \dfrac{h}{4} + \dfrac{2}{3}r^2 h\rho \times \dfrac{3h}{8} = \pi r^2 h\bar{x}$

$\Rightarrow \bar{x} = \dfrac{h}{6}$

Angle TG to vertical is same as axis to horizontal

$\tan \theta = \dfrac{\frac{h}{6}}{r} = \dfrac{1}{3}$ since $h = 2r$

10 Moments about OA:

$3a\rho \times \dfrac{3a}{2} + 2a\rho \times 3a = 9a\rho\bar{x}$

$$\Rightarrow \quad \frac{21a\rho}{2} = 9a\rho\bar{x} \Rightarrow \bar{x} = \frac{7a}{6}$$

Moments about ON:

$$4a\rho \times 2a + 2a\rho \times a = 9a\bar{y}$$
$$\Rightarrow \quad \bar{y} = \frac{10a}{9}$$

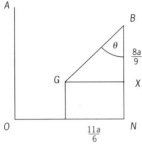

$$\tan \theta = \frac{11}{6} \times \frac{9}{8} = \frac{33}{16}$$

11

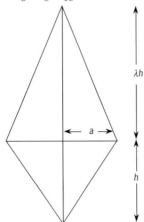

Taking moments about their base, with distances above the base taken as positive gives

Moment whole = Moment large + Moment small

$$\left(\frac{1}{3}\pi r^2 \lambda h + \frac{1}{3}\pi r^2 h\right)\bar{y}$$

$$= \frac{1}{3}\pi r^2 (\lambda h) \times \frac{\lambda h}{4} - \frac{1}{3}\pi r^2 h \times \frac{h}{4}$$

$$\Rightarrow \frac{1}{3}\pi r^2 h (\lambda + 1)\bar{y} = \frac{1}{3}\pi r^2 \frac{h^2}{4}(\lambda^2 - 1)$$

$$\bar{y} = \frac{h}{4}\left(\frac{\lambda^2 - 1}{\lambda + 1}\right) = \frac{h}{4}(\lambda - 1)$$

Required distance, from top of figure, is

$$\lambda h - \bar{y} = \lambda h - \frac{\lambda h}{4} + \frac{h}{4} = \frac{h}{4}(3\lambda + 1)$$

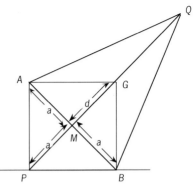

ABP represents the smaller cone in contact with a horizontal surface.

Since $MB = MP = a$,

$$M\hat{B}P = M\hat{A}P = 45° \text{ and } A\hat{P}B = 90°$$

In the limiting position G, the position of the centre of mass of the composite figure, is directly above B, i.e. GB is vertical

$$\Rightarrow G\hat{B}M = 45°, \text{ i.e. } d = a.$$

But we know that $d = \bar{y}$ which we found above,

i.e. $d = \frac{h}{4}(\lambda - 1)$. Putting $d = a = h$ into this gives

$$a = \frac{a}{4}(\lambda - 1)$$
$$\Rightarrow \lambda - 1 = 4 \Rightarrow \lambda = 5$$

This is the limiting position: equilibrium is possible for any value of λ, $\lambda \leq 5$.

12 (a) Moments about plane face

Larger: $\frac{2}{3}\pi R^3 \times \rho \times \frac{3}{8}R$

Smaller: $\frac{2}{3}\pi \left(\frac{R}{2}\right)^3 \times \rho \times \frac{3}{8}\left(\frac{R}{2}\right)$

Remainder: $\left[\frac{2}{3}\pi\left(R^3 - \left(\frac{R}{2}\right)^3\right)\right] \times \rho \times \bar{y}$

Equating, $\frac{2}{3}\pi\left(\frac{7R^3}{8}\right)\rho\,\bar{y} = \frac{\pi\rho R^2}{4} - \frac{\pi\rho R^4}{64}$

$$\Rightarrow \bar{y} = \frac{R\left[\frac{1}{4} - \frac{1}{64}\right]}{\frac{7}{12}} = R \times \frac{15}{64} \times \frac{12}{7}$$

$$= \frac{45R}{112}$$

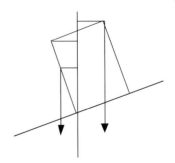

(b) Taking moments about vertical axis through point of contact,

$$28g \times \frac{5R}{8} \sin 8° = mg \times (R \cos 8° - R \sin 8°)$$

$$\Rightarrow m = 2.9 \text{ kg}$$

13 (a) The centre of mass of a circular arc subtending 2θ radians at the centre is $\frac{r \sin \theta}{\theta}$ from the centre on the axis of symmetry. Here, with $2\theta = \frac{\pi}{2} \Rightarrow \theta = \frac{\pi}{4}$,

CoM is $\dfrac{r \times \sin \frac{\pi}{4}}{\frac{\pi}{4}} = \dfrac{4r}{\sqrt{2}\pi}$ from O,

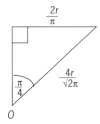

i.e. $\dfrac{4r}{\sqrt{2}\pi} \times \dfrac{1}{\sqrt{2}} = \dfrac{2r}{\pi}$ from OA

(b) From OQ

	Mass	CoM	Moment
Arc:	$\frac{1}{4}(2\pi r) \times \rho$	$\frac{2r}{\pi}$	$\frac{1}{4}(2\pi r)\rho \times \frac{2r}{\pi}$
Line:	$4r \times \rho$	$-2r$	$4r\rho \times -2r$
Total:	$\left(\frac{\pi r}{2} + 4r\right)\rho$	$\bar{x}$	$\left(\frac{\pi r}{2} + 4r\right)\rho\,\bar{x}$

This gives $\frac{1}{4}(2\pi r)\,\rho \times \frac{2r}{\pi} + 4r\rho \times -2 = \left(\frac{\pi r}{2} + 4r\right)\rho\,\bar{x}$

$$r^2 - 8r^2 = \left(\frac{\pi r}{2} + 4r\right)\bar{x}$$

$$\Rightarrow \bar{x} = \frac{-7r}{\frac{\pi}{2} + 4} = -\left(\frac{14r}{8 + \pi}\right)$$

i.e. $\dfrac{14r}{8 + \pi}$ from OQ

(c) From OR

	Mass	CoM	Moment
Arc:	$\frac{\pi r}{2}\rho$	$\frac{2r}{\pi}$	$r^2\rho$
Line:	$4r\rho$	r	$4r^2\rho$
Total:	$\left(\frac{\pi r}{2} + 4r\right)\rho$	$\bar{y}$	$\left(\frac{\pi r + 4r}{2}\right)\rho\bar{y}$

$$\Rightarrow \left(\frac{\pi r + 8r}{2}\right)\bar{y} = r^2 + 4r^2 = 5r^2$$

$$\Rightarrow \bar{y} = \frac{10r}{8 + \pi} \text{ (from } OR\text{)}$$

(d)

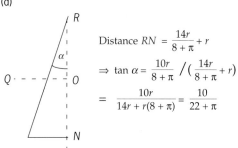

Distance $RN = \dfrac{14r}{8 + \pi} + r$

$$\Rightarrow \tan \alpha = \frac{10r}{8 + \pi} \bigg/ \left(\frac{14r}{8 + \pi} + r\right)$$

$$= \frac{10r}{14r + r(8 + \pi)} = \frac{10}{22 + \pi}$$

14

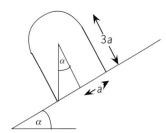

We have to find the distance of the centre of mass of the body from its base (it will lie along the axis joining the centres by symmetry).

Moments about base

Hemisphere: $\dfrac{2}{3}\pi a^3 \times \rho \times \left[3a + \dfrac{3a}{8}\right] = \dfrac{9a^4\pi\rho}{4}$

Cylinder: $\pi a^2 \times 3a \times \rho \times \dfrac{3a}{2} = \dfrac{9a^4\pi\rho}{2}$

Total moment $\left(\dfrac{2}{3}\pi a^3\rho + 3\pi a^3\rho\right)\bar{y}$

$$\Rightarrow \bar{y} = \frac{\dfrac{9a^4\pi\rho}{4} + \dfrac{9a^4\pi\rho}{2}}{\dfrac{2}{3}\pi a^3\rho + 3\pi a^3\rho} = \frac{81a}{44}$$

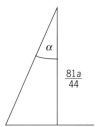

This will topple if

$$\tan \alpha > \frac{a}{\dfrac{81a}{44}} = \frac{44}{81}$$

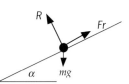

Perpendicular to the plane, $R = mg \cos \alpha$

Parallel to the plane, $Fr = mg \sin \alpha$

In limiting equilibrium, $Fr = \mu R$

$\Rightarrow$ in limit, $mg \sin \alpha = \mu\,mg \cos \alpha$

$\Rightarrow \mu = \tan \alpha$

So it will slide before toppling provided, $\mu < \dfrac{44}{81}$.